SILK GLOVE HEGEMONY
Finnish-Soviet Relations, 1944–1974

Library of Congress Cataloging in Publication Data

Vloyantes, John P. 1918-
 Silk glove hegemony.
 Includes bibliographical references and index.
 1. Finland—Foreign relations—Russia. 2. Russia—Foreign rela-
tions—Finland. I. Title. II. Title: Finnish-Soviet relations, 1944-1974.
JX1555.3.Z7R88   327.471'047   74-27387
ISBN 0-87338-174-2

Silk Glove Hegemony

Finnish-Soviet Relations, 1944–1974

**A CASE STUDY OF THE THEORY
OF THE SOFT SPHERE OF INFLUENCE**

John P. Vloyantes

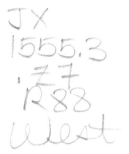
THE KENT STATE UNIVERSITY PRESS

CONTENTS

PREFACE

This book grew out of two separate research interests which in time converged: the study of World War II diplomacy and the effort to develop a framework for analysis of spheres of influence. The former figured in my Ph.D. dissertation and subsequent studies, while the latter has for almost a decade been my primary research interest as a teacher of foreign policy and international relations.

One of the underlying concerns at the Yalta conference and later was the nature and extent of the assertion of Soviet interests in Eastern Europe. The United States was prepared to accept a *de facto* Soviet sphere of influence in this region if the countries could maintain internal self-government as they accommodated themselves to Soviet security interests. Indeed, during the period 1944–45, Czechoslovakia under Eduard Beneš seemed to be a pattern that would characterize this species of sphere of influence, and it was hoped that other countries in this region would fit the mold. Only in Finland, however, did such a pattern develop and endure.

Studies of spheres of influence in World War II stimulated my desire to undertake a broader study of the subject as a phenomenon in international relations; but, as suspected, it was soon learned that almost nothing had been done on the systematic analysis of these relationships. This lack seemed particularly gaping in view of the scope and significance of this occurrence in international relations and the burgeoning efforts to develop theoretical and systematic analysis of the academic discipline.

In the course of the endeavor to develop a framework for analysis of spheres of influence, I was struck by the persisting and recurring significance of *degrees* of influence and the effect of the contemporary forces of nationalsim, self-determination, independence and sovereignty in the face of great power assertions for their own interests. Two contrasting models were devised to reflect these forces: the hard sphere and the soft sphere. Study of these models has led to the conviction that the whole enterprise of spheres of influence analysis would be advanced by improvement of the theoretical models and the classification scheme derived therefrom, as well as the process of change traced in them.

This study of three decades of Finno-Soviet relations was undertaken for the purpose of employing, testing, and refining the soft sphere model. As a result of this first endeavor to examine such a case study in an ample scope of time and detail, it is now possible to delineate more precisely than before the basic features of this typology, especially as indicated in the relations of these two countries. Other case studies of the model would probably reveal variations peculiar to the circumstances, but the results of this case study can be utilized to guide such research. In the course of time, as other case studies of soft spheres are made, research techniques may be improved upon and progress made toward an analytical theory of the soft sphere model.

This intriguing phenomenon has utility beyond examination of specific case studies such as this, for the *process* of softening has been a condition or a source of conflict in many, if not most, spheres of influence. In the course of time, the eastern European Soviet satellites' desire for a softening of their relationships has been a persistent disruptive factor of the system established by Stalin, and the long-run concern of decision makers in Moscow is how to come to terms with the irrepressible impetus for softening. Eventually the Soviet Union may be constrained to accede to formulas more in tune with the soft sphere, and the Finnish example can in some measure be utilized for this purpose.

The Good Neighbor Policy of the United States in the Western Hemisphere provided a set of precepts which exemplified the soft sphere. It has been afflicted with prolonged dysfunction, if not widespread disarray, because of Cold War decision making in Washington that led to renewed intervention, subverting hemispheric institutions to American unilateral preoccupations. In any retrospective assessment of the lessons of the Cold War decades and the unabated desire for independence, and rejection of a regional big brother in Latin America, United States policy makers will have to take cognizance of the suitability of soft sphere principles.

Spheres of influence generally, the soft sphere and the process of softening—as well as hardening—can be of especial utility in the analysis of regional policies of great powers where perceptions of threat, geopolitical hypotheses, strategic doctrines, and economic interests motivate policies. By the same token, spheres analysis can shed light on the policies of small states situated in such regions, which is precisely the condition applicable in the study of Finnish foreign (and domestic) policy.

A collateral value of this study is that it is one of the very few book length publications in English covering postwar Finno-Soviet relations.* Despite its scope, this study does not, and should not, purport to be a *comprehensive* historical description of relations between these two countries for this period. In the first place, the research was undertaken for another purpose, and in the second place such research is at present still handicapped by unavailable Finnish and Soviet official sources and personal data. Needless to say, this study is also limited by lack of these sources; and, until the addition of these materials, description and conclusions will have to be tentative and conjectural. Studies in spheres of influence are hindered by the hesitancy of governments to avow these relationships. Nevertheless, it was deemed possible to proceed with the examination of this case study when it was found

---

*One book length monograph, Max Jakobson, *Finnish Neutrality, A Study of Finnish Foreign Policy since the Second World War*, (New York: Frederick A. Praeger, 1967), is a brief but extremely valuable study by one with rare opportunities for observation and analysis because of his responsibilities in several capacities in the Finnish Foreign Ministry. It should accordingly be regarded as a sort of official history of the period. The Finnish Political Science Association has published two book length collections of scholarly essays on the subject: *Finnish Foreign Policy, Studies in Foreign Politics*, Helsinki, 1963, and *Essays on Finnish Foreign Policy*, Vammala, 1969, which are also extremely valuable sources for study of the subject in English. These are the only book length studies of postwar Finnish foreign policy, although, as will be seen from the citations in this book, many individual articles have been published.

that an impressive and serviceable body of data was available in English.

Concentrated research on this book began in the autumn of 1966, although prior study had sketched in many features of the soft sphere. The methodology for assembling data for this study was first to conduct an exhaustive search for all relevant works published in English, including translations and publications of the Finnish Foreign Ministry and the Finnish Political Science Association; the *New York Times* was combed for the thirty-year period, and considerable use was also made of the *London Times* and *Facts on File*. Two visits were made to Finland at different stages of the research, the first in the autumn of 1967 and the second in the autumn of 1972, for interviews with persons presently or formerly in Finnish politics, those in the Foreign Ministry, public affairs analysts and foreign correspondents, and academic experts on the subject, listed in the acknowledgements below. Some selected works published in German and French were also consulted, and some works were translated from Finnish for use in this study.

Acknowledgements

1. Persons spoken with in two series of interviews in Finland were invaluable both as sources and supplements of data, enlivening many facts, sharpening many perceptions, and illuminating the broad horizon in which this drama has taken place. Sincere gratitude is here expressed to the following for gracious hospitality, generous allotment of time, and candor in discussion:

Karl A. Fagerholm. Prime Minister in three Finnish governments, Speaker of the Parliament, and leader of the Social Democratic Party for most of the period under consideration. Now retired.

Turre J. Junnila. A member of the Fagerholm government in 1958, a career as a member of Parliament and an important figure in the Conservative Party. Has written on Finnish public affairs and foreign policy.

Heikki Brotherus. A noted Finnish journalist and analyst of national and international affairs who was formerly in the Foreign Ministry.

J. O. Söderhjelm. A leading member of the Swedish Party who served in several cabinets before and after the war. One of three living members of the Finnish delegation to Moscow in 1948, which negotiated the Treaty of Friendship, Cooperation, and Mutual Assistance with the U.S.S.R. Now retired.

Lance E. Keyworth. An English journalist, long resident in Finland, and a prominent foreign correspondent in Helsinki. One well informed in Finnish public affairs and able to evaluate them from both the Finnish and outside point of view.

Matti Tuovinen. Ministry of Foreign Affairs. Former Chief of the Press Section. He kindly found time for extensive interviews in 1967 and 1972 and sent relevant issues of *Finnish Features.*

Aaron Bell. An American political science teacher fluent in Finnish and resident in that country for a decade. He was very helpful in planning and arranging the first series of interviews in 1967.

Göran von Bonsdorff. A professor of International Politics at the University of Helsinki who has written on aspects of Finland's foreign policy and Soviet relations with Scandinavia.

Lauri A. Puntila. A distinguished professor of Finnish political history and international relations at the University of Helsinki whose views on neutrality were especially informative. Now retired.

Carl F. Sandelin. Finnish News Agency (S.T.T.), for an interesting description of the leadership of President Paasikivi.

Erik J. S. Castrén. A distinguished professor of International Law at the University of Helsinki, for help in clarifying some legal aspects of Finno-Soviet relations.

2. Although they cannot all be individually mentioned, there were many persons and institutions who provided valued assistance, comment, criticism, encouragement, facilities, and financial support. Sincere thanks is due to all, but the following should be specifically mentioned:

The Faculty Improvement Committee of Colorado State University must be thanked for grants for the initial concentration of work on this subject as well as subsequent study. The Graduate School of International Studies of the University of Denver provided a Research Associates grant for the year 1967–68 which defrayed expenses for a leave of absence to work on spheres of influence and Finno-Soviet relations in research facilities in London and Finland. A sabbatical leave from Colorado State University for 1972–73 made possible a second visit to Finland and time needed to complete the writing of this manuscript. Mr. Pentti Uusivirta of the Finnish Embassy in Washington in 1966 sent copies of speeches, books, and statements useful in this study. Grateful acknowledgement is also due for the use of research facilities in the following libraries: the Library of Congress, the British Museum, the Library of the Royal Institute of International Relations, the Library of the Peace Palace at The Hague, and the Library of Colorado State University. Many librarians invariably provided cheerful assistance and service.

Among teachers, colleagues, and friends I am indebted in various ways to O. Meredith Wilson, who introduced me to the concept of spheres of influence in his lectures on American foreign policy when he was dean of the Liberal Arts College at the University of Utah; to Francis D. Wormuth, G. Homer Durham, and S. Grover Rich of the University of Utah; to Phillip O. Foss, Sue Ellen Charlton, Robert M. Lawrence, William Laux, and Mark Gilderhus of Colorado State University; to Dennis Ray of Los Angeles State College; to Clifton Wilson of the University of Arizona; and to Jerry Lansdowne of Portland State University. John Cranor and Kenneth Warren were two student assistants at Colorado State University who should be remembered with appreciation for diligent and resourceful aid in the task of data accumulation. Special thanks are also due to Mrs. Aino Holma Sarna of London for her translations of selected works from Finnish to English. Countless students were exposed to concepts in spheres of influence in my classes and informal discussions, and I should like to record here thanks for their interest and responses.

This work would probably not have been completed at this time and in this form without the various contributions of the foregoing, but the author alone assumes responsibility for conceptions formulated and positions taken.

A special expression of thanks is due to my wife Gloria for her indispensable contributions of criticism, proofreading and typing the entire manuscript. To this was added her unfailing words of confidence and cheer.

THE CONCEPTUAL FRAMEWORK FOR ANALYSIS

It has been common practice to describe Finland's position in the Soviet orbit as "unique" or "exceptional," and much research has been devoted to supplying historical accounts of and reasons for this uniqueness, and to tracing the nature of Soviet interest in this country.[1] With the aid of spheres of influence analysis, particularly within the context of the soft sphere model, this apparently *sui generis* description can be challenged, and Finland can be classified and explained as an example of a particular kind of sphere of influence. While its status may be unique when contrasted with those of other countries in the Soviet orbit, it is not so when compared, for example, with the status of countries in the western Hemisphere during the era of the Good Neighbor Policy.

Spheres of influence survive in the contemporary international system as a manifestation of imperialism at a time when imperialism is in disrepute and its denunciation part of the international ethos to which all are expected to subscribe. Yet imperialism of one variety or another has been endemic in all international systems with disparities in capability and development. This expression of hegemony, especially by great powers, occurs in different forms and to different degrees as it seeks opportunities and a rationale for its diffusion, but the stirrings of

---

1. See Allan A. Kuusisto, "The Paasikivi Line in Finland's Foreign Policy," *The Western Political Quarterly* (March 1959) p. 49, for a typical reference to the uniqueness of Finland's case.

nationalism now oblige it to be diluted and disguised. Accordingly, a sphere of influence may be little more than a facade for imperialism if it does no more than disguise that imperialism; but if the predominant characteristic of the sphere is both the dilution as well as the disguise, we have the essentials of a soft sphere of influence. The soft sphere concept is one of the main models in the framework for analysis which is presented here for the systematic study of spheres of influence, and the burden of this case study is an implementation and elaboration of the idea.

The main utility of history here is as a source of raw material from which to fashion theoretical constructs. The hard and soft models of spheres of influence make possible a taxonomy which can then be used to chart changes, identify combinations, and distinguish degrees in the analysis of spheres of influence. Equipped with such an instrument, it is possible to perceive better the intrinsic nature and behavior of spheres of influence and great power orbits in international relations and foreign policy. Such an analytical device can help organize facts and relate seemingly disparate happenings, as well as assist in filling the gaps in our knowledge by allowing us to make more sophisticated conjectures and more accurate predictions. The models can facilitate measurement, for they reflect conceptions of degree. They also have special value in the framework for analysis as a whole, for they make it possible to draw upon all of the components and to integrate them into a distinctive device for analysis.

Spheres of influence generally, and the two contrasting models here delineated, can be utilized in the study of regional policies of great powers and can shed light on the policies that small powers in such regions are likely to find necessary or unavoidable.

A framework for analysis can serve as a method for coming to grips in some systematic and comprehensive manner with a study that is wide-ranging and multifaceted. Spheres of influence is such a "macropolitical" subject; but in contemporary writings, although frequently alluded to, it has been treated in only brief, fragmentary, or general terms. The significance of spheres of influence and great power orbits in international politics warrants an effort to develop a framework for analysis.

Complexity makes some repetition and overlapping in the

framework unavoidable and some phases may be more emphasized than others, but care has been taken to maintain internal consistency. The components for the most part have been set forth briefly and in general terms but with some illustrations.

Several manifestations of imperialism up to World War II have much in common with contemporary spheres of influence, and the phenomenon as it is now understood was clearly discernible in the interwar years. Yet, in writings on imperialism before the Second World War "spheres of influence" and "spheres of interest" were terms used to describe a rather specific condition and to distinguish it from other devices of the "new imperialism."

I. Definition of Spheres of Influence

A definition reflecting present usage should be broad, and comprehensive enough to account for variations in manifestations of the phenomenon:[2]

> A sphere of influence is an area into which is projected the power and influence of a country primarily for political, military-strategic, or economic purposes, but sometimes cultural purposes may be added. States within the area are usually nominally independent, but the degree of influence may be so great as to leave little independence; or it may be so indirect and restrained as to permit considerable independence. A sphere may be more or less exclusive, depending upon the degree of independence states within it enjoy.
>
> A sphere of influence can also result from a special position of leadership, initiative, and direction by a great power in association with independent countries, arising out of mutually acceptable relationships which have been established.
>
> A sphere of influence can also result from the activities of private economic entities (with more or less support from home governments) when they become a significant factor in the life of a country.

---

2. The definition and components for analysis of spheres of influence were originally published in John P. Vloyantes, *Spheres of Influence: A Framework for Analysis*, Research Series No. 5, Institute of Government Research, University of Arizona, Tucson, Arizona, 1970. The hard and soft sphere models were first sketched in this publication, but the soft sphere is herein greatly revised and expanded.

II. THE NATURE OF INFLUENCE AND ITS MANIFESTATION IN SPHERES OF INFLUENCE

As the field of international relations continues to mature, one of the attainments should be a greater understanding and formalization of the elusive and complex concept of influence.[3] The systematic study of spheres of influence, including case studies of the soft sphere, can contribute to this end.

All subfields in political science and the other social sciences have probed the implications of influence, but these cannot be fully utilized in international relations because the basic milieu is an international system with its peculiar characteristics, particularly the exertion of influence *by states upon states,* or rather, by decision makers of states upon decision makers of states.[4]

Efforts to define the concept with precision are troubled by its wide compass, covering manifestations and facets closely related to other concepts equally broad. For purposes of this study, however, the range of intensity of influence exerted and responded to is of particular interest. In a scale depicting intensity, the terms *power, control, domination,* and *coercion* would cluster at one end; *intimidation, pressure,* and *leverage* would group in the middle, while *guidance, suggestion* and *inducement* would be found at the other end. Degree can also be indicated by such modifying terms as *strong* or *powerful* influence, *moderate* or *mild* influence, and *subtle* or *gentle* influence as well as *direct* or *indirect* influence.

An excellent general definition of the term "influence" by Henry W. Ehrmann will serve as a prelude to an operational analysis:

. . . whatever causes in any social, and especially political

---

3. See K. J. Holsti, "Foreign Policy Actions: Power, Capability, and Influence," Chapter 6 in *International Politics, A Framework for Analysis* (Englewood Cliffs, N. J.: Prentice-Hall, Inc., second edition, 1972) for an incisive and cogent contribution to this end. See also David J. Singer, "Inter-Nation Influence: A Formal Model," *American Political Science Review,* 57 (1963), pp. 420-430 and Joseph Frankel, "Power, Influence, and Capabilities," Chapter 6 in *International Politics, Conflict and Harmony* (London: Allen Lane the Penguin Press, 1969).

4. Although states remain the most important entities in the international system, due account should also be taken of influence exercised by and upon multistate and nonstate entities in the international system. For example, an alliance system taking the form of a sphere of influence is an entity which affects the behavior of states within and without, as well as other multistate units without.

context, individuals or groups to deviate from a predicted path of behavior. More specifically the term is used to denote changes in behavior of a person or group due to the anticipation of the response of others. In this sense the term connotes the outwardly quiet and possibly gradual exertion of power and persuasion rather than the more demanding legal or overt exercise of power connected with formal authority.[5]

The scale of intensity is useful in tracing and measuring influence as manifested in a sphere of influence, but it is only part of a more comprehensive scheme of operational analysis that first identifies the factors involved in establishing a sphere of influence, then isolates components relating to the exercise of influence, and concludes with a list of ways in which conditioning facilitates the flow of influence and works to perpetuate the system, especially a soft sphere. Most features of the operational scheme can be applied to important decisions affecting an established sphere, as well as in the establishment of one. The outline is as follows:

A. Establishment
   1. Perceived need
   2. Opportunity
   3. Facility

---

5. *A Dictionary of the Social Sciences*, edited by Julius Gould and William L. Kolb, compiled under the auspices of UNESCO. (London: Tavistock Publications, 1964). Ehrmann's discussion concerning the definition of influence in this valuable summary further notes that "Elements common to definitions of influence in various fields of social sciences are (a) that influence will lead to a change or reversal of previous (or predicted) decisions, policies, or behavior; (b) that the 'exercise of influence (influence process) consists in affected policies of others than the self' (H. D. Lasswell and A. Kaplan, *Power and Society*, New Haven: Yale University Press, 1950, p. 71). If social scientists speak of the influence of A over B they note the difference between the way in which B actually behaves and the way he would have behaved if A had not entered into relations with him, or simply did not exist."

"The 'rule of anticipated reaction' which C. J. Friedrich has developed to describe and define influence as a 'very evasive' form of power has found wide acceptance. To him influence is 'apart from power . . . probably the most important basic concept of political science.' But because 'the person or group which is being influenced *anticipates the reactions* of him or those who exercise the influence,' influence operates most of the time 'by changing the conduct of people without any outward appearance of change' (*Constitutional Government and Democracy*, Boston: Ginn and Company, 1946, p. 589)."

B. Implementation
   1. Means
   2. Degree
   3. Effect
C. Conditioning

A. Establishment

1. *Perceived need.* A basic assumption held throughout this treatise is that foreign policy is made by individuals acting for governments and that national needs and interests are thereby susceptible to variable interpretation as perceived by decision makers. Only a few of the factors affecting perceived need can be referred to here, but it should be stressed that it is the seed from which policy sprouts, and effective analysis of the origin of a sphere should probe deeply beyond rhetoric and rationalization to the source of images, fears, and aspirations leading to an assessment of need. Competing national needs must be evaluated, but again the weighing process is subjectively conducted. Perception of need in international relations is often linked to identification of threat, but threat perception should be analyzed in terms of source and degree and these are also susceptible to differing interpretation. For example, as noted below, geopolitical hypotheses such as "regional balance," "vacuum theory," and "domino theory" have guided analysis and decisions regarding national needs.

2. *Opportunity.* If opportunity is present, perceived need can be satisfied; and, obviously, if perceived need is not accompanied by opportunity, the matter ceases to be anything but a dream of national longing or is consigned to ivory tower discourse. Yet, if opportunity is present it can give impetus to the perception of need. Opportunity comes with the existence of favorable factors for the projection of influence, such as weak resistance, nonresistance, or even a welcome of influence. Where there is opportunity, the risks and costs are obviously minimal. There may be other favorable conditions if the country or region is open to influence because it has not been pre-empted by another influencer, or if other states do not take adverse action should influence be exerted. Opportunity is offered by geographic propinquity or other forms of accessibility or by propitious configurations of power, including the existence of a power vacuum. In the contemporary

international system opportunities exist for the rich and powerful as they exploit the economic or military needs of small or under-developed countries. Finally, opportunity may come in the guise of a group seeking to gain or maintain power in a country by foreign assistance.

3. *Facility.* If perceived need and opportunity are present, they will be of no avail without the prospect of success assured by possession of adequate resources and capabilities. If facility exists, however, it may induce perception of need and seek suitable opportunities for the exercise of influence.

In sum, we can succinctly express the establishment of a sphere of influence by the formula:

$$PN + O + F = SI$$

B. Implementation

1. *Means.* In this component are identified the kinds of devices that have been decided upon to exercise influence, including usually a multiplicity of devices which add up to a system of influence. The perceived need and purpose behind the estab-lishment of influence will lead to the choice of means, as will any peculiarities of the situation in the sphere country. Another fac-tor guiding the choice of means is whether certain ones are preferable given the international or domestic concerns of the paramount power.

2. *Degree.* The perceived need and purpose as well as the nature of the opportunities will be reflected in the degree of influence exerted, as will of course the means chosen. Degree of influence can be gauged by reference to the scale of intensity described above. Inasmuch as analysis of degree of influence is an intrinsic part of the description of the soft (and the hard) sphere, it is not necessary to describe it in detail at this point.

3. *Effects.* Effects should be examined after execution of the preceding components of the operation and should especially be weighed in the context of perceived need, means, and degree. The obvious basic question is what happened, not only in the sphere state, although these effects will be the main ones, but also what happened in other countries of the region and what were the effects on the paramount power itself. In addition, probable effects should be traced in other countries of the world, including

other paramount powers with sphere interests of their own. One might ask if the sphere was firmly established or not, and whether there were effects other than those calculated.

At this juncture it is appropriate to conclude the examination of implementation by consideration of a few propositions concerning means, degree, and effect:

1. *First, a paramount power exercises a degree of influence consonant with the effects sought, but modified by the resistance capability of the sphere state.*

This proposition underscores the ever present power factor even in a soft sphere relationship. The power equation between paramount power and sphere state will be crucial regardless of what other factors affect the situation.

2. *Direct influence is of greater effect and degree than indirect influence.*

As a general proposition this will hold, but there may be times when the magnitude of the effect of direct influence is not significant while, on the other hand, the magnitude of the effect of indirect influence may be quite significant. In the former contingency we have a soft sphere condition by direct influence, but in the latter there is a hard-sphere-like effect by indirect influence. There may thus be need for a third proposition:

3. *The distinction between direct and indirect influence in number 2 above should be modified by the distinction between the magnitude of effects, whether or not they be by direct or indirect influence.*

Influence-exerting states and those who are the subjects of influence are both loath to avow its existence, whether direct or indirect, but indirect devices make it possible to mask the occurrence. If avowed, however, the condition becomes more palatable, and it can be claimed that independence and the constitutional processes have been little affected. For this reason indirect influence is idiocratic to the soft sphere. Moreover, the soft sphere by its nature requires the paramount power to eschew influence of significant effect even if it is by indirect means.

C. *Conditioning*

Operationally, the sphere's prospect of success will be enhanced if the flow of influence is facilitated and sustained. This can be accomplished if the ground is prepared by appropriate conditioning, which should really be considered as an elaboration on means. By its essential nature a soft sphere achieves conditioning because the underlying principles upon which it is based give it life and unite the paramount power with the sphere state in common purposes, as will be delineated below. Conditioning can be achieved in the following ways, which are primarily applicable to a soft sphere:

1. By the creation of a benign image of the influencer and its influence by such things as good public relations and effective propaganda, by effective use of media and the assistance of public officials in the sphere state.

2. By a system of effective communication and understanding between the leaders of the countries which underpins their formal and informal discussions. Exchange of visits and periodic conferences would be important ingredients of such a system. (President Kekkonen of Finland and Khrushchev conducted some of their discussions during saunas or hunting trips.)

3. By sincerity in the cultivation of good will and friendly relations through the exercise of restraints or making adjustments and reasonable sacrifices.

4. By kindness, concessions, and rewards to instill good will and gratitude and contribute to the benign image, perhaps to the point of reciprocation.

5. By satisfying needs of the sphere state. The satisfaction of such needs creates dependency that may be difficult to slough off, for the desired satisfaction of economic, technological, military or diplomatic support is a vulnerability offering opportunity to the rich and powerful.

6. By deprivation or some other negative action to induce desired behavior or to signal disapproval.

III. COMPONENTS DERIVED FROM THE POLITICS
OF THE INTERNATIONAL SYSTEM

A. The Setting: General Systemic Factors

The sphere of influence is a multistate unit that may appropriately be designated as a subsystem. It is composed of states that take on certain characteristics and have certain patterns of interaction with the paramount power, with other countries in the sphere, and with countries not part of the sphere. The interaction of paramount powers in spheres of influence situations has a character of its own, and the relationships of a paramount power with states outside of its sphere or with those of another will differ from internal sphere relations.

As a unit in the international system the sphere of influence can at times act more or less as a corporate body; each of these multistate units can make inputs into the system and in turn be affected by the system and the international environment. These actions can be for the purpose of dealing with an "internal" problem as when members of the Warsaw Pact under Soviet leadership dealt with the Czechoslovak situation in August of 1968.

Spheres of influence are symptoms of the basic nature of the international system reflecting the special position and behavior of great states. They also reflect anxieties over insecurity in the international system.

B. Motives and Justification

The motives for spheres of influence stem from basic state interests responding to the nature of the international system, and a primary one has been the protective shell to enhance security. Thus, spheres policies result in the occupation of strategic points, bases, military presence, and the propping up of allied and client states. The possible intrusion of hostile ideologies has brought aggravated anxieties and reinforced the propensity to establish spheres. The watchword "Keep Others Out" is but the other side of the coin with the exhortation, "Go In To Keep Others Out."

Related to the protective shell motive has been the establishment of spheres invoking theories for the maintenance of a world balance of power and regional balances that purport to serve the purpose of security. Such equilibrist conceptions have a direct affinity with geopolitical conceptions, such as the power vacuum and domino theories, which form part of spheres of influence analysis to be dealt with below.

Another political motive involves concern for stability of governments within the sphere: instability is feared because it may invite penetration or intervention by powers who possibly have spheres ambitions. Fear of instability has at times led to a United States policy of support for reactionary regimes, which in turn are loyal to the hegemon. There is thus a mutual reinforcement that stifles reform. The political motive may also be for the purpose of imposing a form of censorship, such as in the case of Finland, which, though independent in practically all respects and not an abject satellite, still must avoid stepping over lines drawn by the paramount power.

The economic motives may be to dominate trade or to exploit the sphere for the advantage of the paramount power. On the other hand, political motives may enlist economic means or may be parallel with economic motives. The main motive may sometimes be difficult to discover, or the motives may be so intermixed that it is difficult to unravel them.

Regions that are near and those that serve for defensive purposes can be more readily justified to the public at home. Such spheres, it may be argued by proponents, are natural, hence justified, thus removing moral qualms and ethical doubts.

C. *Proximity and Distance*

Proximity has been held to endow a sphere with more legitimacy than might otherwise be the case. Besides being more "natural" and supported by public opinion, a sphere that is close can be justified as defensive. If one state has a "legitimate" sphere because of propinquity, why does not another? Proximity itself has not always been sufficient to establish legitimacy and acquire recognition. What seems to count is the respective power position of the states involved, the issue of ideology, and whether the sphere has been successfully established for a relatively long period.

The inhibitions of distance have been so greatly reduced as to raise doubts as to whether distance is any longer an obstacle when technological means are available. The inhibiting factors in Viet Nam were not those of distance. Technology and changes in the international system have ways of outmoding geopolitical hypotheses proposed as universally valid.

It may be asked whether, in view of the swift advance of technology and the growth of such forces as polycentrism, neutralism, and nationalism, there will be less need for spheres and the ability—or even desire—to establish and maintain them. In view of interventions in Czechoslovakia and the Dominican Republic, paramount powers do not yet evince a readiness for change. Paramount powers, however, seem still motivated by concern for who controls population and territory in certain areas, especially those close to home. The probable need to fight by conventional means and the fear that vacuums may be created to tempt others, or of collapse à la the domino theory, help to account for the durability of spheres thinking.

D. *Power Vacuums, Dominos, and Shatterzones*

Power vacuum thinking is intimately bound up with spheres of influence analysis because it serves as a hypothesis on the decline or the intrusion of great powers in particular regions. Power vacuums, like domino thinking, should appropriately be identified as a geopolitical concept because it purports to explain political conditions and processes affecting, and affected by, space.

The great wars and nationalist movements have been the primary causes of power vacuums in the twentieth century. Vacuums reflect transformations occurring in the power configurations of the international system and, like shatterzones, are factors contributing to instability. Apprehensions arise that strategic regions will come into the grasp of rivals, that menacing ideologies will spread, and that regional if not global balances will be upset. The result has been the pursuit of spheres policies to fill the vacuum to prevent others from doing so.

To the extent that vacuum thinking describes the decline and exit of great powers from certain regions, it may be more reliably accurate as an explanation of reality. In the contemporary period, however, there are impediments to new hegemonic powers filling the vacuums, for in the regions where empires formerly held sway are new independent states imbued with the spirit of nationalism. (Even when the new country has a common ideology with, or one similar to, that of a hegemonic state, nationalism may still operate as an impediment.) Yet, under some circumstances—because of needs and weaknesses of regimes in new states—great states may be invited, or find ways to be invited, into a region; and client-state relations may be established as a means of filling the vacuum in some fashion. New countries opting for, and able to maintain, nonalignment have tried to fill their own vacuums.

The domino hypothesis is related to spheres of influence for many of the same reasons vacuum thinking is: the fear that the influence of others will spread to certain areas with the untoward consequences noted above. In response a spheres policy results when a power goes into a country to prevent the initial crucial intrusion or "takeover" by another. The domino hypothesis has also been applied to fear of emulation when a country within a sphere successfully asserts independence or withdraws.

In the United States the domino hypothesis, reflecting Cold War preoccupations, posited a monolithic communist movement with ambitions for expansion and domination through conquest or subversion. It purports to be a basis for predicting the spread of ideology and power and postulates an action and process: if one country in a region "falls," is subverted or "taken over," the adjacent ones will be unable to resist. In the process an "aggressor" will occupy new favorable strategic positions and exploit the advantage of momentum to complete the operation.

Like the vacuum, the domino hypothesis offers insight into the imagery of policy makers, but its validity for accurate description is even more limited than the vacuum. It is abstract, mechanistic, and does not take into account other factors and conditions—either internal or international—that may affect the outcome in each case quite differently. Moreover, in continuing to posit the nature of the communist movement as monolithic it operates on a false assumption.

Vacuum and domino concepts, and, indeed, the necessity for spheres of influence, may reflect the lingering of outdated modes of thinking about security which make security and defense dependent upon control of territory; these concepts may in time become obsolete.

Shatterzone is a relatively little known term among international politics specialists or policy makers. It was coined by some political geographers to describe a type of region in power politics terms. Its usefulness for spheres of influence analysis called for its inclusion in this framework.

The best definition has been supplied by Saul B. Cohen: "A large, strategically located region that is occupied by a number of conflicting states and is caught between the conflicting interests of adjoining great powers."[6] A shatterzone resembles a vacuum in that it is not within the orbit of a great power, and, like the vacuum, it attracts countries seeking to establish influence. A distinguishing feature of the shatterzone is the effect that the intrusion of more than one great power has. Some states in the region attempt nonalignment while others invite the influence of one of the powers; the great powers may contest for influence, and states in the zone may shift from one power to another. Instabilities result from enmity and conflict within countries or among countries in the area; this inhibits cooperation and offers opportunity for the establishment of influence. As tension and trouble areas, shatterzones are a threat to peace, for rivalry may result in hostilities between great powers attracted to the area, or they may be pulled into local quarrels by client states or allies and thus internationalize the conflict.

E. *Great Power Rivalry, Conflict, and Accommodation*

1. *The Roots of Rivalry and Conflict.* Rivalry and conflict have often resulted from competing interests in vacuums and shatterzones and the fear of domino action. An unacceptable expansion may result in war, and an intrusion into an established sphere is viewed as a threat to a vital interest and may result in conflict of crisis proportions. When one power acts to prevent or contest the establishment of a sphere by another, conflict results. Rivalry to exploit a region economically or attract ideological support may likewise cause conflict. Conflicts may result from encroachments into areas beyond those prescribed in spheres of influence agreements. Conflict may also take the form of assistance in a civil war, the outcome of which can affect spheres of influence expansion or contraction. Rivalry and conflict may stem from assertions

---

6. Saul Bernard Cohen, *Geography and Politics in a World Divided* (New York: Random House, 1963), p. 83.

of a rising great power in a region such as Japan before World War II and China after; the United States and Soviet conflicts with China have been aggravated by ideological antagonism.

2. *Bases of Accommodation and Spheres of Influence Agreements.* Spheres of influence have been an expedient in avoiding conflict on either a temporary or long-term basis. The basic principle is simple: there are better reasons to share than to fight for the whole. Also, wider or more weighty considerations might dictate need for a settlement on one front. Like other agreements, formal or tacit, they go through the processes of negotiation, implementation, interpretation, revision, or termination; and the accommodation, if it is to last, requires a more or less continuous process of diplomacy as problems and changes arise.

Accommodation between powers who are involved in a vacuum or shatterzone can take the form of consultation and cooperation to render a degree of stability and lessen the possibility of confrontation. In another context accommodation between paramount powers may take the form of neutralization or disengagement providing for partial or complete withdrawal. Then again, accommodation may be a factor in recognition of spheres, a topic dealt with below.

3. *Recognition of Spheres of Influence.* The basic purpose of legal recognition or less formal political acknowledgement has been to verify and strengthen claims, to commit others to acknowledgement of the position, to restrain states in the sphere from expectation of help from others, and to provide justification for interventions by the hegemon. If these purposes have been fulfilled, the prized status of legitimization has been secured, and *pari passu,* apprehensions of threat and conflict have been diminished.

Recognition does not mean complete abnegation in relations with countries within a sphere. Levels of trade or cultural interaction may be tolerable to the hegemon, but political relationships may not be permitted. Yet, a country in a sphere attempting to follow an independent policy may seek increased relations with nonsphere countries, and this places strains upon the level of tolerance of paramount countries. What may be done varies with the case and decision makers, but interventions have been frequent.

Proposals to ease great power rivalries in the postwar era by delimitation and recognition of spheres of influence have recurringly been offered. These have been accepted in some cases, for the United States seems to have given tacit recognition to the Soviet sphere in Eastern Europe by its refusal to assist the Hungarian regime in 1956 or the Czech regime in 1968. For their part, the Soviets backed down in the Cuban missile crisis in 1962. Spheres delimitation proposals have three sides: 1) the easing of great power rivalry and imparting stability in a region; 2) the fate of states in the sphere is sealed, regardless of their wishes; and 3) the belief that justice is somehow rendered to the hegemonic state which is entitled to its own sphere, especially if other great powers claim spheres for themselves.

The following questions should, however, be raised in analysis of such proposals: Are these not quasi-imperialistic moves counter to the prevailing moods of nationalism and anti-imperialism, and bound to cause trouble? What relations across sphere lines will be permitted? Would this not be a freezing of an international situation, which might later be challenged as changes occur? Would this not result in the probable freezing of the internal status quo in many countries, which might later be challenged? Could there not be parallel or alternative considerations of proposals to neutralize some countries or regions?

4. *Sealing-off, Integration, and Cohesiveness.* Sealing-off and integration result from efforts to maintain an exclusive sphere, and reflect a hard sphere policy. Integration is accomplished mainly by economic devices to tie the countries within the sphere to the paramount power; ideological, political, and even cultural integration may accompany the economic. Cohesiveness in the sphere is achieved by integrating the countries with each other. These processes may serve to maintain hegemony and to exploit the region. Belief that a too-softened or nonexclusive sphere is less reliable for security and gives temptation to withdrawal helps account for sealing-off and integration.

F. Great State-Small State Relationships

As a subsystem, a sphere of influence is a special type of great state-small state relationship, and understanding of great state-small state relations generally should be drawn upon for spheres analysis. Spheres include, for the most part, small or middle-range states, but the designation here will be to "small states."

1. *International Law and Organization.* Spheres of influence and

international law seem to interact to create a vicious circle affecting adversely the position of small states under international law and in spheres of influence. Such interaction may start from either point, but the weakness of international law contributes to the successful assertion of spheres of influence, while the domination of states in a sphere, in turn, weakens international law.

When needed, international law has served the purposes of paramount powers as they extracted or enticed from small states in their sphere unequal and exploitative treaties that bind succeeding governments and endow the paramount power with rights under international law. Yet international law may on occasion be a sword that cuts both ways, for countries within a sphere have at least nominal rights under international law, and under favorable conditions may assert various degrees of independence; e.g., Yugoslavia, Cuba, Mexico, Finland, Romania, and others; the absorbed Baltic states have no such rights.

The United Nations has been a more useful instrument for the assertion of small state interests generally, but it has given little more than verbal comfort to small states within a sphere who were the victims of aggression, intervention, interference, or brutal pressure by a paramount power. While it may be possible to use regional organization, such as the OAS or the Warsaw Pact (which include both the paramount power and smaller countries in the sphere), to advance small state interests and to prevent excesses by the hegemon, they have more often been bent to the wishes of the paramount power to facilitate or legitimize its actions; if expedient, the paramount power may even ignore the regional organization. An organization such as ECLA, however, is constituted to avoid the domination of the paramount power and reflects Latin American interests and conceptions.

2. *Economic Relationships.* Disparity in economic power between great states and small states is among the harsh realities of international life; and paramount powers may use such techniques of control as economic pressure, threats, intimidation, or rewards and enticements. Success varies with the vulnerability and alternatives open to small states and with the question of whether the paramount power utilizes, in addition, political and military power to impose its will.

In addition to the use of economic power as a technique of control, the economic dynamism of the paramount power may be directed toward countries in the sphere as a locus of its economic

activity, with the result that the states may be fastened more securely to the paramount power. This dynamism may be directed, also, to countries outside the sphere, especially developing countries with critical needs, to establish influence or client states.
3. *The Element of Choice.* For some countries there is little element of choice, due to the actual or potential exercise of hegemonic power, especially in a region of propinquity. In other cases there are different degrees of free choice based on alliance relations with the paramount power. In still other instances a regime may seek or be satisfied with inclusion in the sphere because it gains needed support and other benefits.

In the interwar period Romania and Poland tried to avoid the necessity of choosing between Germany and Russia, both of whom aspired to influence in the region. This was described as the policy of "balance" or equilibrium, but it failed in the face of Nazi-Soviet collusion.

Nonalignment also aspires to avoid a choice between contending powers, and has had greater success when the geographic factors have been favorable and, with the lesser pressure of needs and vulnerability, the leaders have found it possible to avoid choosing one side. To evade having to choose one side, it has been found better to avoid trade dependency and to accept assistance from both sides, other countries, and international sources.
4. *Nationalism and Independence.* Nationalism as a motivating force for small powers now undermines superpower designs for spheres of influence as surely as it earlier weakened and destroyed empires. Nationalism nurtures a set of interests which are special and, to a great extent, exclusive. It can readily be seen how a wider unity, especially one that serves mainly the interests of a paramount power, cannot have much appeal. This is the more so if that wider unity reduces independence and sacrifices national interests. Thus a softened sphere or one based upon acceptance of leadership by independent countries is more consonant with nationalism.

As the giants contend with the assertive spirit of nationalism in spheres of influence considerations, it is difficult to assess what the outcome may be. The superpowers confront nationalism in their spheres as a waxing force, and their hold my be weakened; but it is well to note that the superpowers have been persistent, their resources are great, and they have exercised power ruthlessly in their spheres and may continue to do so, especially if they perceive spheres as necessary to their security.

5. *The Growth of Informal Access*. The sphere of influence offers opportunity for influence through informal access, which can supplement older techniques of influence on governments. The definition by Andrew M. Scott in a pathbreaking study on this subject is:

> A technique may be said to involve informal access when it provides a way in which the agents or instruments of one country can reach inside the borders of another country, with or without the approval of the government of that country, and achieve access to that population (or parts of it) or process of that country.[7]

Paramount powers are in the best position to practice informal access in relations with small states in their spheres or out of them, and may, under some circumstances, utilize these techniques to penetrate the spheres of others.

G. *Personality and Decision Making*

The personality of decision makers can have greater effect on spheres of influence in periods of change as they direct its course and pace. As one group of policy makers who have formulated a spheres policy passes from the scene (such as Roosevelt, Hull, Welles, and Duggan, who developed the Good Neighbor Policy) their successors may not feel bound to continue it, or they may decide on modifications.

Actions by policy makers depend in part upon a complexity of factors related to personality and hence are difficult to unravel or assess; e.g., temperament, sensitivity, intellectual background, perceptions and preoccupations regarding the interests of the country, and the influence of close advisers. Some personalities may be more given to accept a softened sphere, for they might more readily resist "quick" solutions by intervention and be more willing to rely on the slower methods of diplomacy. Again, the level of tolerance for independence will differ with decision mak-

---

7. Andrew M. Scott, *The Functioning of the International System* (New York: The Macmillan Company, 1967), p. 192.

ers. Some are more fearful and seek the maximization of security through hard sphere policies; others reject counsels of intervention and reinforce concepts of partnership.

Hull and Roosevelt dreaded spheres of influence but later pursued aspects of it themselves and tried to persuade Stalin to be content with a softened sphere in Eastern Europe. Stalin consistently thought of spheres of influence as realistic, and Churchill was given to spheres arrangements in dealing with power realities to protect British interests. Leaders in small countries may also be effective in shaping the sphere policy that affects them. The leadership qualities of Castro and Tito were probably primary, if not crucial, factors in the successful withdrawal of Cuba and Yugoslavia from their respective spheres.

H. Withdrawal

Withdrawal from a region by a paramount state may be involuntary when it is the result of military defeat, decline of imperial power, or nationalistic efforts. Voluntary exit of a paramount power may follow a neutralization agreement, as in the case of Austria. Voluntary withdrawal may be partial or complete when it stems from decisions to contract involvements abroad. Disengagement is another form of voluntary withdrawal which may be partial or complete, but it may be better to distinguish it from contraction because it sometimes involves agreement with other paramount powers and/or countries in the sphere.

Some unilateral withdrawals in the postwar period by countries in the orbits of the superpowers have succeeded. These were made in order to pursue independent policies, institute reforms, or carry on a revolution not possible while in the sphere of a hostile or unsympathetic paramount state; such were the motives of Cuba, Yugoslavia, and others. The success of these withdrawals depends, in large measure, upon a favorable combination of the following conditions: ability to resist the will of the paramount power because alternatives were available to withstand the effect of economic reprisals; strength in the government, including effective leadership and support of the people; willingness to fight; favorable conditions, including geographic ones, for armed resistance; effective resistance to subversion or corruption; the paramount power's fear of unfavorable internal or world consequences if it intervened forcibly; and lower strategic priorities of the paramount state.

Softening of a sphere resembles a partial withdrawal but differs from a complete withdrawal because it is a change in the character of the sphere rather than the exit of members; but softening or partial withdrawal may be the prelude to complete withdrawal. Hence, opposition to partial withdrawal or softening may be based on apprehension that it will lead to complete withdrawal, the policy makers' fear of vacuums, or fear of emulation to start a dreaded domino action.

Withdrawal raises the question of displacement, and it may mean that a country like Cuba finds it necessary and advantageous to enter the orbit of another paramount power. Yugoslavia, on the other hand, has pursued a policy of nonalignment and has maintained and strengthened its independence.

IV. Typologies and Changes

A. The Hard Sphere

In this model the paramount power reduces the independence of sphere states to the condition of abject satellites or protectorates with one-sided concern for the interests of the superior power. It is an exclusive sphere, considerably sealed off from the intrusion of what may be regarded as undesirable influences inimical to the purposes of the hegemonic state. Thus isolated, it can more effectively be exploited for economic purposes and integrated into the political, defensive, and ideological system of the paramount power. Hard sphere policies are often based on aims to achieve maximum security, and such spheres are usually located in regions regarded as most sensitive to security interests. In hard spheres the hegemonic power is more often prone to open and direct intervention—including forcible intervention or the threat of it—and this may be one of its chief characteristics. Gentler modes of securing compliance such as pressure, "leverage" of various kinds, or intimidation may, however, suffice; but there is little doubt that more direct and stringent measures will be applied if needed. Decision makers following hard sphere policies guard against concessions leading to liberalization and softening which reduce the hold of the paramount power and result in increased independence for the sphere country. In sum, the paramount power has so succeeded in directing the substance and processes of political—and probably economic—life in the sphere state as to impose a crippling degree of dependence and seeming permanence of it.

B. *The Soft Sphere*

The soft sphere is more complex, and its delineation will help in comprehending the hard sphere.

Soft sphere countries experience a greater extent of independence, with sovereignty becoming more real than nominal. This independence is usually manifested by the fact that they have economic and political systems of their own choosing. Their political processes function freely without the threat of interference or dictation, but the paramount power continues to claim a stake in the area and exercises a constant concern for what is done or not done. To this end it devises a system of influence which is indirect and whose effects have due regard for the sovereignty of the sphere country.

An alliance or bloc, such as NATO, uniting independent countries, may take on some of the essential characteristics of a soft sphere because of the acknowledged special position of leadership of the foremost member buttressed by the influence it wields because of the military and economic dependency of the allies. This was more the case in the NATO alliance up to 1955. An hegemonic alliance like the Warsaw Pact, however, integrating a paramount power and its satellites, is both a means to and an evidence of a hard sphere. The soft species may also result, as in the case of Finland, because the exigencies of the situation indicated it to be the most expedient model. A soft sphere may be instituted where strategic-defense concerns are important, even though the region is not greatly exposed to danger. A moderate degree of influence may, therefore, be sufficient for the purposes of the paramount power. In general, lessened international tensions contribute to instituting and maintaining soft sphere policies.

If the aims of the paramount power are primarily economic, (especially the control of trade, which can be achieved with a minimum of political domination), the soft sphere may be established. It should be noted, however, that stress on economic aims does not invariably lead to the soft sphere, for a paramount power may find that its economic objectives can more effectively be attained by hard sphere policies. Then, too, economic exploitation may be only one in a complex of motives behind hard sphere domination, as seemed to be the purpose of Stalin in the Eastern European satellites.

A soft sphere may be rooted in the probability of hostility to, and resentment for, a hard sphere combined with the capability for resistance by the sphere state; maintaining a hard sphere under these circumstances would be costly and vexatious. The soft sphere may be opted for to avoid international complications and undesired responses from other countries, especially those located near by. Paramount power decision makers may take the soft alternative if they are convinced that the system will function satisfactorily; if they are not, they may feel constrained to institute hard policies in some degree. Finally, the soft species can serve as a public relations "showpiece," advertising good will and enlightened international behavior.

Soft spheres are instituted for combinations of the foregoing purposes, with one or more of them forming the primary basis. The main and secondary bases will undoubtedly vary in each case, and it would take research in several case studies to make comparisons denoting the usual primary bases and the usual secondary ones.

In a "pure" exemplification of the soft sphere, expressed in the ideals, but not always the practice, of the Good Neighbor Policy, the paramount power not only renounces intervention, interference, dictation, intimidation, and compulsion in the unilateral pursuit of its hegemonic interests, but proclaims a new day of good will, common interests, and respect for sovereignty and rights. Sphere countries must be persuaded that the conditions are genuine and enduring, while the paramount power needs assurance that its interests, now more broadly conceived, will continue to be served. In contemporary times, as a response to nationalistic sensibilities, a concept of partnership stressing amity, equality, and cooperation characterizes the soft sphere, but despite this there is always an underlying awareness on both sides of who the senior partner is; as noted above, this could undermine the system. A soft sphere is genuine if there is truly a substantive change which endures, and this is more likely to occur when a new set of relationships have been established which condition new perceptions, instill expectations, and guide decisions. The underlying principles are thus *reciprocal advantages, respect for sovereignty,* and a *"mystique"* which unites the paramount power and sphere state in common purpose and ideals. Sceptics, in a *Realpolitik* vein, will be prone to question if hegemonic great powers will long abandon the unilateral pursuit of interests, claiming the soft sphere to be merely an expedient change in form, and consider that the silk glove will be removed at the appropriate moment to reveal the mailed fist.

In reply to such claims it should be pointed out that they really describe what intrinsically differs little from a hard sphere, but has taken on some elements, and the appearance, of the soft. As will be set forth below, the two models here described are abstract constructs and may only exist in approximation in the real world, where complexity has spawned variations in a whole range of permutations combining elements of the two. For a number of reasons, a hard sphere may have had grafted upon it some soft model characteristics, possibly in response to pressure for concessions to reform. This facade type of soft sphere can readily be identified and behavior patterns more easily predicted, for it is to all intents and purposes the same old hard sphere. It is more difficult to identify and predict in the case of a hybrid with substantial hard and soft characteristics, for behavior patterns in such are mixed, going one way or the other depending upon several variables. Also, as hybrids, the soft qualities can temper the hard qualities so that when the latter are manifested they will not have the same effect as in a hard sphere, and vice versa. It could be, however, that old hard sphere ways are too deeply ingrained; and under some circumstances such as international crises, or pressure from a group at home or faction within the decision-making group, the hard policy wins out. Sceptics who dismiss the soft sphere probably base their judgement on observation of behavior in such a hybrid, but by the same token a favorable combination of variables could account for decisions consonant with the soft model.

In still another possibility, a sphere with predominantly soft characteristics could revert to a hard sphere by decisions of the paramount power. Here the sceptical critics are on stronger ground if the reversion is drastic and frequent or permanent; but if the reversion results in only temporary dysfunction through lapses which are not too frequent or drastic, then the essential soft quality of the sphere is preserved. Critics could contend, however, that any lapses prove that the system would be abandoned when it is expedient to do so. This is a good point, but it is here submitted that it should be balanced by another: that distinctions are necessary to denote the nature and frequency of the lapses to determine the *relative* quality of hardness or softness in a sphere over a long period of time.

In relation to the propensity for variations and degrees in spheres of influence affecting the soft sphere, we should account for an inherent dilemma—perhaps flaw—in the soft sphere arising from disparities, often very great, in the political, economic, and military capabilities existing between hegemonic and sphere countries. The dilemma arises from the question of whether relations of reciprocity and equality can be sustained between entities which are not equal in power. Under certain conditions these inequalities may operate to induce subtle or not so subtle undermining of the principles of faithful maintenance of the system, especially when paramount leaders change the rules and invoke the superior capabilities they can call upon. This, again, may be what sceptics have in mind in their doubts about the viability of the system, and surely in some respects this position cannot be gainsaid. It should, on the other hand, be duly acknowledged that the soft sphere system can be, and has been, maintained. In the first place, the relative power of states in international relations is not invariably reflected in their intercourse; indeed, much behavior can be traced to restraint or prudent use of power. In the second place, small states are not always without resources to support their positions, and as indicated above this was one of the factors leading to the establishment of the soft sphere. Accordingly, the following seem most to affect the maintenance of the system: whether enough of the original conditions upon which it was established are still extant; whether new conditions are also conducive to its maintenance; the capability and the determination of sphere state leaders to resist dilutions; the perceptions and temperament of leaders in the respective countries, especially in the paramount power.

The establishment and maintenance of a soft sphere, or for that matter a hard sphere, is, like all decision making, tied to the tenuous and mercurial factor of the personality of decision makers and their advisers in the countries involved. To begin with, it takes the requisite set of perceptions and temperaments on both sides to entertain the notion that a soft sphere is one they can live with—possibly even like—and the one which can be made to function satisfactorily. Operationally, it will fare better if decision makers with tact, restraint, and patience are in authority in the countries | involved and maintain between one another a continuous and effective system of communication. A soft sphere should be founded on two-way trust and confidence, but these are relative concepts and their implementation will vary with the personality and perceptions of those in power. In conclusion, it can readily be seen how this factor affects the preservation or undermining of the system. The topic of changes, already alluded to in other contexts, is thus brought into the picture.

C. *Changes*

Changes in the paramount power which may lead to softening are: diminished apprehension over security, receptive new leadership, prodding or support by public opinion at home, domestic political changes favorable to the softening, or restraints induced by the configurations of international politics. Policy makers may turn to the soft model with the realization that hard sphere intervention and interference lead to pitfalls, pains, high costs, internal division, and disappointing results. Restiveness and assertiveness of leaders and people in sphere countries can lead to unilateral softening or induce the paramount power to adopt a softer policy. Internal sources of strength and stability contribute to a sphere country's capability to resist the imposition of a hard sphere and make possible the assertion of independence it enjoys in the soft one. Unilateral softening, however, triggers responses in the paramount power's level of tolerance for such changes. These responses will differ in each case according to the set of variables present, but the list here will supply some indications: 1) the degree of apprehension over strategic considerations, 2) whether ideological or economic conditions should be preserved, 3) concern for the effect in foreign countries, especially certain ones, 4) concern for the effect in other sphere states of the orbit, and 5) the sphere state's ability to resist the imposition of a hard sphere.

A reversion to hard sphere policies causes disillusionment and undermines the soft system, but a prompt return need not cause permanent damage; frequently recurring or prolonged lapses into hard sphere patterns would probably destroy the system. If, however, soft sphere relationships have been so firmly rooted as to condition the perceptions, instill expectations, and guide decisions, it will probably be a system which survives for a reasonably long time. Like any basic set of relationships between nations, the soft sphere is subject to constant need for affirmation and adjustment in response to changed conditions and new problems, as well as new leadership coming to the fore in the respective countries. There can be the retrogression of stagnation or erosion, or the forward movement of new vigor or new directions inspired by the original spirit.

In the softening process the country, or it may be an entire region, is exposed to an increase in outside relationships, thus reducing the isolating effects of exclusiveness, sealing-off, and integration with the paramount power found in the hard sphere. Yet, having accomplished this, the soft sphere can be the basis for more intimate and extensive relations, as in the Good Neighbor Policy.

Policy makers instituting changes inclining toward the soft sphere would find it difficult and embarrassing later to revert to a hard sphere, for the effect of momentum requires extra effort to reverse the direction. In such a situation, interactions between the sphere state and the paramount power flow through newly established channels, becoming deeply grooved with usage. A new set of policy makers in the paramount power may not feel so committed to a soft sphere policy established by predecessors. Neglect and uninterest may ensue, even to the point of hostility to it. In such a situation, sphere state leaders may wish to exert efforts to stimulate the interest and support of those responsible for policy in the paramount power. It is hard to imagine that a cynical establishment of a soft sphere for the deliberate purpose of a facade will often occur. It is easier to consider a soft sphere or soft sphere policies as instituted in good faith and then violated in the face of "crises" or "emergencies" as perceived, or feigned, by hegemonic decision makers. Finally, it is possible to conceive of a soft sphere so undermined or violated by changes that it is transformed into a hybrid with characteristics of both hard and soft models, or one that has become for the most part a hard sphere; the same process could work to transform a hard sphere into a hybrid or a soft sphere.

D. *Combinations and Degrees*

Combinations and degrees in the analysis of the soft sphere as well as the hard sphere have been alluded to and used as illustrations in all parts of this book, but here the basic processes will be succinctly stated. Human affairs are rarely so ordered as to offer precisely contrasting options; instead, however, they usually reflect an amalgam of relativity in combination and degree. The hard and soft models sketched here are "pure" forms and are offered to facilitate analysis, but in order to achieve greater precision in analysis and classification, we should mark off degrees and combinations of hardness and softness as in a continuum, as illustrated by the following diagram:

Incorporation into the hegemonic state*	Hardness	Softness	Evanescence or withdrawal**

●●●●●●●●●●●●●●●●●●━━━━━━ - - - - - - - - ━━━━━━●●●●●●●●●●●●●●●●

Hybrids

Combinations and Degrees in Spheres of Influence

---

*For example the Baltic States of Latvia, Lithuania and Esthonia were incorporated into the Soviet Union during World War II.

**Yugoslavia withdrew from the Soviet sphere in Eastern Europe in 1948.

With the range of diversity in this complex world, it is possible that for some rare periods of time there will be some fairly "pure" examples of each model. It seems safe to say that a sphere does not remain static but moves, if only by short incremental steps, to one end or the other of the continuum. Finally, we have diversity in spheres of influence in the sense of a large sphere, like Latin America or Eastern Europe, with many countries in a mosaic of various hybrids reflecting different purposes of the paramount power and different conditions in the sphere countries.

E. *The Model of Private Economic Influence*

In addition to aspects of state policy, a fuller understanding of spheres of influence requires analysis of private economic power and of the entities that wield it. In some countries such influence is a major, if not the dominant, fact of national life.

The concepts of vacuum, proximity, facility, opportunity, and perceived need can also serve in the analysis of the flow of private economic power. The flow may be influenced by the needs of the paramount country or the country within the sphere and the area's attractiveness for economic activity; opportunity and facility may also be provided by favorable political conditions.

Private economic influence extends to developed and developing countries alike, but there is greater opportunity to dominate the economic life of a country and exert political influence when the government is weak or internal elites benefit. Vulnerability and needs of countries make it difficult to resist the growth of this power. The home government may be subject to pressure by private economic interests to institute favorable policies and, if need be, to exert political pressure or intervention.

V. Implementing the Framework for Research

The framework can serve to guide research on topics that deal primarily with spheres of influence or for other topics which include spheres as an aspect. In either case the first step in the procedure should be the same: analysis of the topic to determine how the framework can be applied.

The framework as a whole and each of the components and major subunits is a system for collecting, classifying, interpreting, and relating data. Several concepts, the hard and soft models particularly, make it possible also to test data for conformity or deviation from patterns and to establish continuums to chart trends or changes indicated by the data. At appropriate stages in the research the framework can be used to identify problems and issues or to develop hypotheses.

Topics for research derived from the framework may be based on the components or major subunits; each of these is a suitable topic for research as well as an element in the analytic scheme. Beyond this, scores of topics may be found in aspects of one or more of these, and several fruitful comparative studies might be made.

Aside from published and scholarly works, additional sources may be drawn upon for spheres of influence research. First, unpublished data of many kinds by governments, individuals, or other private or public groups; and second, the facts, opinions, perceptions, and analyses of individuals who participate in or observe policy making and those whose business it is to keep informed of this. Utility of these sources depends upon accessibility; they can to some extent be taped interviews, consultations, correspondence, and possibly questionnaires. In yet another sense, game theory and simulation projects, since they are techniques of research, can supply another dimension of data and testing of data and theory.

The development of a framework for analysis is a means of dealing with problems in spheres of influence research, but others remain. Probably the foremost of these are information gaps, because of the sensitive, security nature of the data concerning Soviet and American spheres policies since the end of World War II. A related obstacle is the reluctance of public officials in paramount powers to avow spheres of influence and spheres considerations in policies, so the matter is treated obliquely or the record is obfuscated by generalities and rhetoric. Moreover, policy makers and their advisers acting in terms of regional balances, power vacuum and domino theories, or the supposed menace of ideologies in certain areas, do not usually choose to identify these with a spheres of influence context.

The framework has not eliminated many problems arising from the scope of the subject, for it would be impossible for one researcher to have the linguistic skills and expertise in specialties to research a great number of topics thoroughly. A solution, when practicable, would be to set up group projects.

The task of research would be assisted by the inclusion of spheres of influence implications in the body of theory and scholarly output developing in many parts of the international field and in the related disciplines of history, economics, and political geography.

Several aspects of the framework are basically concepts of

degree and thus readily susceptible to measurement; for example, hard and soft sphere models, sealing-off and integration, and indicators of nationalism. Many kinds of relationships and behavior can also be measured, such as votes of a client state in the United Nations or other international body and the extent and significance of trade or investment of a paramount power in a client state as indicators of economic dependence.

This framework, besides providing a scheme for analysis and guidelines for research, indicates a palpable *need* for research in an important dimension of international politics. The researcher in spheres of influence has an unsurveyed forest to explore into which some faint pathways have been trod by a few pioneers and by others on their way to different destinations. The utility of this framework as a compass is thus apt; but perhaps, too, it may be a lantern to attract others to this neglected but significant study.

Organization and Methodology of This Case Study

The Finnish soft sphere from 1948 to 1958 had evolved into a *system* in the sense of a set of principles to define the nature of obligations and the degree of independence for Finland on the one hand and a pattern of devices for exertion of influence by the Soviet Union on the other. The degree of independence and direction of internal affairs was of such an extent as to characterize Finland definitely as a soft sphere. During this period the system was stabilized as both countries understood and accepted the rules and the limits, reflected in rather definite mutual expectations.

The framework for analysis of spheres of influence generally, and the soft sphere concept particularly, are employed to supply description and analysis of this case study according to the following categories:

1. The origin, development and functioning of the system as it took definite form (Chapters 1-4).
2. The onset of dysfunction; its causes and effects upon the system. Cause of dysfunction removed and restoration of the system (Chapters 5-7).
3. In recent years the effect upon the system of the collapse of the EFTA, the enlargement of the EEC, and Finnish activist neutrality (Chapter 8).

4. The system framed in the broader context of geographic, cultural, and political affinities of Finland in the Scandinavian region (Chapter 9).
5. An examination of the applicability of the Finnish model to Western Europe as proposed in the concept of "Finlandization" (Chapter 10).

CHAPTER ONE

STALIN TRIES ON THE SILK GLOVE

As a prelude to the portrayal of Finno-Soviet relations from 1917 to the end of World War II in terms of spheres of influence, it may be well to depict the abiding significance of these century-long implications by a few broad strokes. Detached from Sweden and annexed by Alexander I, Finland was a pawn in one of the interesting by-plays of great power accommodation of the Napoleonic period. For three generations as the autonomous Duchy of Finland she savored a goodly measure of independence and nationalistic awakening, bearing many resemblances to what has here been described as the soft sphere. This benign species of imperial Russian rule gave way in the late nineteenth century to stringent policies akin to the hard sphere, imposed by the myopic and frightened last tsars and their ministers. Finally, in the wake of the disintegration of the Russian empire and independence for Finland, the country was convulsed by a civil war between "Reds" and "Whites" which would resolve whether there were to be bonds with (and concomitantly influence of, if not possible absorption into) the new Soviet state.[1]

---

1. For a detailed historical treatment of the period sketched above, see Eino Jutikkala with Kauko Pirinen, *A History of Finland,* translated by Paul Sjöblom (London: Thames and Hudson, 1962). See especially Chapter 7, "Finland Becomes An Autonomous State," Chapter 8, "National Awakening in the Shadow of Autonomy," and Chapter 9, "Autonomy Lost and Independence Gained."

The Decision of World War II

In geopolitical perspective, during the aftermath of the first World War in the Baltic region, like the rest of Eastern Europe and the Balkans, conditions favored the assertion of independence and the avoidance of hegemonic domination because of defeats suffered by Austria, Germany, and Russia. The resulting power vacuum was filled by the countries themselves, but French military, political and economic influence was accepted, creating a rather soft sphere in central Europe and the Balkans by the Little Entente. Finland chose to pin her hopes for the maintenance of her newly won independence on a policy of neutrality.

The favorable geopolitical climate lasted until the middle-late 1930's with the revival of German power and its projection into Eastern Europe. As a consequence of the recovery of Russian strength after a decade of Stalinist rule, this country again became interested in developments in Eastern Europe and was prepared to assert her power to deal with the problem of security posed by renascent Germany. In such a situation the prospects for successful preservation of neutrality is dependent upon guarantees given in good faith by both great powers bordering on the region; guarantees by others more distant may not be as valuable.

Eastern Europe and the Baltic in the late 1930's became a "shatterzone"[2] where the ambitions and apprehensions of Britain and France were added to those of the Soviet Union and Germany as the region was transformed into one of rising tensions with a precarious hold on independence for countries in the area.

The Soviet response was in terms of spheres of influence: to expand her position in the region to strengthen her protective shell. Following the Anschluss of Austria, she sought arrangements with border states by which "the Red Army would not have to wait on the border for the enemy, but would advance as far as possible to meet him."[3] Negotiating with the British and French in the summer of 1939, the Russians pressed for approval of such arrangements, but were frustrated by rejection of them by the

---

2. See Saul Bernard Cohen, *Geography and Politics in a World Divided,* p. 83.

3. Max Jakobson, *The Diplomacy of the Winter War, an Account of the Russo-Finnish War, 1939–1940* (Cambridge: Harvard University Press, 1961), p. 10.

border states. Later, however, as the discussions progressed the British and French negotiators felt constrained to accede to the Russian position in principle, and thereby acknowledged tacitly a Soviet Monroe Doctrine in the Baltic.[4] It was the Nazi-Soviet pact, however, that handed to Russia its most tangible claim to a Monroe Doctrine in the Baltic, for instead of contesting for influence in the region, the Nazis and Russians agreed to divide it; Hitler had outbid the British and French, and Finland was consigned to the Soviet sphere. As would be expected in *Realpolitik* bargains of this sort, she was given no choice in the matter, nor was she informed of the agreement.[5]

In the wake of gains under the Nazi-Soviet pact Soviet leaders renewed their approaches to Finland but now sought a rectification of frontiers and a naval base to command the Gulf of Finland. Finnish policy in the negotiations, however, was conditioned by fear of unlimited Soviet desires and by reluctance to abandon neutrality. The negotiations thus came to an impasse. Counsels for concession and compromise among the Finns based on an estimate of limited Soviet desires for essentially defensive objectives were rejected because of residual suspicion of the eastern neighbor and the unpopularity of such a move.

Stalin abruptly chose to settle the matter by force and invaded Finland in November, 1939. We do not know whether he expected an easy victory, but he was undoubtedly dismayed by the heavy Soviet losses and stubborn Finnish resistance. Despite an

---

4. *Ibid.*, pp. 57–93, and pp. 197–198. See also G. A. Gripenberg, *Finland and the Great Powers, Memoirs of a Diplomat.* Translated from the Swedish with an introduction by Albin T. Anderson. (Lincoln: University of Nebraska Press, 1965), Chapter I, "The Last Effort" for a discussion of the interest of Finland in the Anglo-French-Russian negotiations in the summer of 1939. See also William (Lord) Strang, *Home and Abroad* (London: Andre Deutsch, 1956), p. 177, wherein he recounts how Britain and France conceded to the Soviet government a willingness to give them "the right to decide whether any aggression against a Baltic state constituted a threat to the independence or neutrality of that state, such that the Soviet government felt obliged to defend the victim of aggression by engaging in hostilities against the aggressor. Once engaged in such hostilities the Soviet government would be entitled to assistance from France and Great Britain."

5. Raymond J. Sontag and James S. Beddie, editors, *Nazi-Soviet Relations 1939–1941; Documents from the Archives of the German Foreign Office* (Washington: Department of State, 1948). See also Gerhard L. Weinberg, *Germany and the Soviet Union, 1939–1941* (Leiden: E. J. Brill, 1954).

heroic stand, the Finns were in time overwhelmed by the superior resources of their adversary and had to accept a treaty of peace on March 12, 1940, which tendered the objectives Moscow had sought by negotiation, although now somewhat amplified. Finland was a defeated but not a conquered, subjugated, or occupied country.[6] Hitler pursued a "correct" policy, observing the obligations of the Nazi-Soviet pact by refusing assistance of any kind to the Finns.

According to the terms of the Treaty of Moscow, Finland ceded the territory and provided the bases desired, but was unwilling to go all the way and accept a Soviet sphere of influence. One seriously considered alternative to Soviet hegemony was a pact with Sweden, but the Swedes were loath to abandon neutrality. As German plans for attack on Russia matured, Finnish policy makers were drawn into common cause with Hitler, which seemed the logical choice in view of the sting of defeat by the Soviets and resistance to their influence, the failure of an association with the Swedes, and seeming good prospects for German success.[7]

Finland extricated herself from the war with the USSR in September 1944 and again avoided conquest and occupation, but in the armistice she signed were added heavy reparations to the ceded territory and bases of 1940; moreover, an Allied Armistice Commission, dominated by the Soviets, was installed in Finland

---

6. On the diplomacy of the Winter War see especially Jakobson, *Diplomacy of the Winter War,* and C. Leonard Lundin, *Finland and the Second World War* (Bloomington: University of Indiana Press, 1957) for secondary accounts. See also J. K. Paasikivi, *Toimintani Moskovassa ja Suomessa 1939–1940,* Vols. I and II (Porvoo and Helsinki: Werner Söderström, 1958); Gripenberg, *Finland and the Great Powers*; Väinö Tanner, *The Winter War* (Stanford: Stanford University Press, 1957); Ministry of Foreign Affairs of Finland, *The Development of Finnish-Soviet Relations during the Autumn of 1939 Including the Official Documents* (London: George G. Harrap and Co. Ltd., 1940).

7. The period between the Winter War and the Continuation War is treated in detail in Anthony F. Upton, *Finland in Crisis 1940–1941* (Ithaca, New York: Cornell University Press, 1965). See also Finland, Ulkoasiainministerio, *Finland Reveals Her Secret Documents on Soviet Policy March 1940–June 1941. The Attitude of the USSR to Finland after the Peace of Moscow,* with a preface by Hjalmar J. Procope, Minister of Finland to the U.S. (New York: Wilfred Funk, Inc., 1941), and Lundin, *Finland and the Second World War.*

until the treaty of peace was put into effect almost three years later.

The USSR could now fill the vacuum in the Baltic; and while the United States and Britain could challenge it, their resources for a successful challenge were lacking. The Western allies were disposed to approve Soviet insistence on "friendly" border state governments in acknowledgement of their right to provide for security interests in this vital region; but these countries, according to Washington and London, were to be permitted the right of internal self-government—thus we have the main ingredients of the soft sphere.

At Yalta, American negotiators tried to convince Soviet leaders to establish a soft sphere and had reason to believe that some of the Crimea agreements would help to assure it.[8] Under the circumstances Finland concluded that she had no choice but to accommodate herself to inclusion in the Soviet sphere of influence, but indulged the hope that it would be a soft sphere. Other eastern Europeans indulged the same hope but only Finland survived, although Yugoslavia successfully withdrew from the orbit.

Rationale for the Soviet Sphere Policy

Analysis of the Finnish case as it took form in the wake of the decision of World War II should at this juncture probe the answers to two questions, the first of which is: *Why did the Soviet Union want Finland in its sphere of influence?*

The paramount reason for the Soviet desire to include Finland in her sphere of influence was for security-defense purposes. Such Soviet interest in Finland had the historical precedent of serving mainly as a protective buffer. A buffer zone may be neutralized, dominated (as in a sphere of influence) or annexed. Soviet strategists apparently invoked in the case of Finland the same perceptions of threat and defensive strategy as their tsarist

---

8. See John P. Vloyantes, "The Significance of Pre-Yalta Policies toward Liberated Countries in Europe," *The Western Political Quarterly* (June 1958) pp. 209–228, for further reference to American efforts for a soft sphere in Eastern Europe during the Yalta conference.

predecessors.[9] Under these circumstances postwar Soviet political leaders, as well as military experts, considered the projection
of influence into neighboring Finland not only as a *necessity* but as
natural: natural because it was proximate, natural because it was
required, natural because the Soviet Union was a great power,
natural because it had the sanction of history.[10] Specifically, defensive purpose was rooted in the protection of Leningrad, the
second city of the USSR, for if the frontier in the northwest were
to come into hostile hands Leningrad would be gravely
threatened; its loss would be like inflicting a critical wound because of the additional factor of popular morale. Leningrad's
protection was the motive for rectification of the frontier in the
Karelian Isthmus and acquisition of a Russian base at Porkkala,
both terms of the treaty of peace after World War II. Soviet bases
on the Esthonian side of the Gulf of Finland completed defense
preparations.

Reflection on the experience of the interwar years undoubtedly contributed to Soviet determination to achieve security
primarily by dependence upon her own resources and policies,
one of which was spheres of influence. In the first years of this
period Russia was a weakened and partially dismembered state
convulsed by a civil war exacerbated by foreign intervention.
Russian influence declined, collective security and the League of
Nations could not be relied upon, and appeasement was winning
the day in Britain and France—which in Soviet eyes was a
device to steer the Axis to a collision with the Soviet Union.
Eastern European countries were not cooperative and harbored
fear and suspicion, if not hostility, to Russia; their free-handed
neutrality could not be depended upon, especially if a potential
enemy like Germany could bend them to her purposes by coercion or blandishment. All this had been especially true of Finland
during this period, and Soviet leaders had not forgotten it.

Moscow's decision to include Finland in her sphere of influ-

---

9. See Kalevi J. Holsti, "Strategy and Techniques of Influence in Soviet-
Finnish Relations," *The Western Political Quarterly* (March 1964) pp. 64–68,
wherein he stresses the defensive interest of the Soviet Union in Finland and
continuity of tsarist perceptions of defensive strategy.

10. The United States has also found it natural for the same reasons to project
its influence into the neighboring Caribbean region.

ence, as in the case of other countries who were also included, was to prevent all of them from drifting as though free agents. In the case of Finland she would probably again opt for an unencumbered neutrality and veer toward the Scandinavian countries, Western Europe, Britain, and probably even the United States. The Soviets could find little prospect of Finland's turning to the East. Traditional Soviet suspiciousness of certain forms of Scandinavian cooperation was combined with Soviet distrust of a too independent Finland, which would be fostered by these Scandinavian ties. Inclusion in the Soviet sphere, on the other hand, would render her pliant and cooperative for Soviet purposes.

In 1944–45 Finland had really no other option if the Soviet Union perceived it was a necessity to enclose the Finns within her sphere of influence. Finland was defeated and weakened, the defeat of Germany excluded a possibility of her being drawn in that direction, a postwar Scandinavian defense system was not in existence (nor was it ever to be established), and the United States and Britain were distant and had already tacitly conceded Russian security interests in the region. If the Soviet Union chose, she could enfold Finland into her sphere of influence; *opportunity* hence settled any doubts on the part of Moscow.

Economic motives were probably weighed in Russia's decision to absorb Finland into her expanding orbit; but they were perhaps of less importance than security considerations, for by the terms of the armistice and the peace treaty she could collect reparations without bringing that country into the sphere. But, in spheres of influence considerations, economic means may be enlisted to support security objectives, and vice versa. If Finland were in the Soviet sphere, economic and trade dependency would bind her more securely and could be a means of mounting pressure or practicing manipulation for desired ends. Scant consideration, if any, of ideological motives seems to have applied in Moscow decision making.

Rationale for Silk Glove Hegemony

The second question to be answered is: *Why did the Soviet decision makers decide upon the soft sphere policy in the case of Finland?*

Until there is available sufficient evidence to make possible more solid historical judgement, we shall have to rely on the fragments available and "circumstantial evidence." Spheres of influence analysis may shed additional light on Soviet motives, helping to discern and assess patterns in the policies adopted. For example, we may logically infer that because the soft sphere was adopted, several of the motives usually leading to the adoption of that model were the ones that applied.

A decision as basic as the one to follow the soft sphere policy in Finland was certainly founded on a combination of mutually reinforcing reasons, the most telling one of which was the fact that security interests could just as well be attained by a soft sphere. Soviet leaders felt assured, especially after 1948, that the soft sphere was workable and that by devices of indirect influence the desired results could be achieved. Exigencies of the war contributed to the decision, for the fact that Finland was not subjugated and occupied made satellization more difficult. The fact that the Finns themselves wisely decided to expel the German troops prevented the Soviet Army from rolling over the country. If Finland had been occupied by the Soviet Army in 1944, she would probably not have become a soft sphere. Stalin would have been presented with an irresistible temptation to satellize the country completely; Soviet foreign policy objectives tend to be determined by existing opportunities. Internal political factors also provided sources of strength to discourage forcible satellization, and Soviet leaders were probably mindful of potential repercussions in Scandinavia if Finland were converted to a hard sphere.

Finland's location is important to Soviet defense because of the country's location at a confluence of the northern extremity of eastern Europe and the eastern extremity of the Baltic-Scandinavian region where lie Leningrad, the Soviet Union's second city, and a great urban-industrial complex. Yet, although Soviet security concerns dominate her interest in Finland, it was assigned a lesser priority than other parts of eastern and central Europe. The first and most telling reason for this is that the northeast became less exposed and vulnerable to invasion by Germany or from Western Europe because of absorption of the Baltic states and the satellization of Poland and East Germany. Secondly, Swedish neutrality reduced danger by providing a buffer to the region. Moreover, Soviet perception of danger had been mitigated by annexation of the Karelian Isthmus and the base at Porkkala, and Germany's power had been diminished by partition and disarmament.

Soviet leaders apparently settled on the soft sphere after an assessment of the situation as it stood between 1944 and 1948, before the North Atlantic Alliance came into being. We may conclude that Soviet decision makers reasoned that although Finland was important to Soviet security, satellization was *not necessary* because sufficient provision could be made for defense with Finland in a soft sphere, especially if it was a credible soft sphere. If the combination of factors were not so favorable and Finland's vulnerability exposed the Soviet Union to greater threat, there might have been less faith in a soft sphere, for a hard sphere policy seems to be adopted when there is priority on the maximization of security.

The turn of events in the crucial last months of the war worked to the advantage of Finland, for her timely withdrawal from the war in September 1944, eight months before the end, and Finnish assumption of responsibility to rid the country of Germans still there led to diversion of Soviet forces to the south. An unoccupied Finland prevented the recurrence of the pattern which in the rest of eastern Europe made it possible to assist local communists and directly assert Soviet power. Persons and groups in Finland were not liquidated under a foreign occupation, and the orderly transition of political power remained in Finnish hands.

As Stalin weighed the decision for a soft sphere, he may well have realized that if he imposed a hard sphere by forcible satellization he would have to put up with a sullen and resistant people who had to be conquered and stay conquered.[11] Unlike the Slavic countries of Eastern Europe, the Finns would not accept Soviet satellization in the guise of panslavism where Soviet troops came as liberators; there was no Finnish anti-German animus to appeal to. Stalin undoubtedly understood that for Sweden a Finnish soft

---

11. Risto Hyvärinen, "The Defense Forces in the Service of Neutrality," *Introduction to Finland, 1963.* Prepared with the cooperation of the Press Bureau of the Finnish Foreign Ministry (Porvoo and Helsinki: Werner Söderström, 1963), p. 64. The large lake and forest region is especially suitable for guerrilla resistance. Söderjhelm in his interview in September 1972 vividly related to the author how Stalin and Molotov during the negotiations of the Treaty of Friendship, Cooperation and Mutual Assistance in Moscow in the spring of 1948 conveyed how they distinguished the Finnish case but wanted to remove any threat from that quarter. They in effect said, "but we don't want any trouble with you; we don't want to fight you; keep nice and clean and strong; don't have any troublesome revanchism and then we can get along."

sphere would serve as a welcome buffer to retain her alliance-free policy, and Sweden's desire to retain her traditional neutrality must certainly have contributed to Moscow's decision in favor of the soft sphere. Thus from the point of view of both Stockholm and Moscow, to say nothing of Helsinki, the soft sphere policy was the best choice. It must be borne in mind that the period under consideration is from September 1944 to April 1948 when the Russo-Finnish Treaty of Friendship, Cooperation and Mutual Assistance was negotiated. Stalin's consideration of adverse Swedish reaction was on general principles.

Later in 1948 and in 1949 there were some sharp Scandinavian responses to the Czechoslovak coup on March 18, 1948, which may have helped to induce Soviet restraint toward Finland. A conference of representatives from Sweden, Norway, and Denmark to discuss a Nordic defense treaty did not convene, however, until October 15, 1948, and the United States Senate did not pass the Vandenberg Resolution in preparation for the North Atlantic Treaty until June 11, 1948, after the Finno-Soviet pact had been signed.[12] These discussions could not, therefore, have been instrumental in inducing Stalin to opt for the soft sphere in March-April 1948 when the pact of 1948 was negotiated and ratified, signaling the dénouement of the soft sphere. To be sure, after April 1948 the possibility of Sweden's joining NATO or forming a Nordic alliance would reinforce Moscow's decision to be moderate toward Finland. By the same token, if Sweden were drawn into the North Atlantic Alliance, the USSR would reconsider its Finnish policy.[13]

Soviet decision makers may also have concluded that it was

---

12. *Facts on File,* 1948, p. 85. On March 18 the premiers of Norway, Denmark and Sweden speaking from the same platform declared that their countries would resist Communist bids for power regardless of domestic or external pressure. *Ibid.,* p. 331: The three countries established a Defense Ministers Committee in Oslo, October 15. *Ibid.,* p. 148: The U.S. Senate passed the Vandenberg Resolution by a vote of 64 to 4. See Chapter 8, "Finland, the Soviet Union and the Scandinavian Subsystem."

13. See Åke Sandler, "Sweden's Postwar Diplomacy: Some Problems, Views and Issues," *The Western Political Quarterly* (December 1960) pp. 924–933; Joseph B. Board, Jr., *The Government and Politics of Sweden* (Boston: Houghton Mifflin Company, 1970), Chapter 8, "Foreign Policy and Defense"; Nils Andrén, *Power Balance and Non-Alignment, A Perspective on Swedish Foreign Policy* (Stockholm: Almquist and Wiksell, 1967), pp. 56–57 and 136–137.

relatively safe to institute the soft sphere because Finland's inclusion in the Soviet orbit was tacitly "recognized" by the United States, Western Europe, and the Scandinavian countries, which "recognition" served to "legitimize" the situation and reduce apprehension that efforts would be made to change the status quo.[14]

As Soviet leaders appraised the internal political situation in Finland, they probably assessed additional sources of strength to support the maintenance of independence and resistance to satellization. In the first place, 75 to 80 per cent of the people belonged to political parties which were independent, well organized, well led, and dedicated to preserving national independence. The Social Democrats and the Agrarians, two of the three major parties, entered into temporary cooperation with the Communist Party and its left wing socialist associates forming the SKDL, which was the third major party.[15] Neither the Social Democrats nor the Agrarians nor the Conservatives and other minor parties comprising about a quarter of the electorate showed any inclination to collaborate with the SKDL on a full-fledged program oriented toward closer integration with the Soviet Union. Resistance to satellization was likewise aided by the strength of Mannerheim and Paasikivi in the period immediately after the armistice.

Related to the character of leadership for internal strength is the factor of convincing reassurance desired by Soviet leaders that Finland would be reliable as a soft sphere; for, as will be borne out, they have invariably insisted that the assurances were only as worthy as the individuals in authority. President Paasikivi and his line should here be described, but this will be dealt with in the context of the terms of the "fulfillment" below.

Lastly, the soft sphere was probably deemed expedient in Moscow because of confidence in devices of indirect influence, to be traced in Chapter 4.

The "Fulfillment"

Stalin's decision to institute the soft sphere probably also took account of the context of suitable preconditions which were terms

---

14. See Introduction on recognition of spheres of influence.
15. See Chapter 3, pp. 68–74, on the formation and composition of the SKDL.

of guarantee that the system would be functional. For Finland it was 1) the price to be paid for defeat in war, and 2) the price to be paid for the moderate treatment of the soft sphere. Under the fulfillment, Finnish-Soviet relations, firstly, would be grounded upon a new "spirit" or "attitude" which would animate Finnish policy; secondly, they would be based upon a "legal" order of substantive changes and commitments fixed by the Armistice of 1944, the Treaty of Peace of 1947, and the Treaty of Friendship, Cooperation, and Mutual Assistance of 1948. The latter will be the subject of the following chapter.

The spirit by itself was necessary, but if a wise and steadfast leader could inspire and articulate it as well as be the guiding hand for its implementation, the precondition would be doubly assured. Such a man was Juho Kusti Paasikivi, the architect of Finland's postwar foreign policy, the keystone of which was a new orientation toward the Soviet Union. Paasikivi enjoyed the unique position of being the Finnish public figure most trusted, in Finland as well as in the Soviet Union, to assume responsibility during the crucial first twelve years after the war.[16] For Paasikivi the fundamental political fact of life was self-evident: that Finland's future independence required simply and unequivocally the correct assessment of the basic geopolitical facts. Soviet Russia, the victorious great power that had defeated Finland, was the immediate neighbor to the east and nothing could alter this. In any contest for the assertion of influence in Finland the USSR

---

16. The study of Paasikivi and the Paasikivi Line provides, more than anything else, insight into the fascinating Finnish case. Söderhjelm, who served with Paasikivi, related in 1972 that he understood the Russians and they understood him; that he was somewhat of an anomaly among Finns with his fluency in Russian and specialization in Russian history and literature. See John H. Hodgson, "The Paasikivi Line," *The American Slavic and East European Review* (April 1959); Kuusisto, "The Paasikivi Line in Finland's Foreign Policy"; Marvin Rintala, Chapter V, "The Politician in Politics: J. K. Paasikivi" in *Four Finns* (Berkeley and Los Angeles: University of California Press, 1969); Axel Von Gandolin, "Der Staatspräsident J. K. Paasikivi und die 'Paasikivi Linie,'" *Politische Studien* (Munich) Vol. 10, No. 116 (December 1959); Reinhold Svento, *Ystäväni Juho Kusti Paasikivi* (Porvoo-Helsinki: Werner Söderström, 1960); J. K. Paasikivi, *Paasikiven Linja, I Puheita Vuosilta, 1944–1956* (Porvoo-Helsinki: Werner Söderström, 1962), and two interviews with Paasikivi by Alfred Joachim Fischer, "The Thoughts of a Statesman," *The Norseman* (January-February 1948) and "A Visit to Juho Paasikivi," *The Norseman* (November-December 1954).

enjoyed decisive advantages: proximate location over the United States and Britain and preponderance of power over Sweden. In living beside a giant, the instinct for preservation required the keenest perception of realism.[17] Paasikivi reasoned that "Russian interest in us is purely strategic,"[18] and he rejected the notion of others that ideological and economic motives were behind a Soviet desire to snuff out Finnish independence. He urged that Soviet leaders should be persuaded that the security of their country would under no circumstances be threatened by Finland. He would cultivate Soviet trust in Finland by strict observance of all agreements and prevent suspicion by carefully avoiding involvement in disagreements among the great powers or exploitation of their divisions and quarrels.

Paasikivi was convinced, moreover, that formal and official political assurances would not be sufficient, for the new policy had to be made credible beyond any doubt to Soviet policy makers. Accordingly, political parties and their leaders had to accept in good faith the new Soviet image. As early as December 6, 1944, in the first postwar independence day observance he declared that:

> ... there are obtainable in the future good and faithful relations with our great neighbor. Distrust must be thrown out, friendship established. It is my conviction that in accordance with the rights of our people, Finnish policy must be led in the future in such a way that it will not move against the Soviet Union. Peace and harmony in addition to neighborly relations of confidence with the great Soviet Union is the first objective of the government.[19]

Paasikivi adamantly insisted that the Finns really had to change old modes of thinking which dwelt not only on irredentist resentments and hatred of the Russians as a "hereditary foe," but also on contempt of them as cultural inferiors. He insisted that criticism of the USSR in the press be muted in order to avoid

---

17. A thought vividly expressed by Dr. Fagerholm in the interview of October 1967.

18. Fischer, "Thoughts of a Statesman," p. 22.

19. J. K. Paasikivi, *Paasikiven Linja*, Vol. 1. (Porvoo and Helsinki: Werner Söderström, 1956), pp. 9–12.

offending Russian sensibilities and thus aid the establishment of the new orientation.[20] The Paasikivi Line and its author became the symbol of the new relationship to both Finns and Soviets.[21]

The Paasikivi Line set the parameters of Finnish foreign policy and committed the country to a basically pro-Soviet policy, but one which had certain limits because she was not an ally. Indeed, the Line pledged that Finland would avoid involvement in the disagreements of great powers, which included the USSR. Moreover, Paasikivi never failed to go on record recalling the cultural affinities with the other Scandinavian countries—to be pro-Soviet did not necessarily mean Finland had to be anti-Scandinavian. The Line worked as a means of insuring Finnish independence, but by the same token it should be reckoned as a *condition* of independence. Soviet policy makers could utilize it for criticism or pressure upon governments and politicians if there were violations of the spirit, as interpreted by Moscow.

The legal fulfillment was designed for three purposes: to provide for strategic and security interests of the USSR by annexations and leasing of a base, to obtain indemnification for war losses, and to establish conditions deemed suitable for the exercise of Finnish independence as a soft sphere. The terms would be binding under international law, and if not observed by Finland the Soviet Union would have a legitimate basis for criticism, pressure, interference, or even intervention. Nevertheless the legal fulfillment set the limits, on paper at least, for Soviet influence. Despite the heavy burden of the terms for a war-weakened

---

20. Sigyn Alenius, *Finland between the Armistice and the Peace* (Helsinki: Werner Söderström, 1947), p. 32, and Shirl H. Swenson, *The Finnish Paradox—An Analysis of a Peripheral State's Struggle against Soviet Integration*, unpublished Master of Arts thesis, Georgetown University, 1954, in the Library of Congress, Washington, D.C. In his interview in October 1967 Mr. Sunderlin recalled how Paasikivi, who was at times hot-tempered, shouted and banged the table in his effort to pound into the heads of Finns the new attitude toward the Russians. Paasikivi in time symbolized the effort to change the image of the Soviet Union, but the author in his two visits noted a few incidents, still part of the culture in Finland, showing an inclination to dislike and look down on their "eastern neighbor."

21. For an example of Soviet acceptance of the symbol see L. Bezymensky, "A Policy Tested by Time—Twenty Years of Soviet-Finnish Relations," *New Times, A Weekly Journal of World Affairs* (Moscow), No. 35, September 2, 1964, pp. 10–12.

small country, it might be borne if enough independence were preserved.

Under the armistice agreement of 1944 the USSR sought essentially the same objectives included in the Treaty of Moscow, signed in March 1940, which ended the Winter War; the 1947 Treaty of Peace also differed little from the armistice terms.[22] Continuity in the basic tenor of the agreements supports the view that Soviet objectives vis-à-vis Finland had remained basically strategic since 1939. Finland ceded the Karelian Isthmus, which included the city of Viipuri and the Petsamo region in the north, an action which resulted in the necessity of absorbing about 400,000 refugees, reckoned as about ten per cent of the population. Reparations totaling $300,000,000 had to be paid in six years, and the base at Porkkala, located twelve miles from Helsinki, was leased by Russia with rights of access for fifty years. The Finnish Communist Party was legalized, and all pro-Hilter organizations of a fascist type were to be dissolved, as were "other organizations conducting propaganda hostile to the United Nations, in particular to the Soviet Union, and [which] will not in future permit the existence of organizations of that kind."[23] The armistice charged Finland to conduct a trial of the "War Responsibles," which included Väinö Tanner and seven other distinguished persons in public life who held office from 1939 to 1944. The trial was held between November 15, 1945, and February 21, 1946, and was actually a political purge desired by the Soviet Union to cleanse the body politic of leaders in whom they could have no faith.

Under the armistice agreement the Finns assumed responsibility to disarm German forces remaining in the country and to

---

22. The texts of these agreements are included in Anatole G. Mazour, *Finland between East and West* (Princeton: D. Van Nostrand, Inc., 1956), Appendix VII, Treaty of Peace between the Republic of Finland and the Union of Soviet Socialist Republics, March 12, 1940; Appendix X, Armistice Agreement between the USSR and Finland, September 19, 1944; Appendix XI, Treaty of Peace between the Allies and Finland, February 10, 1947. For a legal analysis of these agreements see Erik Castrén, "Peace Treaties and Other Agreements Made by Finland," especially pp. 55–61, in Finnish Political Science Association, *Finnish Foreign Policy, Studies in Foreign Politics,* Helsinki, 1963.

23. Article 8 of the Treaty of Peace between the Allies and Finland, 1947.

hand over the prisoners to Russia. It took seven months to disarm two hundred thousand well equipped troops, which was like a third episode of World War II in loss of life and destruction in Lapland. Yet, the effort yielded a valuable dividend for it was accomplished without assistance from Soviet forces.[24]

In the Treaty of Peace Finland agreed to "cooperate fully with the Allied and Associated Powers with a view to insuring that Germany will not be able to take steps outside German territory towards rearmament,"[25] reflecting continued Soviet fear of a renascent Germany and providing a means for scrutiny of Finnish activities.

Armistice terms for all of Germany's defeated allies and associates included an Allied Control Commission charged with executing the armistice under the general direction of the Soviet High Command. The Commission for Finland was under the chairmanship of Andrei Zhdanov. Among its functions detailed in the Annex to the Armistice was to "make the necessary investigations and the collection of information which it requires"; it also had the "right to visit without let or hindrance any institution, enterprise, or port" for information necessary to its function.[26] When the peace treaty went into effect in September 1947, the Allied Control Commission terminated its functions, to the relief of the Finns, for it was a thorn in their side, facilitating meddlings which were especially odious under Zhdanov. The Commission, according to Sunderlin in his interview with the author in October 1967, had occupied two big hotels in Helsinki and still had some people in Finland until 1952 when reparations were paid.

During the crucial formative period after the end of hostilities, the whole country was in a sense on trial to determine whether the soft sphere would work. In addition to the leadership of Paasikivi the Parliament functioned under a three-party coalition: the Agrarians, a centrist party of smallholders led by Uhro

---

24. Max Jakobson, *The Diplomacy of the Winter War,* p. 258.

25. Article 20 of the Treaty of Peace between the Allies and Finland, 1947.

26. Paasikivi had to meet almost daily with Zhdanov, whom he characterized as "not known as a friend of Finland." H. Peter Krosby's review of Juho Kusti Paasikivi, *President Paasikivis Minnen, 1939–1940* (Helsingfors: Söderström and Co., 1958), p. 213, in the *American Slavic and East European Review,* Vol. XVIII (October 1959), pp. 474–475, and Fischer, "A Visit to Juho Paasikivi," p. 387.

Kekkonen, the Social Democrats, led mainly by Karl A. Fagerholm, and the SKDL, a front organization composed mainly of the Communist Party and dissident left Socialists. Hertta Kuusinen, firebrand daughter of Otto Kuusinen, the grand old man of Finnish Communism exiled in Russia, and Mauno Pekkala, leader of the dissident socialists, were prominent in the SKDL. The "Red-Green" coalition functioned to provide a regime with a broad consensus for political stability, and inclusion of the SKDL with its 25% of the vote probably helped to reassure Stalin that internal political responsibility would not be exercised by elements hostile to the Soviet Union. Although enjoying an important position in the government, the SKDL did not exercise a dominating role.[27]

The Finnish craft had weathered rough seas for three and a half years until the Treaty of Peace was signed. The year 1948 dawned with its trials, but was to be crowned by successes in the firmer rooting of the soft sphere.

---

27. See Alenius, *Finland between the Armistice and the Peace*, pp. 10–33, for a summary of government and politics during this period.

CHAPTER TWO

DÉNOUEMENT OF THE SOFT SPHERE:
THE TREATY OF 1948

Before the soft sphere could be defined in more positive and lasting terms, the nature of Finland's role in the Soviet
security system had to be spelled out. The issue seemed to have
been resolved earlier by provisions of the armistice and peace
treaty as well as by the spirit of the Paasikivi Line; but in the early
months of 1948 Russia was taking several steps to tighten her
defenses in Eastern Europe, including the negotiation of defensive pacts with Rumania[1] and Hungary, which seemed to call for
consideration of how Finland might fit into the picture. Moscow's
moves to shore up defenses in eastern Europe were in response to
the quickening pace of polarization taking place at this time, but
for Finland it raised the issue of how deeply she would be drawn
into the Soviet orbit, which was being transformed into a hard

---

1. "Treaty of Friendship, Co-operation and Mutual Assistance Between the
U.S.S.R. and Rumania, Moscow, 4 February 1948," U. N. *Treaty Series*, Vol. 48, No.
745, pp. 189–201. The treaty between the USSR and Hungary was signed on 18
February, 1948, *ibid.*, No. 743, pp. 163–175. The defensive alliance tenor of the
Russo-Rumanian pact was set in Article 1: "The High Contracting Parties agree to
take all joint action in their power to obviate any threat of renewed aggression by
Germany or any other power which might be associated with Germany either
directly or in any other way." Under Article 2, if either of the parties should " . . .
be involved in hostilities with a Germany which might seek to renew its policy of
aggression, or with any other state which might have been associated with Germany in a policy of aggression, either directly or in any other way, the other High
Contracting Party shall immediately extend to the Contracting Party involved in
hostilities military and other assistance with all the means at its disposal."

sphere. Under the circumstances, there were uncertainties over the future of the soft sphere, even though technically it would survive if Finland signed a defense pact, as had Rumania and Hungary, for she would still retain her institutions of internal self-government.[2] If, on the other hand, Finland were able to avoid integration into the defense system of the Soviet orbit, uncertainties over the future of the soft sphere could for the time being be dispelled. Concern for the future of the soft sphere was high, but the prospect of a defensive pact was more keenly feared, for it would dash one of Paasikivi's fondest hopes and a basic principle of his Line: that Finland would avoid taking sides in great power conflicts.

In a letter dated February 28, 1948,[3] the day after the Czechoslovak coup, Stalin broached the question of a Soviet-Finnish defense pact directly to President Paasikivi, proposing a treaty modeled on those concluded with Hungary and Rumania. A Finnish delegation was invited to conduct negotiations in the USSR, but in a gesture of *politesse* Stalin stated he was willing to meet in Helsinki if it was more convenient. Soviet leaders obviously preferred to continue the pattern of the Rumanian and Hugarian pacts because they contained the kind of commitments desired. Apparently Soviet defense and foreign policy experts had concluded in early 1948 that the role of Finland in the security system of the USSR and Eastern Europe had not been fully defined; the proposed treaty would have converted Finland's role from a passive to a more active one. Stalin's proposal, it could be argued, was a plausible and not wholly unexpected move when seen from Moscow's view of Finland's strategic

---

2. As an ally of the Soviet Union, Finland, a small state, would be allied with a giant, and the fact that she was already in the Russian orbit would work to increase the prospect of its becoming a "hegemonic alliance" which would tend to weaken the soft sphere. See Peter J. Fliess, "Hegemonial Nature of Alliances," pp. 106–133 in *International Relations in the Bipolar World* (New York: Random House, 1968).

3. See the *New York Times,* February 29, 1948, p. 4, for the text of the letter. It was written in a terse but not ungracious manner and was probably meant as a courtesy to Paasikivi that Stalin himself sent the letter. It proposed to "establish conditions for radical improvement in the relations between our countries with the aim of strengthening peace and security" and assumed that Finland, like the other countries, was interested in a pact against possible German aggression.

importance and when assurances in the Paasikivi Line concerning Finnish regard for the security interests of her neighbor are recalled.

Paasikivi probably did not perceive the proposed pact as intended to satellize Finland—as many in Finland and the West feared—but as designed to fit her into the Soviet security system. Realistically, negotiations were unavoidable, but he would concentrate his efforts to limit to a minimum the nature and extent of his commitments. Finnish policy makers were not unaware of Soviet interest in a treaty, for the matter had been raised on at least three previous occasions,[4] and Paasikivi had publicly stated a year earlier that "Finland would fight with all her resources against any aggressor seeking to strike the Soviet Union across Finnish territory."[5] Stalin had made a shrewd move, for it put the Finns on the spot of having to confirm by concrete commitments their professed obligation for Soviet security and the new way of thinking about the Soviet Union; Paasikivi and the Finns, as will be seen, were equal to the occasion.

Finnish political leaders had actually hoped to move in the opposite direction toward neutrality, as much as was consistent with the Paasikivi Line. The soft sphere would be better sustained by neutrality than alliance, so the delegation to Moscow would strive to reduce as much as possible military obligations in negotiations while seeking confirmation of Finland's desire to remain outside of great power conflicts. In his letter accepting the invitation President Paasikivi noted he was doing so on "the assumption that during the talks the contents of the proposed treaty would be subject on all sides to amendments."[6] The necessity of discussing the matter in cabinet meetings and with committees of Parliament, which under the constitution would have to ratify any treaty negotiated, incurred delays before the departure of the delegation; but the time served to generate support for the position of the government and to indicate to Finnish public opinion

---

4. Zhdanov mentioned the possibility of a defense pact with Mannerheim as early as January 1945 and raised the question again with Paasikivi in May of that year; Molotov broached the subject with a Finnish delegation visiting Moscow in November, 1947. See Max Jakobson, *Finnish Neutrality, A Study of Finnish Foreign Policy since the Second World War* (New York: Frederick A. Praeger, 1969), p. 37.

5. *New York Times*, February 14, 1947, p. 8.

6. *New York Times*, March 15, p. 1.

that there would be no undue haste or inadequate preparation for the journey to Moscow.

Paasikivi's objectives in the negotiations were "to limit commitments to the barest minimum required to remove the historic Russian fear of Finnish collusion in an attack against Leningrad."[7] In view of this the treaty should be designed "only to repel an attack directed against the territory of Finland or against the Soviet Union through Finland." Finnish military responsibility should be restricted to the defense of her own territory, and such action would be undertaken primarily by Finnish forces. Assistance by Soviet forces would be given only if requested by Finland or on the basis of an agreement between the two signatories. The instructions specifically rejected any general commitment to political consultations.

In Moscow the Finnish delegation braced itself for sessions of hard bargaining, as they expected the Soviet negotiators to press for a pact as outlined by Stalin, and there was no surprise when Molotov at the outset offered terms for such a treaty. Mauno Pekkala, Prime Minister and head of the Finnish delegation, replied that his government could not agree to such a treaty because the position of Finland differed from that of Rumania and Hungary and she preferred to remain a neutral country free from any world power blocs. In his rejoinder Molotov asked if the Finnish representatives would submit proposals of their own for an agreement, and they promptly offered a draft based on their instructions.

---

7. On instructions to the delegation, the author is indebted to Dr. Söderhjelm for the interview in September, 1972; Jakobson, *Finnish Neutrality*, pp. 40–41, and Svento, *Ystäväni Juho Kusti Paasikivi*, p. 32. Svento, who was a member of the delegation, Deputy Foreign Minister, and a left wing Social Democrat who had joined the SKDL, was a close associate of the President. The delegation was also composed of M. Pekkala, the Prime Minister, a left wing Social Democrat who joined the SKDL, Carl Enckell, the Foreign Minister, a nonparty professional who was also close to the President; Söderhjelm, a member of the Swedish Party and a lawyer who had headed the Ministry of Justice; Kekkonen, leader of the Agrarian Party and a rising political figure in postwar Finnish politics; and Yrjö Leino, a Communist member of the SKDL, who took charge of the important Ministry of Interior in the "Red-Green Coalition." In the opinion of Söderhjelm he and Kekkonen were the most effective members of the delegation, for Pekkala was ill, Enckell was old and tired, Svento was withdrawn and meditative, and Leino was often inebriated.

It was then Molotov's move in a crucial stage of the exchanges, and one can imagine the feeling of relief and elation when he accepted the Finnish draft as a basis for negotiations and expressed no objection to its basic provision limiting the application of the treaty to the defense of Finnish territory.[8] In current American idiom it was a "new ball game," but Molotov thought it necessary to achieve sufficient certainty on two points and offered an amendment that in the event of such an attack against Finnish territory, Soviet assistance would be sent automatically. Another amendment sought "a provision for mutual consultations on measures to remove a *threat* of attack against Finnish territory."[9] With Molotov's amendments, on the heels of his concession to base negotiations on the Finnish draft, the negotiations entered a delicate phase, for it would be difficult to reject the amendments out of hand. As negotiations centered on the two points, the Finnish delegation, which was divided and hesitant, sent Söderhjelm and Kekkonen back to Helsinki for additional instructions.

The Soviet proposals under consideration would tend to render Finnish defensive action and the need for it subject to a more active role than desired by Finland, which hoped to keep it as much as possible a primarily *Finnish* activity. Moreover, under the second amendment there might be differences between the signatories on what constituted "a threat of attack against Finnish territory," which could be a source of embarrassment or pressure on Finland. In Helsinki, Paasikivi's new instructions were, in effect, to stand firmly by the original instructions: Soviet military assistance could be accepted only in the event of need and by prior agreement, and the scope of possible consultations was to be limited to measures against an actual attack and not the threat of one. Further instructions were for specific inclusion of Finland's desire to remain outside of great power conflicts of interest and for the treaty to be for a duration of ten years instead of the twenty as proposed by the Soviet delegation. In Moscow the full

---

8. In his interview with the author, Söderhjelm related how he believed that Molotov and Stalin were prepared from the beginning to "go on different lines" and to accept the Finnish conception of the treaty because they considered the Finnish case to be *different.*

9. Jakobson, *Finnish Neutrality,* p. 41, italics supplied.

delegation, anxiously anticipating tough bargaining, was again relieved when Molotov gave in on all essential points;[10] the final text bore very close resemblance to the proposed Finnish draft and was signed in Moscow on April 6, 1948.

Some provisions of the pact, which was officially titled "Agreement of Friendship, Cooperation, and Mutual Assistance Between the Republic of Finland and the Union of Soviet Socialist Republics, April 6, 1948,"[11] but which will hereafter usually be referred to as the "pact" or "treaty of 1948," will be quoted at this point and followed by discussion of problems in interpretation.

In the preamble, after an expression of the general principle that the parties were "convinced that the strengthening of good neighborhood relations and cooperation . . . lies in the interest of both countries," the concept of neutrality, so highly prized in Finland, was acknowledged in the words: "Considering Finland's desire to remain out of the conflicting interests of the great powers. . . ."

Articles 1 and 2 expressed the main purpose of the treaty:

> *Article* 1. In the eventuality that Finland, or the Soviet Union through Finnish territory, becomes the object of an armed attack by Germany or any state allied with the latter, Finland will, true to its obligations as an independent state, fight to repel the attack. Finland will in such cases use all its available forces for defending its territorial integrity by land, sea and air, and will do so within the frontiers of Finland in accordance with obligations defined in the present agreement and, if necessary, with the assistance of, or jointly with, the Soviet Union.
>
> In the cases aforementioned the Soviet Union will give Finland the help required, the giving of which will be subject to mutual agreement between the Contracting Parties.

---

10. *Ibid.* On this crucial phase of the negotiations, Söderhjelm recalled in his interview with the author that Paasikivi was rather distressed over the Molotov rejoinder, but the decision was made to stand firm. He added that in his view Molotov readily accepted the Finnish response because he *wanted a treaty* and that to the Soviet Foreign Minister the specific words did not matter all that much. Söderhjelm also described the atmosphere at the informal sessions where the Soviets were good hosts, conveyed a sense of cordiality and wanted to get along. Stalin at one point said, "We don't need you—we have enough timber."

11. For the full text of the treaty see Mazour, *Finland between East and West,* Appendix XII, pp. 280–282.

Article 2. The High Contracting Parties will confer with each other if it is established that the threat of an armed attack as described in Article 1 is present.

Under Article 4 the parties agree "not to conclude any alliance or join any coalition directed against the other," and in Article 6 they "pledge themselves to observe the principles of mutual respect and integrity and that of noninterference in the internal affairs of the other state."

Finland, in ratifying the pact,[12] entered into some definite but limited obligations to the Soviet Union; the agreement stipulated the contingencies for invoking the obligations and the manner of executing them. From the Finnish point of view the basic features of the instrument seemed clear enough, but in order to enlighten public opinion at home and allay its fears, as well as to enlighten world opinion on the limited nature of the obligations, several official and semi-official statements were made. President Paasikivi made one of the most cogent of these statements in a broadcast three days after the treaty was signed:

> Should Finland be involved in military operations such as are presupposed in this treaty, and should she on this account require assistance, then . . . such assistance will be given by the Soviet Union. As for the kind and extent, as well as—and above all—the need for this assistance, the Finnish government will come to agreement with the Soviet Union.[13]

---

12. Hodgson, "The Paasikivi Line," p. 156, and Jakobson, *Finnish Neutrality*, p. 44. Parliament ratified the treaty by a large majority: 157 in favor, 11 against, and 30 abstentions. Despite the overwhelming vote and reason for satisfaction that Finnish objectives in the negotiations had been achieved, "the debate preceding the vote clearly revealed the reluctance and misgivings of the majority of members," which reflected opposition to having any treaty. Opposition and abstention came from parties of the right: the National Progressive Party and the National Coalition Party. The favorable vote reflected confidence in Paasikivi and recognition that, realistically, there was no other choice.

13. See Gripenberg, "Finnish Neutrality," *Introduction to Finland, 1960*, edited by Urho Toivola and prepared with the assistance of the Press Bureau of the Finnish Ministry of Foreign Affairs (Helsinki: Werner Söderström, 1960), pp. 62–63. See also Fredrik Valros, *Finland, 1946–1952* (Helsinki: Valtioneuvoston Kirjapaino, 1953), pp. 10–12, where he notes that the Fundamental Law Committee of Parliament reported that in its view "the said necessity must be established by each of the two states." The Committee on Foreign Affairs stated that the

Paasikivi's statement was designed to set at rest anxieties over the nature of, and conditions under which, Soviet assistance and the need for it under Article 1 would be given. This statement then became the interpretation Finland preferred. The President also felt it necessary to spell out what was meant by "established" in Article 2. In his interpretation the obligation to confer would come into force only after threat of attack on Finnish territory had been established in the view of *both* parties. The attack, or threat of it, would have to be of a military character.[14]

President Paasikivi's interpretation of the obligations in Articles 1 and 2 have been consistently held in Finland, as was indicated by President Kekkonen, a member of the delegation to Moscow in 1948, in a speech in November 1965. "The pact," he emphasized, "is not hinged to any automatically released mechanism;" he continued stressing how limited Finland's obligations were and drew a distinction between the pact of 1948 and a "treaty of military alliance proper":

> Firstly, there is the territorial scope of the pact. Finland has engaged itself to defend the inviolability of its territory within its own boundaries, which it would certainly do in any case, treaty or no treaty. But this self-evident point was included in order to clarify the nature of the pact. In the event of an attack on the USSR by another route than over Finnish territory we will not, under the pact be involved in the war. On the contrary, we will take every conceivable step to remain neutral.[15]

It seems evident that the Finno-Soviet Treaty of Friendship, Cooperation and Mutual Assistance signaled the dénouement of the soft sphere for Finland. Lingering doubts and new exigencies of polarization weighed by Soviet policy makers were, it seems, resolved in favor of the soft model, for when presented with alternative Finnish proposals, they chose to move in that direction. The Soviets, who were in the asking position, wanted some-

---

contracting parties would in due time decide together the time and nature of the assistance.

14. Gripenberg, "Finnish Neutrality," p. 63.

15. Ministry of Foreign Affairs, Helsinki, *Finnish Features*, No. 41/65. "Speech Delivered by the President of the Republic, Uhro Kekkonen, to a Meeting of the Foreign Policy Youth Association on November 29, 1965," p. 6 (cited hereafter as *Finnish Features*).

thing from the Finns and had initiated the process of negotiation, while Paasikivi's realism indicated he should not refuse. Events have proved that the Soviets were disposed to negotiate, not dictate. In the Soviet view Finland was a friendly country under Paasikivi; indeed, by 1948 Moscow had already marked him as the indispensible man in the soft sphere system and one whom Stalin respected and trusted.[16] If the negotiations failed, Paasikivi and his Line would appear to be discredited, and the Soviets would not want this; if, on the other hand, the negotiations succeeded, Paasikivi and his Line would be strengthened, and the Russians would surely want this. There was, to be sure, pressure to negotiate, but as time would tell the Finnish position would actually be improved by the treaty. In these circumstances the treaty of 1948 became a Soviet *confirmation* and *application* of the soft sphere concept, while for Finland it was a *clarification* and *formalization* of her obligations to the Soviet Union under the concept.

Unlike the treaties with Rumania and Hungary, the pact of 1948 established a loose and limited association with the Soviet security system, but one which, nevertheless, would serve Soviet geostrategy. Although in time the Finns were to prize the treaty as the neutrality component in it gained fuller regard, Soviet policy makers prized it equally well as an element in their security system and a vital part of their relationship with Finland, which accounts for frequent favorable Russian references to it and desire for its perpetuation. Like all durable relations in foreign policy, the cement of common interest seals its vitality. Spheres of influence, especially the soft sphere, prosper better when a mystique unites in common interest the paramount and sphere states; this, it seems, has been achieved in goodly measure by the Paasikivi Line and the pact of 1948. The silk glove seemed to fit, and made possible a handclasp of greater mutual interest, especially when the neutrality feature was enhanced.

Finnish Neutrality and the Pact of 1948

Articles 1 and 2, if not the treaty in general, deal with obligations laid upon Finland in the interest of Soviet defense, but from

---

16. Fischer, "A Visit to Juho Paasikivi," p. 387.

the Finnish standpoint the most valued provision was the one wherein Moscow acknowledged in the preamble her "desire to remain out of the conflicting interests of the great powers." Inclusion in a treaty at this time of one of Finland's cardinal aspirations placed it in a legal instrument which to this day remains the only juridical expression of it, but as part of the preamble it does not require the degree of substantive obligation it would have if included among the explicit undertakings in the main body of the treaty.[17] In international law the preamble is regarded as an indication of the objectives and purposes of the parties, and Finland's desire to avoid involvement in great power conflicts is rather like a statement of principle. But it could be claimed by Finland that the preambular statements' inclusion in a treaty created a legal obligation for the Soviet Union to take into account her *desire*. Any Finnish claim on a legal basis cannot really go much beyond this, for the preamble, in addition to having a status inferior to specific provisions in the body, can have utility as one of the contexts for interpreting the articles of the treaty.[18] There was, however, no article in the body following up the principle expressed in the preamble, but it could be, if necessary, resorted to in the interpretation of the pivotal Articles 1 and 2, to be further considered below.

1948 and some years thereafter were not, however, a propitious time to advance the acceptance of neutralism, and neither side in the cold war was disposed toward tolerance for neutrals. Moreover, Finland's geopolitical position as the immediate neighbor of a great power makes it more difficult to pursue a neutral policy than for countries like Sweden or Switzerland to do so. In addition her neutral aspirations were clouded by provisions of the treaty of peace, which granted the naval base at Porkkala to the Soviet Union for fifty years with rights of transit.

By 1956, however, the times were more auspicious for the growth of Finnish neutrality, which had been planted in the

---

17. See Charles Rousseau, *Principes Généraux Du Droit International Public* (Paris: Editions A. Pedone, 1944), Tome 1, p. 186.

18. Article 31, Section 2 of the Vienna Convention of the Law of Treaties, 1969 codified existing practice on the use of the preamble for interpretation of specific provisions. See also D. P. O'Connell, *International Law* (London: Stevens and Sons, 1970), 2nd edition, Vol. I, p. 260.

preamble and should be regarded as the crowning achievement of President Paasikivi before his retirement. Finno-Soviet relations, reflecting improved world conditions as well as confidence in the system of the soft sphere, which had been in effect for a decade, led the Soviet policy makers to move more positively to recognize Finnish neutrality. In their most important concession ever to Finland, Soviet forces were withdrawn from Porkkala on January 26, 1956, two years before the date for the renewal of the treaty of 1948, and claim to the base was relinquished. A month later at the Twentieth Congress of the Soviet Communist Party, Finland was referred to for the first time in an official statement as a neutral country. A year later an interpretation of the pact of 1948 appeared in a work published by the Research Institute for International Relations in Moscow edited by two professors, one of them legal advisor to the Soviet Foreign Office. In it the treaty of 1948 with Finland was distinguished from other bilateral treaties the USSR had entered into with countries in Eastern Europe and included the following:

> Finland is bound to resort to action only if the attack touches her territory, land, sea or air. Finland binds herself only to undertake action within her own frontiers. Support is given in case of need by the Soviet Union, and this should occur on the basis of an agreement between the parties to the pact. If the Soviet Union is subject to an attack which does not affect the territory of Finland, Finland is under an obligation not to join any coalitions or enter into any alliances which are directed against the Soviet Union, that is to say to preserve her neutrality. All of this indicates that the treaty between the Soviet Union and Finland is rather a pact to guarantee neutrality than a treaty for mutual assistance in the proper meaning of these words.[19]

The shift in Soviet policy signaled the opportunity for Finland to develop more fully the neutrality component as one of the main pillars of foreign policy and to seek identification of and

---

19. The study, published in 1957, was edited by S. B. Krylov and V. N. Durdenevski, *Meždunarodnopravovyje formy mirogo sosuščestvovanija gosudarstu i natsij.* See *Ulkopoliittisia Lausutoja ja Asiakirjoja, 1963,* p. 15, an annual publication of the Finnish Foreign Ministry of various statements related to foreign policy hereafter cited as UAL. See also Gripenberg, "Finnish Neutrality," p. 66, and Aimo Pajunen, "Finland's Security Policy," p. 17 in *Essays on Finnish Foreign Policy,* published by the Finnish Political Science Association, Vammala, 1969.

recognition for it in the appropriate international circles. Accordingly, in official communiques Prime Minister Macmillan for Britain and President Kennedy for the United States acknowledged in 1961 Finnish aspirations for neutrality.

In defining Finland's commitments in the treaty in the light of her hopes to keep out of great power conflicts, it should not be forgotten that if she is attacked or the Soviet Union is attacked through her territory, or there is a threat of armed attack with either of these objectives in view, then Finland has certain clear obligations which are subject to mutual agreement with the Soviet Union. This would obviously mean that Finland was unable to maintain her neutrality and she would have to envisage possible *joint military defense* of Finnish territory; the choices of nonresistance or siding with the attackers are precluded. Under these defined contingencies, the *casus foederis* would operate and Finnish neutrality would be terminated. There is no obligation under the treaty, however, if the Soviet Union is attacked from any other quarter, and Finland's desire to remain neutral in such an event has been acknowledged. Indeed, under Soviet and Finnish interpretations she would be *required* to remain neutral. Finland's desire to keep out of great power conflicts also protects her against pressure from Moscow for political involvements; she must by the same token eschew activities the Soviet Union, or for that matter any other country, might brand as violative of neutral behavior. Thus, as long as the 1948 pact in its present form binds Finland, it should be described as a *qualified* neutrality, for it has the dualism of neutrality together with limited military commitments.[20]

---

20. For a discussion of the dualism in the treaty and the qualified nature of Finnish neutrality, see Peter Lyon, *Neutralism* (Leicester: Leicester University Press, 1963), pp. 97-99. Lyon is probably one of the academic authorities on the subject who have drawn criticism of Finnish authorities and spokesmen for preoccupation with "abstract" or "pure" forms of neutrality, thereby denigrating the Finnish version of it. See also Nils Andren, "Scandinavian Perspectives: The Future of the Scandinavian Security System," *International Journal* (Canadian Institute of International Affairs), Vol. XXIV, No. 2 (Spring 1969) p. 34: "Finland although clearly within the Soviet orbit is not a member of the Warsaw Pact; it has gradually succeeded in acquiring recognition as a sort of neutral. . . . Since 1948 Finnish neutrality has been qualified, however, by the conditions of the Treaty of Friendship and Mutual Assistance with the USSR." In light of analysis to be made hereinafter, these authorities may have somewhat overdrawn the extent of the qualified character of Finnish neutrality.

In regard to such dualism it should be noted that neutrality and limited military obligations are complementary, as most Finnish analysts are wont to stress, for the neutrality of Finland, if it is respected, enhances Soviet security by reducing dangers and stabilizing the situation on the northwest frontier. Finnish neutrality also assures the Soviet Union that her neighbor would offer no encouragement to potential enemy forces expecting aid as they struck at the USSR through Finland. Not only through neutrality would there be no Finnish assistance, but if attacked, Finland would defend her territory and possibly take Soviet assistance. In the course of time the neutrality component tended to wax as the military component waned. The way neutrality served Soviet security interests inclined Moscow to be favorably disposed toward it, and as Finnish neutrality became internationally credible it would obviate the need to fulfill the military commitments.

There can be no denying the fact that if Finnish neutrality fails to protect Finland or the USSR, her neutrality will have terminated, but this would also be the case if any other neutral were so attacked. Finland under the pact of 1948 would in effect become an ally of the Soviet Union. Official and other Finnish spokesmen have written extensively and with remarkable consistency to dispose of the putative incompatibility of the desire for neutrality with military obligations in the pact[21] and in the period since the return of Porkkala have increasingly characterized Finland as a neutral country. Max Jakobson in a typical statement argued that

---

21. Max Jakobson, who has for years held several positions of importance in the Foreign Ministry, has written *Finnish Neutrality,* cited throughout this book, and many of President Kekkonen's speeches on neutrality and related subjects which have recently been published in *Neutrality: The Finnish Position,* edited by Tuomas Vilkuma with a preface by Jan-Magnus Jansson and translated by P. O. Jansuu and L. E. Keyworth (London: Heinemann, 1970). See also statements by former Foreign Ministers Ralf Törngren, "The Neutrality of Finland," *Foreign Affairs,* Vol. 39, No. 4 (July 1961) pp. 601-609; Ahti Karjalainen, "The Foreign Policy of Finland," a speech in Stockholm before the Foreign Policy Association of the University of Stockholm, December 2, 1965, 6 pp., distributed by the Embassy of Finland, Washington, D. C., and K. G. Idman, "Quelques Observations sur la Coéxistence Pacifique et le Traité D'Amitié entre L'U.R.S.S. et La Finlande," *Revue Générale De Droit International Public,* October-December 1959, Tome XXX, No. 4, pp. 639-648. See also L. A. Puntila, "Finland's Neutrality," by a distinguished professor of political history, in *Finnish Foreign Policy, Studies in Foreign Politics* (Helsinki: The Finnish Political Science Association, 1963), pp. 218-227.

the obligations of the treaty were a "necessary precondition for securing the confidence of the USSR, without which our neutrality would have been built on sand." He continued, ". . . assistance comes into the question only after an armed attack against Finland's territory, or via Finland's territory against the USSR, has taken place—in other words not until Finland's neutrality has actually failed and the country has become involved in military operations." Under these circumstances he concluded, "A neutral state has a generally acknowledged right to receive assistance for the defense of its territory from whatever assistance is available."[22]

Soviet policy makers for their part place the highest priority on the relationship with Finland established by the treaty and never tire of stressing the need to maintain it. We may thus conclude that the USSR has acceded to enhancing the neutrality component and has no objection to Finland's designation as a neutral; but her insistence on preserving the treaty obviously indicates that she would oppose termination of the military obligations of Finland under it, limited as they may be.[23] Yet, despite the existence of a military obligation in the treaty, it can be argued that Finland has achieved *de facto* a remarkable degree of authentic neutrality because of the stability of the situation in Scandinavia, the major source of danger.[24] Additional salutary features are the toning down of the cold war and degrees of détente in international relations generally. Furthermore, the program of "active neutrality" by which the Finns have sought to assume United Nations peacekeeping responsibilities and to host conferences such as the SALT talks and the preparatory talks for a

---

22. *Lecture by Mr. Max Jakobson, Director for Political Affairs, Ministry for Foreign Affairs at the Meeting of the Foreign Policy Association of the University of Lund, Sweden, on November 13, 1963*, p. 6. Made available to the author by the Press Bureau of the Foreign Ministry, Finland.

23. After the return of Porkkala, Finnish policy makers probed the possibility of instituting a more complete form of neutrality as enjoyed by Switzerland with formal guarantees of the great powers, but this would have resulted in rescinding the military obligations of the pact of 1948 and was opposed by the Soviet Union. See L. A. Puntila, "Finland's Neutrality," p. 224. For other references to the USSR's view of neutrality see Chapter 6, pp. 111–125 and the postcript, p. 200.

24. See Chapter 9, "The Primary External Relationship: Finland, the Soviet Union, and the Scandinavian Subsystem."

European security conference in 1972-1973 also contribute to the image of Finnish neutrality.

Under the treaty as well as the subsequent evolution of Finland as a neutral, she is set off from the Warsaw Pact countries, and her independence and soft sphere status have been more firmly anchored. There should be no doubt about why there is such unremitting stress laid upon neutrality and Finnish efforts in the Scandinavian-Baltic region to prevent international tensions that might endanger it.

CHAPTER THREE

DÉNOUEMENT OF THE SOFT SPHERE: INTERNAL DEVELOPMENTS, 1948–1949

In the wake of—if not concomitantly with—success on the diplomatic front in 1948, resources had to be summoned for internal challenges, especially the vitalization of Finnish democracy; if this were achieved, independence and nationalism—hallmarks of the soft sphere—would have fertile soil in which to grow.[1]

The success of democratic reconstruction and the maintenance of independence required a basis of residual economic vitality[2] and sacrifices to make it possible to pay the seemingly impossible burden of the *real* costs of reparations, which were nominally set at $300,000,000 in terms of the 1938 value of the dollar but have variously been estimated at $570,000,000, $720,000,000, or $949,000,000.[3]

---

1. See p. 18, Introduction, on nationalism and independence in the framework for analysis of spheres of influence.

2. On the sources of economic strength in postwar Finland see J. William Fredrickson, "The Economic Recovery of Finland since World War II," *The Journal of Political Economy* (February 1960) pp. 17–36.

3. In reference to the real costs of reparations see Arthur Spencer, "Finland Maintains Democracy," *Foreign Affairs* (January 1953) p. 301, wherein he cites the opinion of Professor Bruno Suviranta, a foremost authority on reparations, writing in *Nordiska Foreningsbanken's Quarterly Review*, No. 3 (August 1952) p. 77, that the final payments were worth $226,500,000 reparations dollars, which he estimates is equivalent to $570,000,000 1953 dollars on the assumption that the Finnish mark is overvalued. The Bank of Finland, using official exchange rates, gives a total of $720,000,000. In Suviranta's calculation the whole Finnish war

Professor Jaakko Auer has provided a vivid graphic illustration of the quantity of goods Finland rendered to the Soviet Union under the reparations agreement. Excluding the ships, reparations goods took 343,635 loaded railway cars:

> A train that formed that number of cars would reach from Helsinki over the Mediterranean to Africa. In addition to these goods Finland supplied the Soviet Union with 514 new ships. The gross register tonnage of this "fleet" was about 359,000; and if the vessels had been placed in a straight line, one tightly with another, the "length" of the "fleet" would have been about 20 miles.[4]

Valuable assistance, especially from Sweden and the United States, helped Finland to meet heavy delivery schedules in the first phase of reparations. The Soviet Union, too, first helped to lighten the burden by extending the time of payment from six to eight years and by flexibility in certain critical situations. As they strained to fulfill the first year's commitments, the Finns were mindful that "the punctual accomplishment of war reparations deliveries was regarded as one of the most fundamental conditions of her national independence."[5]

Reparations stimulated sections of the economy and had a lasting beneficial effect that was well established by 1948. Four-fifths of the goods delivered to the Soviet Union were products of the shipbuilding, machinery, and metals industries, and "by the time the last payments were made in September 1952 these industries had undergone a transformation that had raised them to a level few could have foreseen in 1939."[6]

---

indemnity, including reparations, amounted to $949,000,000. See also Jaakko Auer, "Finland's War Reparation Deliveries to the Soviet Union," *Finnish Foreign Policy*, pp. 66–83. John H. Wuorinen, *A History of Finland* (New York: Columbia University Press, 1965), has a good short discussion of the reparations problem, pp. 388–392.

4. Auer, "Finland's War Reparations Deliveries to the Soviet Union," p. 76.

5. *Ibid.*, pp. 82–83.

6. Wuorinen, *A History of Finland*, p. 402. See also Nils Meinander, "Finland's Commercial Policy," in *Finnish Foreign Policy*, pp. 132–133. Reparations influenced the character of post-reparations trade between Finland and the Soviet Union, for "Finland continued to deliver ships, machines, and other products of heavy industry as normal export goods to Russia." See also Bartel C. Jensen, *The*

In 1948 during the crucial Parliamentary election campaign, the Soviet Union cancelled one-half of the payments still due, which amounted to $73,500,000 or 24.8% of the original sum.[7] By mid 1948, the fourth reparations year, Finland had paid 67.5% of the amount due. During the 17 month life of the first Fagerholm government, beginning in July 1948, about one-half of the remaining total was paid, leaving a comparatively manageable burden to be met. With the end of reparations in sight a lift to Finnish morale must surely have accompanied a sense of pride and confidence in the economic future—all grist for the mill of independence, nationalism, and democratic revitalization.

Yet, if Finland was to embark upon a period directed toward achieving internal stability and vitality, certain urgent political problems had to be dealt with. First among them was to restore Parliament to its influence in the life of the nation;[8] secondly, traditional freedoms had to be reinstituted, including freedom of the press,[9] and organizations such as VALPO, the police arm of

---

Impact of Reparations on the Post-War Finnish Economy (Homewood, Illinois: Richard D. Irwin, Inc., 1966) pp. 16–19. Finland as the debtor had to expand greatly her industrial potential. After the completion of payments it was feared that the new industries "would have to be shut down, their capital written off and their skilled workers thrown into unemployment, or they would have to go on producing for the Soviet Union, who as the sole buyer would be able to specify her terms." Some of these uncertainties were set at rest, however, by the negotiation of the Finno-Russian trade agreement concluded under the Fagerholm government in June 1950. Under the agreement the Soviet Union would purchase, during the five year period ending December 31, 1955, basically the same commodities she had received in reparations during the previous five years.

7. The reduction was claimed by the SKDL to be a fruit of their efforts and was widely interpreted as an effort by Moscow to influence the result of the election. This may have in part been the reason for the Soviet action, for the SKDL, having its difficulties, could have benefited from outside support; but the Soviet Union had also good reason to reward the Finns for prompt deliveries and was aware of the weight of the burden. Moreover, reductions were also at this time made in the payments of Hungary and Rumania.

8. "The stresses of war, the influence of the Allied Control Commission and the activities of the Popular Democratic cabinet had all tended to reduce the power of the Diet." Spencer, "Finland Maintains Democracy," p. 305. See also M.E.R.L., "Finnish Outlook," *World Today* (March 1950) p. 165.

9. Freedom of the press extended to domestic issues but was "subject to penalties for publication of material calculated to disturb friendly relations with other powers." The provision was obviously designed to prevent offending Soviet

the Ministry of Interior, had to be curbed or abolished. A source of uncertainty, if not anxiety in some quarters, was the powerful Communist Party and its associates in the SKDL:[10] What were their aims and what would be their role in the democratic reconstruction? In particular, what influence would they wield in new governments, what would be their relations with the Social Democrats, and how much power would they have in the labor unions?

The legalization of the Communist Party and its role in Finnish politics after the armistice may retrospectively be described as its most propitious moment. The general mood of the first two years favored its rise to great, but not decisive, power. Russia had dealt with defeated Finland better than had been feared, and "many Finns supported the party which seemed to offer the best chance of obtaining reasonable treatment from their mighty neighbor. . . ."[11] In the "period of peril" the SKDL rode the crest of this wave and seemed to be forging ahead in a manner that portended "far reaching changes on the broad front of labor, politics, and government."[12] United in the three party "Red-Green" coalition with the Agrarians and Social Democrats, which

---

sensibilities and charges from Moscow that the Finns were not sincere about the new orientation in relations with their neighbor. Raymond Daniell, "In the Forepaws of the Russian Bear," *New York Times Magazine*, May 22, 1949, p. 11. See also Mazour, *Finland between East and West*, pp. 174–175: The "security law" which enabled authorities to evade fundamental constitutional laws and to infringe basic rights of individuals terminated with the treaty of peace when ratifications were exchanged in September 1947, which was only three months before the December local government elections.

10. The Finnish People's Democratic League (Suomen Kansan Demokraattinen Liitto, SKDL) was formed in October 1944, not with the purpose of creating a new party, but as an organization to serve as a clearinghouse and a means of cooperation for individuals and organizations sharing common principles and goals. The most important group was the Finnish Communist Party, but an influential segment of splinter groups were the Finnish Women's Democratic League, the League of Finnish Comradely Associations, and the Academic Socialist Society. Mauno Pekkala and Reinhold Svento of the Socialist Unity Party were Prime Minister and Deputy Foreign Minister respectively. See Jaakko Nousiainen, *The Finnish Political System,* translated by John H. Hodgson (Cambridge: Harvard University Press, 1971), p. 26.

11. Spencer, "Finland Maintains Democracy," p. 303.

12. Wuorinen, *A History of Finland,* p. 434.

governed from March 1945 to July 1948, the SKDL enjoyed an edge over its partners with the Prime Minister and six portfolios in the Ministry, including the powerful Ministry of Interior. Until December 1947 the SKDL-Communist forces seemed to be headed toward continuing and dominant leadership.[13] Many Finns, observing the rise to dominance of Communist led movements in eastern Europe, wondered what sort of future their Republic might have, even though the soft sphere had been assured by direct Finnish-Soviet negotiations on the diplomatic front.

In the period under consideration it would be useful to sketch the relations between the Communist-SKDL and the Social Democrats in order to account for their significance in domestic political developments that affected the turn of political events. In the interwar years the Social Democrats under the leadership of Väinö Tanner resembled their counterparts in other Scandinavian countries as revisionist Socialists of the Second International; the party was wedded to the parliamentary tradition and its leadership was nationalist as well as socialist and democratic. As a nationalistic Finnish party it shared the aversion to the USSR and would have nothing to do with Finnish Communists. For part of this period it was the largest party in the country when it controlled the labor unions and was influential in the cooperative movement.[14]

After the war, old line Social Democratic party leaders opposed unity, or even cooperation with, the newly-legalized Communist Party, whose fortunes were ascending. The decision taken at the party congress on November 25 to 29, 1944, to elect leaders opposed to a common front resulted in a split of the party, with a minority joining the Communists in the SKDL. Again, in March of 1945 a proposal to form a common ticket for parliamentary elections was rejected.

Following the first postwar election in 1945, the Socialists relented and accepted an SKDL proposal to join in the tri-party "Red-Green" coalition with the Agrarians. The coalition was

---

13. *Ibid.*

14. Nousiainen, *The Finnish Political System,* pp. 25, 30, 42. See also Nils Andrén, *Government and Politics in the Nordic Countries* (Stockholm: Almquist and Wiksel, 1964), pp. 83–84.

composed of the three largest parties with almost identical strength.[15] Exigencies of party and national interest seemed to require for all three parties the expediency of collaboration on a limited basis. The coalition held until the campaign for election of a new parliament in 1948 despite difficulties and frictions, but its last year was very shaky.[16] During the year of uncertainty under consideration, the Presidency was a factor for influence and stability in internal politics as well as in foreign policy; although this should be counted among the contributions of Paasikivi's leadership, it is also due to the broad and independent authority of the President under the constitution, where executive power is shared by the President and cabinet.

The turning point in postwar domestic politics can probably be traced to the local elections held in December 1947 after the peace treaty had gone into effect and the Allied Control Commission had departed. The returns marked significant, but not disastrous, losses for the SKDL. As the high tide of Communist-SKDL power appeared to ebb,[17] it was undoubtedly a factor in the collapse of the Red-Green coalition and the Socialist resolve to terminate even this temporary and tenuous collaboration with them. The time from the weakening of the coalition, the setback of the SKDL, through the parliamentary election campaign in July of 1948 was an interval of multiple crises that crowded the scene in rapid succession and raised the pitch of expectation and apprehension to such an extent that without strong leadership

---

15. The Finnish Parliament (Eduskunta) is a 200 member unicameral body elected on the basis of a proportional representation system called the d'Hondt method after its creator, a nineteenth century Belgian jurist. See *Finnish Features*, No. 41/66, and Nousiainen, *The Finnish Political System*, pp. 165–166. The election of 1948 gave the Social Democrats 50 seats and the largest popular vote, but it was now evident that the division in the party and legalization of the Communists reduced their strength from over 80 before the war. The SKDL and the Agrarians each got 49 seats.

16. Eric C. Bellquist, "Finland: Democracy in Travail," *The Western Political Quarterly* (June 1949) p. 221. A six week government crisis was caused by the resignation of the Agrarian members of the cabinet, although they were persuaded to remain. The coalition's demise occurred in May of 1948 when the Social Democrats formally denounced it. See Valros, *Finland, 1946–1952*, p. 18.

17. Thornstein V. Kalijarvi, "Finland Since 1939," *Review of Politics* (April 1948) p. 224. In 529 communes the Communists-SKDL lost 345 seats against a gain of 705 seats by the right and center parties.

and a heritage of steadfastness and grit (*sisu*), the results could have been disastrous for Finland.

The first of these was Stalin's letter on February 22, 1948, to Paasikivi proposing a treaty patterned on those of Rumania and Hungary, and ended on April 28 with ratification of the treaty by Parliament. The second crisis to stir the nation immediately followed the first. It is the story of the alleged coup attempted by activist revolutionary elements of the Communist Party modeled on the successful Czechoslovak coup in February. The plans were scotched, the story goes, when Yrjö Leino, the Communist Minister of the Interior, on the evening of March 19, the night before he was to leave with the Finnish delegation for Moscow to participate in negotiations on the pact of 1948, called on General Aarne Sihvo, the Finnish Commander in Chief, at his home and revealed the plot.[18]

The third crisis involved Leino's dismissal from the cabinet. As a leading Communist he held the key Ministry of Interior in

---

18. Details of this event, insofar as known or avowed—or indeed, if they really exist—still seem shrouded in mystery. For obvious reasons the governments of Finland and the USSR have done nothing to remove the mystery; Finnish Communist Party leaders deny the entire story. Although accounts of an attempted coup and its frustration existed shortly after the time, the implication of Leino and his revealing the plot to Sihvo are based mainly on an account by Arvo Tuominen, who until the Winter War was Finland's No. 1 Communist and later became a prominent Social Democrat. Tuominen, who had originally recruited Leino for the Communists, relates how Leino told him the story in 1949. See Arvo Tuominen, *Hemligt Ränkspel Pa Jorden Och Jorden* (Helsingfors: Werner Söderström, 1958), pp. 252–256. General Sihvo later confirmed the account of his conversation with Leino, but Hertta Kuusinen, who at the time was Leino's wife, called it "utter nonsense." See Bellquist, "Finland's Democracy in Travail," p. 218, for a secondary account as reported in 1949; for a full length article see Hans Peter Krosby, "The Communist Bid for Power in Finland in 1948," *Political Science Quarterly* (June 1960) pp. 229–243. Immanuel Birnbaum, "The Communist Course in Finland," *Problems of Communism*, No. 5, Vol. VIII (September-October 1959) p. 44, relates that "other well informed participants in the political events of the postwar years hold that the decision not to press for an experiment in 'people's democracy' originated in Moscow and not with Leino." Leino's own account of what happened during the fateful evening has not been made public, for the publication of his memoirs was postponed since the autumn of 1958 at the "request of the Finnish government acting in response to a demand for suppression voiced by the Soviet Chargé d'Affaires in Helsinki." See Austin Goodrich, *Study in Sisu, Finland's Fight for Independence* (New York: Ballantine Books, 1960), pp. 108–111.

the Red-Green coalition. The action creating the crisis was a vote of censure on Leino passed by Parliament on May 19, 1948, for an action he had taken on April 21, 1945, four days after he had taken office as Minister. Acceding to a request of the Allied Control Commission he turned over to the USSR twenty persons, ten of whom were Finnish citizens and ten of whom were Russians with long residence in Finland on Nansen passports.[19] Leino failed to refer the matter to the cabinet and took action independently, which, in the decision of Parliament, was the point at which he had exceeded his authority; he did, however, report to President Paasikivi after the persons had been delivered to Soviet officials. Leino refused to resign even though Article 36 of the constitution requires that Ministers "must enjoy the confidence of the Diet." President Paasikivi three days after the vote of censure, acting to uphold the constitution, released him from membership in the government.[20] The Communist leaders immediately called a general strike, which threatened to tie up transportation and other vital services, but only about 7.4% of organized labor heeded the call.[21] In a move to placate the Communists, Eino Kilpi, a Socialist Unity member of the SKDL, was chosen to replace Leino, and Hertta Kuusinen was appointed Minister without portfolio. In the Leino Affair the Communists had suffered another serious blow, and the actions of Parliament and the President contributed to the preservation of constitutionalism and democratic vitality.

On the heels of the crises and crucial decisions, the campaign for the election of Parliament was in full swing. Among other things, the election would test the extent of popular support for the Communist-SKDL in light of setbacks and controversy, departure of the Allied Control Commission, and the new context of relations with the Soviet Union. A hard fought and spirited campaign brought a record turnout of voters: 78.4% of qualified

---

19. *New York Times*, May 5, 1948, p. 17: These individuals were wanted in Moscow on charges of espionage and "anti-Russian terror acts."

20. See Hodgson, "The Paasikivi Line," pp. 156–158, for a good summary account of the relevant details. See also *New York Times*, May 20, 1948, pp. 10 and 11, and May 24, 1948, p. 1. The censure motion was introduced by the Conservative Party and was passed by a vote of 80 to 60. In the parliamentary debate Leino explained that the Allied Control Commission forced him to deliver the persons.

21. Bellquist, "Finland's Democracy in Travail," p. 218.

voters went to the polls, an increase of almost 5% over the 1945 total,[22] which resulted in a sharp decline of 11 seats for the SKDL, a gain of 5 for the Social Democrats, 7 for the Agrarians, and 4 for the Conservatives. Two of the smaller parties, the Swedish and the Progressives, a liberal party, lost 1 and 4 seats respectively.[23] Power in Parliament had shifted to the center with a moderate gain for the Conservatives. (Social Democrats should be classified as left center and Communist-SKDL as far left.) It was a free election in the traditional sense of Western parliamentary democracy, an accurate gauge of national opinion, and a confirmation of Finnish independence. It was expected that despite its losses the SKDL would be included in the new government, for none of the three major parties had a substantial lead. Adhering to parliamentary tradition President Paasikivi, after counsulting with Uhro Kekkonen, the new Speaker, and the various Diet groups, invited Karl August Fagerholm, the former Speaker and Social Democrat, to form a new cabinet.

Fagerholm as Prime Minister designate endeavored to reinstitute basically the previous coalition composed of six Social Democrats, six Agrarians, and four SKDL, which reflected their reduced strength. The latter, however, refused to accept, and countered with insistence upon more representation and control of the key Ministries of Foreign Affairs, Interior, and Trade, laying special claim to Interior. Discussions were discontinued when the SKDL rejected Fagerholm's counter offer of five cabinet posts, not including the influential ones desired.[24] Negotiations also failed to install a Social Democratic-Agrarian coalition, which left the alternative of forming an all-Social Democratic cabinet with the retention of C. J. A. Enckell, nonparty, as Foreign Minister, whose inclusion indicated that the foreign policy line of President Paasikivi would be continued under a friend and supporter. President Paasikivi, who had suggested the all-Socialist cabinet in order to end the impasse, readily

---

22. *Ibid.,* p. 220.

23. *Facts on File,* July 4–10, 1948, pp. 219–220.

24. John H. Hodgson, *Communism in Finland* (Princeton: Princeton University Press, 1967), p. 231. Fagerholm related to Hodgson that one of the SKDL demands he considered impossible was that they be given the Interior or Foreign Ministry.

approved the solution, and the new government took office on July 29. It had the support of the Conservatives, the Swedish Party, and the Progressives, which with the Socialist seats accounted for a total of 106 votes out of 200.[25] A possible consequence of the absence of the SKDL was the establishment of a practice conformed to in the succeeding government under Kekkonen and all cabinets until 1966.[26]

In approving the new government, Paasikivi may have expected Soviet coolness, skepticism, suspicion, or even hostility to a government so composed and supported—and so opposed—but felt obligated to accept one brought about by the election and the parliamentary processes taking their natural course. With the prestige of his person and office, Paasikivi undeviatingly supported the new cabinet, which was probably another reason the Soviets felt obliged to accept the Fagerholm coalition. It may thus be concluded that the conduct of the election, the results, and the choice of a new Prime Minister and cabinet all indicated that the political processes in Finland were functioning as in the soft sphere model. Furthermore, when it is considered that these processes resulted in a reduction of Communist influence in Parliament, their exclusion from the government, and the creating of a new cabinet which might be distrusted and criticized by the Soviet Union, there should be little doubt of the actuality of independence the Finns enjoyed in 1948.

During the life of the Fagerholm government of 1948 the Agrarians were for the most part lukewarm or hostile and in crucial votes sided with the SKDL, which was in opposition. It might thus be described as a "Pink" government with "White" support, but with tepid "Green" support or opposition, and outright "Red" opposition.

The soft sphere system had survived the first of two trials in

---

25. On the formation of the first Fagerholm government see Bellquist, "Finland's Democracy in Travail," p. 222; Valros, *Finland, 1946–1952*, p. 19; and M.E.R.L., "Finnish Outlook," *World Today*, p. 166. The members of the cabinet are listed in *Facts on File*, July 25–31, 1948, p. 246.

26. After 1948 the clearinghouse character of the SKDL changed to function more like a political party proper and as an instrument of the Communist Party, which retained its own organization. In 1955 the Socialist Unity Party, which was a component of the SKDL, resigned leaving the Communists the only part left in it. Nousiainen, *The Finnish Political System*, p. 26.

1948 when the political process functioned in a manner reflecting internal independence and democracy. The second trial would be the response of the Soviet Union to the new government, after having decided not to interfere in the campaign, the election, or the formation of the cabinet. Moscow's attitude was in general one of passive acceptance, with some cordiality and even gracious concession on the one hand, some coolness, warning, criticism, accusation, and pressure on the other, but no hackles of fear and anger were raised that would lead to denunciation and rejection, such as in 1958 and in 1961.

The first sign of negative response to the Fagerholm government was coolness, indicated when the Soviet Ambassador did not pay customary respects to the new Premier.[27] Later, Soviet press and radio joined Finnish Communist criticism and accusation charging the government with dreams of restoring a fascist regime that received instructions from abroad, that threatened rights and freedoms of the Finnish people, and that undermined Soviet-Finnish relations.[28] In December of 1948 and early 1949 the attacks intensified as Moscow media criticized the release because of good behavior of V. Tanner and E. Linkomies, two of the "War Responsibles," from prison after serving half of their five and one-half year sentences. The Soviet government itself then exerted direct pressure in notes demanding the disbanding of rifle clubs, the punishment of two policemen who had mistreated Soviet citizens, and denounced two plays whose performances were regarded as "a manifestation of a spirit of hostility and revenge against the Soviet Union."[29] Soviet media attacks upon the Fagerholm government were in part a reflection of the influence of Finnish Communists in shaping Soviet perceptions of Finnish politics. Fagerholm in riposte denounced the Communist charges as lies and accused them of covering their tactical

27. Hodgson, "The Paasikivi Line," p. 158. Lt. Gen. G. M. Savonenkov, the Soviet Minister to Finland, continued his coolness by ignoring invitations to functions and had yet to meet Fagerholm as the new Prime Minister by the end of October. *New York Times,* October 30, 1948, p. 3.

28. Bellquist, "Finland's Democracy in Travail," p. 223; October 2 over Radio Moscow citing the *Literary Gazette,* and October 20 a commentator writing in *Novoye Vremya.*

29. *Ibid.* Bellquist cites the Helsinki press of December 8, 1948; the two plays were "Les Mains Sales" by Sartre and "The Jaeger's Bride" by Sihvo.

error of scuttling the cabinet negotiations for their inclusion in the government.

Reflecting on the other hand Soviet acceptance of the new government, a successful negotiation of a postwar trade agreement in Moscow was in November and December accompanied by gracious receptions and entertainment; a further manifestation of good will was the alleviation of $600,000 of fines for delayed deliveries of reparations goods, two-thirds of the fines which had been levied.[30]

The soft sphere system in 1948–1949 survived the second test in view of the fact that the Soviet government did little more than allow Moscow media attacks and exert some mild pressures on the new government. It seems reasonable to conjecture that Soviet decision makers, after scanning and coding the information and weighing the alternative of rejecting the Fagerholm government, came down in favor of accepting it and adopting a wait-and-see policy to determine if the level of Soviet tolerance would be breached by future events.

Fagerholm, for his part, upon announcing the program of his government the day after it was formed, declared that it would continue "the foreign political trend of the preceding cabinet" and that its "leading aim" was to strengthen the country's international position "with Finland's independence and sovereignty as a starting point" upon the basis of the peace treaty, United Nations principles, and the Finno-Soviet treaty of 1948.[31] Here was assurance, to be affirmed by later assurances, that the Paasikivi Line as the spirit and the legal basis of the soft sphere would be continued in full force regardless of the change of government. The Soviet government accepted the assurances and apparently found that they were adhered to substantially in good faith. Soviet decision makers, as noted, also probably took due regard of the fact that the Fagerholm cabinet had the unwavering support of President Paasikivi.

Two additional factors may also be adduced to explain the Soviet decision: Paasikivi as President was the dominant and,

---

30. *Ibid.,* pp. 225–226.

31. *Ibid.,* p. 225. The full text was reported in all leading Helsinki newspapers on July 31, 1948.

beyond question, the dependable force in Finnish government as far as Moscow was concerned, and there seemed to be no threat to his position from the new government; indeed, Fagerholm had his steadfast support. The second factor was that in 1948–1949 Tanner and his faction, who were to become anathema in Moscow, had not yet re-established their control over the Social Democratic Party. Fagerholm, on the other hand, was a critic and opponent of *Finnish* Communists, but even at that Moscow may have realized that his terms for their inclusion in his cabinet were reasonable.

The list of substantive reforms of the first Fagerholm government should be headed by the abolition of "VALPO," the state police, headed by Leino and shaped into an instrument to serve his purposes as Minister of Interior. The publication of a report of an investigation into its operations by the new government (which the previous government had received but failed to publish) caused a sensation, for it revealed that Ministers were shadowed and their telephones tapped, that the organization had exceeded its powers, that most of its members lacked educational qualifications and many had criminal records.[32]

Significant economic and social welfare legislation included a new family allowance for each mother with children under 16 years of age.[33] In November of 1948 a bill was signed providing a five-year plan for housing to cost at least 27 billion marks during the next decade.[34] Restrictions on the issuance of passports were modified and a limited travel allowance was permitted.[35]

The Fagerholm government lasted for seventeen months, which, given the hostility from within the Parliament by the two other major parties, and Soviet press and radio from without, was in itself a major accomplishment.[36] The historic significance of

---

32. Valros, *Finland, 1946–1952*, p. 20; Spencer, "Finland Maintains Democracy," p. 305; M.E.R.L., "Finnish Outlook," p. 167.

33. See Bellquist, "Finland's Democracy in Travail," p. 225, who cites *Suomen Socialidemokraati*, July 25, 1948, wherein it was estimated that there were about 1,142,500 such children in Finland and that the total annual expenditure would rise to 8,200 million marks.

34. *Ibid.*, where *Helsingen Sanomat*, November 24, 1948, is cited.

35. Valros, *Finland, 1946–1952*, p. 20.

36. Andren, *Government and Politics in Nordic Countries*, Appendix 2, indicates it has been one of the most durable of postwar Finnish governments.

this government was to preside over the "democratic reconstruction."[37] A corner had been turned to a clearer and wider path where democratic institutions and national independence became so firmly rooted that they could only be undermined or destroyed by intervention from without. The internal ground had thus been prepared for the effective functioning of the soft sphere; the second phase of its dénouement had been concluded. Thus, as the soft sphere took durable and definite form, so did the Soviet system of influence, to which attention should next be turned.

---

37. Two contemporary observers expressed far more than usual praise for an outgoing cabinet: Spencer, "Finland Maintains Democracy," p. 305, concluded that the authority of Parliament "was raised to new heights," and M.E.R.L., "Finnish Outlook," p. 165, was convinced that the outgoing government had "rendered Finland signal services, if indeed, it did not alone secure the country's future as a free and democratic state."

CHAPTER FOUR

THE SYSTEM OF SOVIET INFLUENCE

At this point there will be a further examination of the general principles involved in the means, degree, and effects of Soviet influence and from there an identification of specific techniques which have been formulated to this end.[1] The basic principle guiding exercise of the system of Soviet influence in Finland was the expectation that her independence as a soft sphere would operate in approved ways, but more especially would *not* operate in ways disapproved. It is difficult to resist the impression that although the Paasikivi Line underlay postwar policy, and the government was bound by obligations in the treaty of peace and the pact of 1948, Finnish independence was not fully trusted. This in part stemmed from the residuum of distrust on both sides and the apparent Soviet belief that the primary ingredient in the effective functioning of the Finnish system was quality of leadership in power.

The study of systems of influence in soft spheres is largely the

---

1. The study of the techniques of Soviet influence in Finland has been the subject of systematic and penetrating studies, and this chapter is indebted to them. See Kent Forster, "The Finnish-Soviet Crisis of 1958–1959," *International Journal* (Spring 1960) pp. 147–150, and "The Silent Soviet Vote in Finnish Politics," *International Journal* (Summer 1963) pp. 341–352; Hodgson, "The Paasikivi Line" and "Postwar Finnish Foreign Policy: Institutions and Personalities," *The Western Political Quarterly* (March 1972) pp. 80–92; Holsti, "Strategy and Techniques of Influence in Soviet-Finnish Relations"; and Kuusisto, "The Paasikivi Line in Finland's Foreign Policy."

study of techniques of indirect influence. The techniques of indirect influence have aimed to bring about certain conditions, to prevent others from occurring, and to maintain certain ones intact. Moscow has strived withal, however, to foster an image of a "reasonable," "restrained," "cooperative," and even "benevolent" great power coexisting with its little neighbor, instead of a dominating, imperialistic, hegemonic "big brother."

The Paasikivi Line, which charts the basic course of Finnish attitudes and behavior toward the USSR, should be identified as *the* primary mode of indirect influence. As such, its significance cannot be overestimated, and its effects are very great indeed; but as a technique of influence which is indirect it is subtle and inoffensive as well. To the Finns it has become *their* policy, one upon which the great majority of people can unite, and in political life it has become unquestioned doctrine.[2] Among other things, the Line is a pro-Soviet position which Moscow expects and welcomes. Such hearty mutual endorsement is a main pillar of the soft sphere and the Soviet system of influence. To the Finns, however, it is more than a mode of influence, for it sets limits that protect their independence. The Line also endorses neutrality and recognizes Finland's affinity with Scandinavia.[3]

The Primary Technique: A Pair of Doctrines

It will be recalled that the chief purpose of Soviet influence in Finland was to maintain a policy favorable to Soviet security and strategic interests. Previous chapters have traced how the peace treaty, the pact of 1948, and the Paasikivi Line were all geared to serve this interest and thus became the basis for the new postwar relationship, which might be designated as the "settlement" or the "fulfillment." Soviet leaders felt the need for constant vigilance to prevent the undermining of the relationship by persons and groups who would do so by utilizing the freedom and indepen-

2. See Holsti, "Strategy and Techniques of Influence in Soviet-Finnish Relations," p. 71. All noncommunist parties support the line; to question these principles "is considered political suicide." Dr. T. Junnila in his interview with the author in October, 1967.

3. See Hodgson, "The Paasikivi Line," pp. 149–150, wherein he notes that one of the most important components of the Line is what Paasikivi called *"puolustustaho"* or the will and desire to defend one's rights and independence.

dence of Finland. Thus, in the Soviet view, the soft sphere was not to be the means of destroying the objectives for which it was established, and they felt constrained to judge when and from whom the danger arose. In particular, they were on guard against a recrudescence of prewar anti-Russian attitudes and "outpost of the West" mentality.

Issuing from such preoccupations (at times obsessions) were a pair of devices for influence: one, to prevent persons and groups with such discredited and feared attitudes from gaining political power in Finland, and the other to approve and assist persons and groups with attitudes congenial to the maintenance of the system, in both cases as seen by Soviet leaders. Thus we have the doctrine of distrust-rejection-opposition matched by the doctrine of trust-acceptance-assistance. The two doctrines could work to inject Soviet influence in subtle or not so subtle guises, steering or interfering in the internal political processes of Finland. If the Finnish political system "absorbed" the influence because it was subtle and caused little objection or disruption, the soft sphere system would be little affected; indeed, the system would accommodate itself readily to this kind of influence. If, on the other hand, the influence were of great magnitude and its effects serious, a crisis and attendant dysfunction of the system might follow.

The first step in implementing the doctrine of distrust-rejection-opposition was to include in the armistice an insistence upon a trial of the "War Responsibles" alluded to above. Even before the trial, in order to carry out the Soviet intention and instill confidence in Finnish desires for better relations, Paasikivi as Premier, in January 1945, urged "that leading politicians of the last years and persons chiefly responsible for the entry into the unfortunate war and for a policy which was inconsistent with the interests of the country should retire from public life."[4] Strong pressure from Paasikivi continued and brought the withdrawal of several politicians who were anathema to the USSR.[5] The Soviet press, however, was not content to leave matters to chance, for *Pravda* and *Izvestia* issued warnings that the results of the trials would have consequences beyond Finland's borders and

---

4. Alenius, *Finland between the Armistice and the Peace*, pp. 24–25.
5. See Hodgson, "The Paasikivi Line," p. 154.

would test whether "Finland is determined to eradicate all traces of Fascism."[6]

An example of trust-acceptance-assistance was the Red-Green coalition, in which the Communists and their left Socialist associates in the SKDL played a prominent role in the government established in cooperation with the Social Democrats and Agrarians. The smoothest operation of this doctrine, however, was the Soviet support of Paasikivi as Premier and later as President for the first dozen years of the postwar period. Under the twin doctrines the Soviets had a gallery of rogues but also a pantheon of heroes. In Paasikivi they had a hero whose qualities and stature among the Finns no one else could equal at that period of time. In Moscow he was respected, his policies were welcomed, his leadership was acknowledged and trusted. He was thus suited for the role of prime mover in Finland under the soft sphere concept. Indeed, Stalin and the Soviet leaders were probably willing to accede to the soft sphere because Paasikivi was available and could be trusted. If Passikivi had not been on the scene, the Soviets might have insisted upon someone from the SKDL, but they had no one to match his stature.

As the years slipped by, the institution became in goodly measure the lengthened shadow of this man, and when he passed from the scene the Soviet decision makers felt they had to find another Paasikivi in order to be confident the system would still work. This was probably an important reason for their elaboration of the doctrine of trust-acceptance-assistance. During his period in power, important concessions and assistance were rendered to Finland, such as the adoption of the Finnish delegation's draft for the pact of 1948 and the return of Porkkala. These concessions worked to shore up his position, assure the Finnish people of the correctness of his policies, and facilitate acceptance of Soviet influence—probably a motive in the "assistance" aspect of this doctrine.

The issue of applying the doctrines very likely arose, in 1948, in the case of Fagerholm and his government. It seems reasonable to infer on the basis of evidence available that the case fell midway between the two, but perhaps a little more toward the trust-acceptance-assistance doctrine. The inconclusive nature of the

---

6. *New York Times,* March 13, 1945, p. 8, and March 17, p. 4.

case probably inclined Stalin to accept Fagerholm, without much trust, and to indulge in some harassment and opposition. He accepted him conditionally, waiting to see how trustworthy he would be. He was probably reinforced in this attitude by Paasikivi's firm backing of Fagerholm. For his part, Fagerholm gave unequivocal assurances by word and deed that the "fulfill-ment" would not be disturbed.[7] It seems that in the application of the doctrines for this case Stalin settled on an operating principle: when the case is in doubt, adopt the doctrine of trust-acceptance-assistance on a trial basis. This seems consistent with the soft sphere expectations.

The period after Paasikivi's re-election in 1950 to a second term as President was also a period of Kekkonen's rise in political stature. As early as 1943 he could point to the change in his views as they began to coincide with those of Paasikivi.[8] By 1956 Kekko-nen was the leading politician of the Agrarian Party and had served as Premier in more governments than anyone else. When Paasikivi announced his retirement that year, the battle lines were drawn for the contest between Kekkonen and Fagerholm to de-termine who would be his successor. Fagerholm could claim a position in Finnish politics at least equal to that of Kekkonen, for he had been Prime Minister and Speaker of the Parliament as well as the leading postwar Social Democratic politician up to that time. The President in Finland is elected by a majority vote of a 300 member electoral college chosen by a system of proportional representation. Fagerholm had strong support, not only from his own party but from the National Coalition, the Liberals, and the Swedish Party, and stood a good chance to win the presidency. Kekkonen had the support of his own party. This left the matter in the hands of the SKDL, for if Kekkonen got their support, he had a chance to win. In the decisive third ballot between Fagerholm and Kekkonen as the only two candidates under the rules, the SKDL threw their support to Kekkonen and assured his election in the closest vote possible for victory: 151 to 149.

---

7. See Chapter 3, pp. 73–78, for discussion of the first Fagerholm govern-ment in a broader context.

8. See Kekkonen, *Neutrality: The Finnish Position,* for the text of "Good Neigh-bourliness with the 'Hereditary Enemy,'" a speech given at a meeting organized by the Swedish Agrarian Union in Stockholm, 7 December 1943, especially pp. 29–30.

Moscow watched the campaign with keen interest. Paasikivi had become a legend, and the Soviet leaders desired to see his role perpetuated by someone they trusted. Moscow's choice was obviously Kekkonen, and we can infer that the SKDL in resolving its doubts was either steered by Moscow or chose to read the mind of Soviet leaders. At any rate, in commenting on the election *Izvestia* recorded delight over the outcome.[9] Finland had another President, but it would take a decade before Moscow could relax with the assurance that he enjoyed the same broad base of support as Paasikivi. Fagerholm's defeat obviated the need for Soviet decision makers to anguish over whether they would accept him or not.

Soviet leaders marked with keen interest and alarm the return to political power of Väinö Tanner, the grand old man of the Social Democratic Party and one of the foremost Finnish political figures of the interwar years. Found guilty as one of the "War Responsibles" he was released on good behavior in 1948 after having served half of his five and one-half year sentence, which was the practice under Finnish law. In the Soviet perception of him, Tanner was the chief rogue and the one who represented the greatest menace to the "fulfillment" and "settlement," which would be undermined or overturned if he came to power. Leaders in the USSR branded Tanner as one of the prime movers in the war against the Soviet Union and blamed him for much of the anti-Soviet animus before, during, and after the conflict.[10] In

---

9. See Hodgson, "The Paasikivi Line," p. 164, for quotation of a passage from *Izvestia*.

10. See *ibid.*, p. 168. See also Marvin Rintala, "Väinö Tanner in Finnish Politics," *The American Slavic and East European Review* (February 1961) pp. 84–98, and Rintala, *Four Finns*, Chapter III, "The Bureaucrat in Politics: Väinö Tanner," pp. 47–70; also Jakobson, *Diplomacy of the Winter War*, for the role of Tanner in the negotiations of autumn 1939. To some extent the ill-will of the Soviet leaders might have come from the pre-World War I period when Tanner was a Menshevik. Bolshevik contempt for European Social Democrats in the interwar years is also well known. When Tanner met Stalin in the autumn of 1939 during the negotiations which preceded the Winter War, he remarked to Stalin, probably in a jocular manner, that he had been a Menshevik. Paasikivi, however, got on rather well with the Soviets because he would speak to them in Russian and had a better gift for *politesse* in diplomacy than Tanner, whose career had been as a party boss for so many years. The author is indebted to several of the persons interviewed in Finland for discussion of the personality of these two great men of Finnish politics.

Paasikivi the Soviets found a strong figure about whom there was
no doubt, but Tanner was a strong figure about whom there were
grave doubts, if not certainty of his menace. He was charged with
desires for revanchism, designs to restore relations with the Germans and with being a tool of American-Western imperialism.

In 1951 Tanner had again been elected to Parliament, and by
1957 he had re-established his power in the party when elected
Chairman by defeating Fagerholm by one vote, 95 to 94, after a
bitter contest. Tanner inspired a group of followers, notably the
eloquent, energetic and magnetic Väinö Leskinen, who was expected to succeed to the leadership after the aging Tanner retired. Tanner and his followers, in coming to power, divided the
party, and a group led by Emil Skog withdrew and made common
cause with the SKDL.

Soviet apprehensions mounted as Tanner and his followers
made big waves in the Finnish political pond, but a flare of anger
greeted President Kekkonen's invitation to Tanner to form a
government in 1957 after he had been elected Chairman.[11] Soviet
displeasure in 1957 was but a prelude to the outbursts of wrath in
1958 and 1961 directed at the Social Democrats, especially Tanner and his protégés, and did not subside until Tanner retired in
1963, Leskinen disavowed his former views, and a new leadership
took the helm and changed policies. These are all events in the
climactic period from 1958 to 1966 in Finnish-Soviet relations, as
well as in domestic political life of the country, which can be traced
in the main to the doctrine of distrust-rejection-opposition. But
there were two strings to the Soviet bow, and they shot the arrow
of trust-acceptance-assistance toward the goal of establishing
Kekkonen as the new Paasikivi. The next three chapters examine
the events and the application of the doctrines in detail.

Do's and Don'ts for Finland

Decisions were called for from time to time concerning the

---

11. See Forster, "The Silent Vote in Finnish Politics," p. 346, where he notes
that the Soviet response was an abrupt suspension of trade negotiations with
Finland then in progress and a denunciation of Tanner. See also Hodgson, "The
Paasikivi Line," p. 169, who quotes the Soviet response published in *Izvestia* on
October 26, 1957. Hodgson speculated that Kekkonen invited Tanner to form a
government, knowing he would not succeed, in order to puncture his inflated
hopes.

appropriate things for Finland to do or not to do in the context of her relations with the Soviet Union as defined in the formative years of the soft sphere. Moscow wanted a hand in these decisions and interpretations and found various ways to convey her wishes. Helsinki, we may conjecture, found at times that it was wiser to ascertain the inclinations of Moscow if there was any doubt. In another sense, however, it was not always necessary for the Soviet Union to convey its wishes explicitly. It is a test of the effectiveness of influence if neither pressure nor suggestion is necessary, because the one who is influenced anticipates the reactions of the influencer. This is the best way to disguise influence, and, of course, in international relations sovereignty and national sensibilities can be respected thereby.

In Finnish-Soviet relations, however, direct indications often seemed necessary, for the Soviet press and radio were frequently used to indicate approval as well as disapproval, warning, criticism, or even demands to the Finnish politicians or public; the campaign of harassment and criticism in 1948 against Fagerholm and his government has been previously noted. Sometimes it was deemed appropriate for the Soviet government to make a direct representation to the Finnish government—which might or might not be public. Statements in the media were often made by journalists, but stronger insistence was conveyed if made by Soviet officials.

One of the earliest examples of Soviet indication that a Finnish action should be avoided was in the summer of 1947 when the Finnish government was invited to participate in a conference of European countries in Paris to discuss their needs under the projected Marshall aid plan of the United States. Moscow dispatched an official note to the Finnish government with the admonition that if the invitation was accepted it would be considered an act hostile to the Soviet Union. Here was one of the few instances of *direct* influence, and Paasikivi, if for no other reason, had to abide by the pledge in his Line "to do nothing in conflict with the interests of the Soviet Union." This was one of the most painful decisions made under Soviet pressure in view of Finland's known need for economic assitance.[12]

---

12. Mazour, *Finland between East and West*, p. 175. Even though a majority of Parliament's Foreign Affairs Committee had given an affirmative response to the

An aspect of Soviet policy more pronounced in the Stalinist era of the period under consideration was the pressure on Finland to restrict her diplomatic and economic relations with Western countries and even Scandinavia. Finland, like the Eastern European satellites, would thus to some extent be "sealed-off" from countries outside of the Soviet orbit. Such "sealing-off" reflected Moscow's suspicions and included an element of the hard sphere policy for Finland.[13]

In addition to Soviet interdiction of participation in the Marshall plan, there was a Soviet veto of Finnish membership in the United Nations, probably because it was favored by the United States and the Western bloc which vetoed membership of countries sponsored by the USSR. Finland and other countries came into the United Nations in 1956 as part of the East-West "package deal." In 1952, however, a more serious exclusion occurred when Finland chose not to accept membership in the Nordic Council when it was formed, probably anticipating negative reactions in Moscow, and applied instead to participate as an observer. But in a few years, with some changes in the international situation and Soviet reassessments, she could now see a green light and applied for full membership.[14] Thus in the Soviet system of influence Finnish decision makers had to be aware when a positive response could replace an adverse one, and vice versa.[15]

Two examples of "don'ts" in the period of delicate relations

---

invitation, the government declined it, explaining "that Finland had not yet exchanged treaty ratifications with the Soviet Union and could not undertake any obligations unless her political stability was more firmly established." See also Kuusisto, "The Paasikivi Line in Finland's Foreign Policy," p. 44.

13. See Holsti, "Strategy and Techniques of Influence in Soviet-Finnish Relations," p. 71. Despite the sealing-off policy with its hard sphere overtones, a general policy of relaxation begun under Stalin in 1948 and up through 1956 is readily discernible. In 1952, for example, a United States-Finnish agreement for a Fulbright program was concluded. See also Kuusisto, "The Paasikivi Line in Finland's Foreign Policy," pp. 44–45.

14. See Chapter 9, "The Primary External Relationship: Finland, the Soviet Union, and the Scandinavian Subsystem."

15. This seemed to be the case in April 1970 when President Kekkonen in an abrupt *volte-face* declared that under present circumstances Finland would not sign the projected "NORDEK treaty" for a Nordic Economic Union to include Norway, Denmark, Sweden, and Finland. See Karl E. Birnbaum, "Soviet Policy in Northern Europe," *Survival,* XII, No. 7 (July 1970) pp. 231–232 and 229.

occurred in the autumn of 1958 with direct objection by Soviet officials on some relatively inconsequential matters: 1) a particularly uncomplimentary cartoon of Khrushchev was suppressed and 2) the Finnish government announced that the memoirs of Leino were to be withdrawn from publication until further notice.[16]

A few years later, however, in a matter of great moment to the life of the country, persistent and resourceful negotiations yielded a Soviet concurrence when Moscow was convinced that economic interests compelled Finland to seek an agreement with the EFTA countries even though, from the Soviet point of view, the organization was subject to suspicion as not really very different from the EEC, which was little more than an arm of the NATO block. Finland, in negotiations with EFTA countries, did not accede as a full member but joined with them in creating a new free trade association composed of the seven EFTA countries as one party and Finland as the other. Collateral Helsinki-Moscow negotiations preserved Soviet rights under Most Favored Nation clauses in Finno-Soviet trade treaties.[17] The red light flashed unequivocally against any link with EEC, which Moscow regarded as having a *political* character, Finland's membership in which

---

16. See Forster, "The Silent Vote in Finnish Politics," p. 347. In September 1972 these memoirs were still unpublished and the author was given the general impression by one who had read them that nothing new or startling was contained in them, but some persons who were identified would be spared embarrassment by continued withholding of publication. The Kremlin, however, has not withdrawn objections.

17. See Klaus Törnudd, *Soviet Attitudes toward Non-Military Regional Cooperation,* Commentationes Humanarum Litterarum XXVIII, No. 1 (Helsingfors: Societas Scientiacum Fennica, 1961), pp. 169–178. See also Meinander, "Finland's Commercial Policy," pp. 136–138, where he notes that the neutral character of the Scandinavian members in EFTA may have been a factor in Finland's association with EFTA. See also Holsti, "Strategy and Techniques of Influence in Soviet-Finnish Relations," pp. 72–73, where he notes that Finland had to clear possible USSR objection to her association with EFTA on the grounds that it would violate Article 4 of the pact of 1948 by which she pledged not to join any alliance or coalition directed against the Soviet Union. See Treaty Series No. 105, 1961, *Agreement Creating An Association between the Members of EFTA and the Republic of Finland* (with Protocol) Helsinki, March 27, 1961 (London: H. M. Stationery Office Command 1549).

would violate her obligation to keep out of the conflicts of great powers.[18]

Concessions and Gifts

Akin to the need for approval of the paramount power is the technique of timely concessions of something desired, but perhaps withheld, from the sphere state. Concession is a positive action which helps to sustain the basic attitude in the soft sphere system; it conveys by tangible means the ideal of "partnership" and "good neighborliness" and not the narrow unilateral pursuit of interest by the hegemonic power. It can redound to the benefit of the paramount power by an increase of good will and greater sensitivity for the interests of the latter in the sphere state, for it serves as part of the conditioning process to ease the flow of influence.

Concession can be defined as a gift as well as an inducement for reciprocity; such was the case in the evacuation of Porkkala, which helped induce Finnish agreement to renew the pact of 1948 for an additional twenty years, a move ardently desired by Moscow. Sometimes concession is virtually unavoidable, in the sense that harm would result if it were not given, as when Finland's economic interest seemed to require an arrangement with EFTA; the same could be said of her membership in the Nordic Council. Concession could be used to shore up the position of favored Finns such as Paasikivi and Kekkonen, who could then argue the wisdom of the postwar change in Finnish policy and their being entrusted with leadership.

Soviet accession to the Paasikivi version of the pact of 1948 was a significant diplomatic concession affecting the character of relations between the two countries in the formative stages of the soft sphere, and the reduction of reparations in 1948 helped to lighten the burden on Finland imposed by the treaty of peace. Another concession was to reduce the weight of the peace terms,

---

18. See Törnudd, *Soviet Attitudes toward Non-Military Regional Cooperation*, pp. 152–162, where he refers to abundant Soviet criticism of the EEC which uses both political and economic arguments to attack almost all aspects of the Community. See also Holsti, "Strategy and Techniques of Influence in Soviet-Finnish Relations," pp. 72–73.

such as the arrangements concluded regarding the Saimaa Canal. In the summer of 1962 a treaty was negotiated for lease to Finland of the Soviet-owned portion of the canal which had been ceded to the Soviet Union in the treaty of peace as part of the Karelian Isthmus. The concession has added significance in light of the fact that it was the first time the USSR relinquished part of its territory for use by another state, and could be taken as a clear indication of its confidence in the relationship with Finland after the Note Crisis and dysfunction it caused had just passed.[19]

Pursuant to the discussion in Chapter 2, we can count as a concession Soviet interpretation of the position of Finland as a neutral under the pact of 1948.[20] Finally, it is possible that in part the Soviet termination of the status of the Karelian-Finnish S.S.R. as a Union Republic and the transfer of the long time Finnish communist exile Otto Kuusinen to duties of theoretical analyst and adviser in Moscow was a concession to Finland.[21]

Once concessions have been made, it is difficult, and in some cases impossible, to revoke them, and a new status quo is constituted, incorporating them into the system to anchor the soft sphere more firmly. If the atmosphere is conducive, concession-

---

19. See *Finnish Features* No. 63/62 for a text of the treaty, and Erkki Savolainen, "Saimaa Canal," pp. 138–141 in *Introduction to Finland, 1963*. This Soviet concession and President Kekkonen's pursuit of it drew criticism in Finland that renovation of the waterway, which had not been used since the war, would be too costly for the benefits to be derived. Kekkonen justified the move by emphasizing the special benefits to eastern Finland, where economic conditions needed some improvement. See *New York Times*, November 26, 1962, p. 34, and November 28, p. 4.

20. See pp. 58–64 above.

21. After 1940 the elevation of the Karelo-Finnish Autonomous Republic to the status of a Union Republic "was obviously a political move directed against Finland because the Karelians were a minority of the population in this very backward unit": Frederick C. Barghoorn, *Soviet Russian Nationalism* (New York: Oxford University Press, 1956), p. 77. The change back to an Autonomous Republic took place in mid 1956 when the Soviet Union made the other important concessions to Finland. Stalin's heirs had abandoned the policy of attempting to attract Finnish citizens into the USSR by immigration to the Karelo-Finnish S.S.R. "and decided it was time to be realistic and incorporate the Karelo-Finnish minority within the Russian Republic to which they were already bound closely economically": John N. Hazard, "The Soviet Federal System," p. 306, in *Soviet Politics and Government, A Reader,* edited by Randolph L. Braham (New York: Alfred A. Knopf, 1965).

giving can become somewhat of a habit for the paramount power, while for the sphere state it may become an expectation.

The means, degree, and effects of the Soviet system of influence up to 1958 can best be described as a predominantly soft sphere. This was especially so after 1955 when a liberalization resulted from some significant concessions, induced in part by an improved international climate but more particularly by confidence of Soviet policy makers that the system worked according to expectations and that Soviet interests were served by it.

The Paasikivi Line, which undergirded the new dispensation, was acclaimed in both countries. Some of the burdens of the peace treaty had been fulfilled (reparations), lifted (Porkkala), or revised (Saimaa Canal); and the pact of 1948 in commitments and provision for neutrality and subsequent interpretations thereof, going far toward accommodating the Finnish point of view, was also reciprocally acclaimed. Presidential and parliamentary elections were conducted in accordance with the constitutional processes of the country, and governments were formed and maintained (or dissolved) with adherence to parliamentary practice. The Fagerholm government of 1948 was subjected to some harassment and criticism, but the Soviet government refrained from a degree of influence that would precipitate a crisis and probable demise of the government. Likewise the election of Kekkonen in 1956 by a razor thin margin indicated the free functioning of the political system.

Behind the whole edifice stood the towering figure of Paasikivi, and even after he retired it seemed likely, for a few years at least, that the system would function without him. Indeed, by 1958 it seemed that the system had been stabilized, with a good prospect for durability in conditioning perceptions, instilling expectations, and guiding decisions in both countries. Thus reciprocal advantages, respect for sovereignty, and even in some measure a "mystique" united the two countries in common purpose. These are hallmarks of a soft sphere, which characterized the Finno-Soviet relationship. The comfort of optimism was thus indulged in, but it soon gave way to gloom as discord and disturbance afflicted the system.

CHAPTER FIVE

CRISIS AND DYSFUNCTION:
THE NIGHTFROST, 1958

The least that could be said for the Soviet system of influence evolved by 1958 was that it operated with sufficient efficacy to satisfy Soviet purposes and provide a basis for a chastened but pragmatic Finland to "live with" unavoidable Soviet hegemony. By 1958, however, one fundamental of the system had not been definitely ascertained: What was the level of tolerance in Moscow for the free functioning of the Finnish political system, and under what circumstances would Soviet leaders determine that they should be constrained to interfere to forestall undesired developments? Once interference had been decided upon, a parallel fundamental had also to be ascertained: What particular means would be chosen, how great a degree of influence would be exercised, and what would be the desired effects? If the measures chosen resulted in effects of such magnitude as to disturb significantly the internal operation of the Finnish political system, this should be identified as dysfunction. To be sure, Soviet leaders could argue that the system had ceased to function properly, which would justify the measures taken; but Moscow probably made these arguments privately, for it has been loath to acknowledge interference.

The breached level of tolerance, Moscow would undoubtedly argue, was an exceptional circumstance requiring exceptional measures; if the magnitude of the effect caused dysfunction, it would have to be borne and could be justified from the Soviet point of view. Achievement of desired results would signify it was safe for relaxation and a return to the "normal" system of influence; dysfunction would in this contingency be only a temporary lapse and, the Soviets might further argue, help to rid the system of undesirable elements clogging its efficiency. In 1958 it was not, however, foreseen how prolonged the dysfunction would be nor how many crises would jar the system. Indeed, the matters causing the dysfunction were uncertainties in Moscow over major developments in the Finnish body politic that were largely dispelled in 1968.

The Soviet response to Fagerholm's government in 1948 provided some indication of reaction by Moscow to "questionable" developments in Finnish politics when Stalin decided to apply the doctrine of trust-acceptance-assistance in a doubtful case. The election of Kekkonen as President over Fagerholm by one vote spared Moscow the necessity of deciding if Fagerholm was a fit successor to Paasikivi. In 1957, however, an invitation to Tanner to form a government triggered a vehement reaction in Moscow, foreshadowing the crisis of the Nightfrost.

The point at which the level of Soviet tolerance was breached and intrusions made to affect the course of politics in Finland should in retrospect be viewed in the light of two pervasive factors underlying Finnish politics and Finno-Soviet relations: the void left by Paasikivi and the postwar obtrusion of Tanner and his followers as a force to be reckoned with. The Nightfrost and the Note crises of 1958 and 1961, respectively, as well as the conciliation of the Social Democrats with Moscow culminating in 1968 can all be seen more vividly in the light of Soviet anxieties—real or imagined—induced by these two factors. The anxieties stemming from the first factor were over uncertainties as to how the system would function without the strong hand of a leader confronted with no serious opposition. With the passing of Paasikivi the play of Finnish politics was less constricted, and Kekkonen found opposition and obstacles as he strove with Soviet blessing to assume the mantle of his predecessor. Had he succeeded quickly and easily to establish himself as the new Paasikivi, Soviet anxieties would probably not have risen to the pitch they did.

The victory of Tanner and his followers for control of the Social Democrats in 1957 in itself distressed Moscow, but when joined with uncertainties due to the exit of Paasikivi and the possibility that the Tannerites and Conservatives would make common cause, it probably lowered the threshold of tolerance and disposition for restraint.

These developments not only cast a shadow over the smooth

functioning of the system of Finno-Soviet relations, but were to affect significantly internal political rivalry between the Agrarians and the Social Democrats; President Kekkonen, although an Agrarian, was expected by a tradition of his office to stand aside from partisan conflict. Coincident with the rise of Tanner the Agrarians and Kekkonen posed as those best suited to exercise political power because they could best serve the country's interest due to their "realistic" and "correct" assessment of Finno-Soviet relations and responses from Moscow. Indeed, at times there were intimations that the Social Democrats as a whole were unworthy to assume responsibility and would do harm to the country if they did. In these circumstances rivalry between these two largest parties in the country intensified, replacing an earlier practice of restraint and cooperation. The Agrarians gained an advantage over the Socialists and Moscow found opportunity and facility to play one against the other, making possible the exercise of influence to a degree Soviet leaders might have hesitated to employ if they were confronted with a united and firm Finnish reaction.

The Nightfrost: Origins and Nature of the Crisis

The Nightfrost came after the parliamentary elections of July 1958 and the formation in late August of a government under Fagerholm, a moderate Social Democrat who had opposed Tanner in his election to Chairman and was, of course, not one of the "Tannerites." Fagerholm's government was one resulting from the free play of election and parliamentary processes and was based on a substantial majority of 137 out of 200 members of the Diet. A coalition of five parties was formed including two of the three leading parties: Social Democrats claimed 5 cabinet posts, including the Prime Minister; Agrarians also had 5, including the Foreign Minister, Johannes Virolainen. The National Coalition (Conservatives) were included in a government with 3 members, which placed them in a prominent position after the big two; the coalition was rounded out to include one member each from the Liberals and the Swedish Party.[1] In accordance with the practice

_____

1. See *London Times,* August 30, 1958, p. 5, for the composition of the governments. Agrarian J. Virolainen assumed the posts of Deputy Prime Minister

of the parliamentary group of the Social Democratic Party it determined which of its members would serve in the government. Thus V. Leskinen and O. Lindblom, members of the Tanner faction, were given two of the Social Democratic posts.[2]

Reaction in the Soviet press to the composition of the government was that it included a strong if not decisive element of the most distrusted, rejected, and opposed groups: the Tannerites and the "extreme Right-wing Coalition Party, which together with the Social Democrats now has an opportunity of shaping its policies."[3] Moscow's pre-election apprehension over these two groups that ". . . have been angling to form a reactionary government with representatives of the Leskinen-Tanner group as the leading force" seemed to have been borne out.[4]

What grew to be Soviet vexation over the composition of the new government was early indicated by suggestions which their Ambassador in Helsinki proffered at the time of its formation,

---

and Foreign Minister, and Leskinen was given the Ministry of Social Affairs. Other members of the cabinet were: Interior, A. Pakkonen, Agrarian; Justice, S. Hogstrom, Swedish Party; Finance, P. Hetemaki, Conservative; Defense, T. Viherheimo, Conservative; Trade, O. Hiltunen, Social Democrat; Communications, K. Eskola, Agrarian; Education, K. Kajatsalo, Finnish Peoples Party (Liberals); Agriculture, M. Miettunen, Agrarian. See *London Times*, July 12, 1958, p. 5, for the results of the election.

2. In an interview with Dr. Fagerholm in Helsinki in October 1967, he explained to the author that the practice has since been dropped, and expressed the opinion that it is not a wise procedure because it might tie the hands of the government. Dr. Junnila in the interview in September 1972 was of the opinion that Fagerholm had to take Leskinen.

3. See *International Affairs* (Moscow) (10), October 1958, pp. 97–98 where D. Borisov commented on the new Finnish government. He stated erroneously that it included five members of the "Tanner wing." The Tannerites and National Coalition together had five members, a third of the cabinet, which could account for a goodly degree of influence, but it would take at least three more to give them a majority, which would not be very easy for they would have to come from the other Social Democrats, the Swedish Party, or the Liberals. Fagerholm, the two other Social Democrats and the five Agrarians, however, could command in such a delicately balanced government only a bare majority. The Agrarians could have checked any rash moves by threatening to resign and bring it to an end.

4. See *International Affairs* (Moscow) (12), 1957, "World Events," "Aggravation of Political Struggle in Finland," by P. Krymov, pp. 131–132. The article also noted the division within the Social Democratic Party and the Social Democratic-Agrarian cooperation which preceded the rise of Tanner.

but pressure commenced soon after it was installed and mounted in intensity until Fagerholm resigned about three months later, on December 4. As the pressure heightened there seemed little doubt that it was intended to force the resignation of the government. Displeasure was a first response from Moscow and was registered by the failure of Ambassador Lebedev to follow diplomatic custom as the doyen of the diplomatic corps in Helsinki to pay a courtesy call on the new Foreign Minister. A stronger note of disapproval followed, with the recall of the Ambassador, who departed without the customary farewell visit to the Finnish President. Critical articles sprouted in *Izvestia* and *Pravda* written by Soviet correspondents in Helsinki, and before long Finnish diplomats in Moscow encountered obstacles in making appointments to see Foreign Ministry officials. No replacement of Lebedev was sent, and the Chinese Ambassador also left Helsinki.[5]

There were throughout no formal communications to the Finnish government from the Soviet government, but their actions and omissions conveyed the intended meaning. The Soviet attitude raised the issue in Finland of whether the Fagerholm government was a liability because of strained relations with the eastern neighbor. As in 1948, Fagerholm carefully avoided any moves which would confirm Soviet suspicions, and he forthrightly declared loyalty to the Paasikivi Line.[6]

It took the intensification of economic pressures, however, to convey the seriousness of Soviet intentions, and in time these pressures brought the situation to a head. Delays in signing an agreement on fishing rights in the Gulf of Finland were accompanied by suspension of discussions on the large rouble credit and lease of the Saimaa Canal. "Technical grounds" were offered for the halting of plans for construction by Finland of a power plant on the Soviet side of the north Karelian frontier. Then came postponement of the regularly scheduled autumn meeting of the

---

5. These events are well known and were reported at the time in the *New York Times* and the *London Times*. See Holsti, "Strategy and Techniques of Soviet Influence in Finland," pp. 75–77, for a good summary and documentation. See also Forster, "The Finnish-Soviet Crisis of 1958–1959" and Turre Junnila, *Freiheit im Vorfeld. Finnlands Kampf um Sicherheit und Neutralität.* Translated from Finnish by Marta Römer (Vienna: Europe Verlag, 1965), pp. 93–100.

6. *New York Times,* November 23, 1958, p. 1.

Finno-Soviet Scientific and Technical Cooperation Committee in Moscow because of travel plans of several Soviet committee members. A much heavier blow fell when the Finnish trade delegation, scheduled to travel to Moscow to negotiate the 1959 bilateral trade agreement on October 27, was left waiting without an invitation. Further severe blows were inflicted when three large manufacturers of metal and other products for export to the Soviet Union were informed that, despite contracts, deliveries scheduled for the rest of the year had to be curtailed. As the government tottered in its last week of existence because of impending Agrarian defection, it was announced that the Soviet Union suspended imports from Finland and postponed payments totaling 23 million roubles, estimated to be 4 per cent of the annual Finno-Soviet trade. Unemployment increased to a record 100,000, a matter of special concern for the Social Democrats.[7]

Other than capitulation and resignation only, two alternatives seemed to be available to Fagerholm which would be consistent with preservation of the soft sphere system:

1. To reshuffle the cabinet but maintain the coalition. Such a move would have required the support of all parties in the government, especially the Agrarians, as well as the support or neutrality of the President. Additionally, it would have needed the concurrence of the Tanner faction, one or both of whose cabinet members would have to resign.

2. To stand firm. For this there would also have to be the support of all coalition parties, but especially the Agrarians. Support of the President or at least his neutrality would also be necessary.

The role of the President, the Agrarians, and the Tanner faction were obviously the crucial variables in preventing a collapse of the government.

In view of the unavoidable necessity of assuaging Soviet misgivings, gaining the support of the President, and maintaining

---

7. On the subject of the economic pressures see Kent Forster, "The Finnish-Soviet Crisis of 1958–1959," *International Journal* (Spring 1960); Austin Goodrich, *Study in Sisu, Finland's Fight for Independence*, pp. 140–141; Branco Lazitch, "Succès de La Politique Sovieto-Communiste en Finlande," *Est et Ouest*, July 1–15, 1966, p. 3; *New York Times*, November 23, 1958, p. 1; *London Times*, December 1, 1958, p. 8.

the adhesion of *all* the Agrarians to the cabinet, the better of the two alternatives would have been to reshuffle the cabinet. At the very least Leskinen would have had to be replaced in such a reorganization, but a reduction of Conservative members from three to two would better assure success of the move. Fresh political backing for the government could have helped it to withstand Soviet pressure more firmly. Moscow would then have had to bear the onus of deciding whether to continue the ban on the government. President Kekkonen and the Agrarians would also be placed in a position of embarrassment if they withheld support from such a reshuffled government. In the context of the soft sphere system, a successful reshuffling would have ended the crisis and forestalled the impending dysfunction of the system.

Reshuffling, however, was not given serious consideration, probably because it would have encountered, or actually did encounter, stiff opposition of the Social Democratic Parliamentary group, where Tanner's faction had a majority.[8]

Under the circumstances, the only course left for Fagerholm was to stand firm. He pinned his hopes—slim as they were—on the chance that enough Agrarians, including J. Virolainen, who as Deputy Prime Minister and Foreign Minister was the key Agrarian in his cabinet, would want to maintain Social Democratic-Agrarian cooperation, which had been a feature of Finnish politics before the rise of Tanner. The policy of standing firm would mean continued hostility and pressure from Moscow; such unrelenting hostility would, in turn, lead to coolness toward the government by President Kekkonen and those Agrarians who would follow his lead. The Agrarians, too, were divided, with the President able to sway a large group to his side. Thus, behind the scenes the two main parties of the Fagerholm government, the Social Democrats and the Agrarians, were divided and these

---

8. Dr. Fagerholm did not refer to reshuffling in his interview, and Dr. Junnila, who was a member of the Parliament from the National Coalition Party, which was a coalition member, recalled that reshuffling was definitely not tried; Professor Bonsdorff was of the same opinion. This seems to confirm the anticipation of rejection by the Social Democratic Parliamentary group and Leskinen's strong position therein, for the Tanner faction outnumbered the others in the Parliamentary group.

divisions prevented the success of the policy of reshuffling or the policy of standing firm. To all intents and purposes the government was doomed unless by a miracle the President decided to follow a "hands off" policy and let his fellow Agrarians decide for themselves.

The stage was set for the culmination of events stemming from the parliamentary election of 1958, if not of events a year earlier when Tanner and his followers won control of the Social Democratic Party. If the Agrarians decided to stand firm, the Russians would be confronted with a show of unity which would require them to reconsider just how menacing the Fagerholm government really was. Kekkonen, to no one's surprise, decided against neutrality, a move which was readily surmised when A. Karjalainen, one of the Agrarian leaders closest to the President was quoted as saying: "The longer the current weakening of our foreign relations continues . . . the more precipitous will be the changes that will be required." Other leading Agrarians outside of the government spoke in the same vein.[9] Pressure on Virolainen, who seemingly was reluctant to resign, had probably brought him around, as indicated when he was reported to have declared at an Agrarian Party meeting that he and other party members would resign. At a meeting of the Foreign Policy Committee of the Parliament this seemed to be confirmed when the Foreign Minister declared that "difficulties with Russia had become overwhelming."[10]

The government was obviously crumbling when the Agrarian Party Parliamentary group struck what may have been the final blow by authorizing all ministers belonging to the party to resign.[11] On November 28 Fagerholm acknowledged his failure and placed responsibility squarely on the Agrarians for the government's collapse:

---

9. *New York Times,* November 23, 1958, p. 1. The quotation was taken from the Agrarian Party newspaper *Maakansa.*

10. *London Times,* November 26, 1958, p. 9. There was common agreement among three well-informed persons interviewed in Finland in 1972 that Virolainen was under pressure to resign, one saying flatly he "was told" to resign. The question was not raised with all who were interviewed; no one gave a contrary opinion.

11. *London Times,* November 28, 1958, p. 9.

No other conclusion can be drawn from this situation than that the Agrarians want to dissolve the government. This will remain their responsibility. I have tried to discuss reconciliation so that the country will not be thrown into a typical crisis. This is the best government in which I have worked.[12]

A week later Virolainen resigned and was followed by the four other Agrarian ministers; the resignation of the government, which followed, was a mere formality.[13]

The pivotal position of President Kekkonen and the Agrarian Party in the demise of the Fagerholm government is difficult to deny. Although an equal partner in the coalition, the Agrarians stood to gain by the dissolution of the government to make way for their own exercise of power as the party best suited to be trusted with a "sensitive" and "sensible" approach to the national interest.

From the beginning President Kekkonen was known to be cool to the Fagerholm coalition, and this coolness grew as the crisis intensified. In addition to possible political motives of the President and the Agrarians, they may well have had genuine misgivings over the situation which caused strained relations with the eastern neighbor, undermining the basis of confidence which Moscow stressed in the soft sphere system. To Agrarians the adverse Soviet response to inclusion of Leskinen and Lindblom in a government was predictable.

On the other hand, as far as the Social Democrats and others were concerned, the issue raised by the Nightfrost was whether the Finns could order their own internal affairs under the system

---

12. *Ibid.,* November 29, 1958, p. 5.

13. *Ibid.,* December 5, 1958, p. 9. Virolainen offered no reasons for his action; the other ministers gave as their reasons the resignation of Virolainen and vaguely referred to difficulties "over other matters important to the country." Dr. Fagerholm in an interview with the author in October 1967 explained how he hoped Virolainen would not resign and that Social Democratic-Agrarian cooperation would be revived. He felt that his government deserved to be supported and said that it was one of the best the country ever had. He also said to Gordon Shepard in 1959 that his government "was a working alliance of all of Finland's democratic parties, Conservatives included." Gordon Shepard, "Finland's Mortgaged Democracy," *The Reporter,* November 26, 1959.

after having given renewed assurances that the Paasikivi Line, the treaty of 1948, and the treaty of peace would be faithfully adhered to. Confidence in a government, Socialists insisted, should be based on *what it does;* they also argued that all Finnish political parties in the postwar years had fully accepted the principles of the Paasikivi Line and should accordingly be trusted with responsibility.

Social Democratic-Agrarian differences over the issue of confidence in persons actually amounted to conflicting Finnish interpretations over the level of tolerance the Soviet Union had a right to insist upon and the degree of Soviet influence affecting domestic political processes these two parties believed the country should accept. Such differences between the two major parties of the Fagerholm government offered Moscow the option of a "harder" policy in the crisis of the Nightfrost.

Socialist-Agrarian differences over the rise of Tanner and his faction, as well as their inclusion in the government, actually lay behind the divergent responses to the issue of Soviet confidence. To Kekkonen and the Agrarians it was regarded as a deplorable occurrence which threatened to upset the structure built by Paasikivi. The soft sphere system provided extensive independence, neutrality, and expanded ties with Scandinavia. The Soviet condition of acceptable persons, Kekkonen would argue, was crucial in safeguarding these achievements and should be willingly consented to as a good exchange. Why should the system be jeopardized, he would further argue, when Soviet reactions were palpably predictable? Finally, Kekkonen and the Agrarians viewed with alarm the Tannerites as a provocative political force and a liability that should not be supported.

Fagerholm, the Socialists, and other Finns could argue that the internal political processes were sacrosanct because they were prerogatives of the measure of independence Finland was to be assured under the soft sphere system. The Tannerites' and Conservatives' strength in Parliament resulted from the free functioning of these internal political processes and should be tolerated for this reason. It would be inconsistent and unfair to allow these processes to function only when they brought results that could be approved. Soviet leaders were obligated, under the system, as the Socialists saw it, to accept in good faith Fagerholm's assurances regarding his government's dedication to the Paasikivi Line and should reserve judgement on anyone's loyalty to the Line until concrete decisions violating it had taken place.

As a result of the Nightfrost, the system, as it had developed up to 1958, was deprived of a test of what the Soviet reaction would be in the face of united Finnish resistance. Strengthened by such unity, the issue could have been defined as a predominantly internal matter. In the face of uncertainties, the Soviet leaders could adopt Stalin's precedent of 1948 when he opted for the doctrine of trust-acceptance-assistance on a wait-and-see basis.

Moscow's reaction to such a steadfast position, however, would have depended upon how determined the Russians were to strike at a regime which had admitted Tannerites and "Coalitionists" from the right to a considerable degree of influence, which was the main difference between the Fagerholm government of 1948 and that of 1958. Moscow would probably have had to precipitate a much greater crisis to bring down a government backed by parliamentary unity and the support of the President.[14] To be sure there would have been coolness and criticism and hawklike watchfulness in Moscow for any misstep, but the level of pressure would not have been escalated to the point of dysfunction in the system.

The consequence of the resignation of Fagerholm was that the operation of one of the basic functions of government, the dissolving of a cabinet, took place because of the influence of the Soviet Union. It was the logical result of defining the issue in terms of confidence in persons, in both the Soviet Union and Finland. The influence exercised was indirect, for no specific or direct action of the Soviet leaders constituted interference in the Finnish political process. The role and actions of the President and the Agrarians were strictly consistent with law and political practice in Finland,

---

14. Kekkonen occupied the foremost position in Finland politically and constitutionally as well as having the favor and confidence of Moscow. If in the face of steadfast support of the government by the President the Russians were still determined to bring the government down, it would also have cast a shadow over their relationship with Kekkonen as their most trusted, accepted, and assisted Finn. We can conjecture, however, that he knew better than anyone in Helsinki how adamant Soviet distrust, rejection, and opposition to the government was. Persons interviewed in Finland usually referred to Kekkonen's coolness to the government *from the beginning*, and one of them was of the definite opinion that the President could have saved it if he told the Russians it was an internal matter.

but the *probable reason* their actions were taken was because of known attitudes and anticipated reactions in Moscow.[15]

The soft sphere system as it had developed by 1958 was one wherein the free conduct of Finnish internal politics and parliamentary practice was not interfered with, but in the Nightfrost it was found that independence in these matters was, after all, conditional. An infusion of elements of the hard sphere took place at this time because of the *magnitude of the effects* of Soviet influence, even though indirect.[16] This is where the dysfunction occurred, because it was a *departure from and disturbance of the system as it had functioned.*[17] Specifically, it now seemed certain that a matter such as the composition of a cabinet, as distinct from any policies or actions it might take, was subject to Soviet approval. This is the limit, the Soviet leaders in effect conveyed, of the Soviet level of tolerance for Finnish independence. Moscow's doctrine of distrust-rejection-opposition had its counterpart in Helsinki, held by those who accorded priority to Soviet confidence in persons who exercise authority. The line between internal and external matters, which is usually difficult enough to draw, could be meaningless in a spheres of influence situation reflecting anxieties of the paramount power, even in a soft sphere system.

The Nightfrost depicts the dilemma in a soft sphere arising from disparities in power between the sphere country and hegemonic power when the latter invokes its superior capability

---

15. See Goodrich, *Study in Sisu, Finland's Fight for Independence,* p. 141, where the President was reported as "convinced that friendly Finnish-Soviet relations—a 'question upon which our destiny rests'—demanded a new government; a government whose composition would be acceptable to the Kremlin." In an interview in May of 1963 President Kekkonen disavowed Soviet pressure and interference in the Nightfrost, but acknowledged that "there was doubtless tension then in the relations between the USSR and Finland . . . the Soviet government was obviously alarmed . . . by the possibility of disturbance in the confidence between Finland and the USSR." He added that despite this, "The USSR by no means forced us to choose the road that we chose. . . . In making our decisions we naturally took into account how they affect our relations with other states." This of course indicated behavior in anticipation of Soviet reaction. See *Finnish Features* No. 29/63, "Interview with U. Kekkonen by Mr. A. E. Pederson, U.P.I., May 5, 1963."

16. See Introduction, p. 8.

17. *Ibid.,* pp. 4, 8, 19, 26.

to undermine the system.[18] Soviet decision makers acceded to the soft sphere on the condition and expectation that it would function satisfactorily;[19] the Nightfrost indicates that they would institute hard-sphere-like policies causing dysfunction of the system in the belief that these conditions and expectations were threatened. Even though a soft sphere has been instituted, "the paramount power continues to claim a stake in the area and exercises constant concern for what is done or not done."[20] The Nightfrost indicates such an assertion and vigilance by Moscow. Paramount powers, in the same vein, "need assurance that their interests, although broadly conceived under the soft sphere, will nevertheless continue to be served."[21] The Nightfrost also indicates Soviet leaders believed that such assurance was threatened.

From the vantage point of the sphere state, the Nightfrost gave rise to uncertainties, insecurities, and some disillusionment because the distinctive mark of the soft sphere is internal self-government. Sphere state "political processes function freely without the threat of interference or dictation"[22] and "sphere countries must be persuaded that the conditions are genuine and enduring."[23] The Finns found that they could not run their internal affairs if they were run in certain ways.

There was obviously a crisis of the Finno-Soviet system in 1958, for it had not functioned as either party had expected. The system was in need of readjustment and reaffirmation in response to the problems caused by Tanner's rise. The fact that his faction had achieved the balance of power in the Social Democratic Party and that two of his protégés, including Leskinen, held the reins of power together with three Conservatives in a new government brought the matter to a head. A "peaceful settlement" of some sort would have been preferable to the shock of crisis which disturbed not only Finno-Soviet relations but domestic Finnish politics and intra-Social Democratic politics as well.

---

18. *Ibid.,* p. 25.
19. Chapter 2, p. 41.
20. Introduction, p. 22.
21. *Ibid.,* p. 23.
22. *Ibid.,* pp. 22–26.
23. *Ibid.*

Reshuffling of the cabinet, while not such a settlement, might have made it possible to head off the storm that broke, and time would have been provided for an opportunity to deal with the problem diplomatically.

It is difficult to say, however, what manner of solemn pledges would have mollified the Soviet leaders and gotten them to see Tanner and his faction (as well as the Conservatives) in less menacing terms. Most Finns believed that Moscow's fears were exaggerated and had overlooked aspects of Tanner's record which could not be objected to, but in the postwar period, as earlier, he had taken a rather "anti-communist" stance[24] and apparently did little to relieve Soviet misgivings. He was by temperament and political experience one who was used to having his way.[25] Not only did he do little to dispel Moscow's apprehensions, but he added fuel to the flame by confirming the worst of their suspicions a few days prior to the formation of Fagerholm's government in 1958. In a major speech he warned that Finnish independence was threatened and the possibility of the country's becoming a satellite could not be ignored. Russia, he continued, was the source of the danger and always had been a dangerous neighbor to Finland.[26]

Thus, when viewed from the Soviet perspective, the formation of the Fagerholm government was an alarming development culminating from dangerous tendencies in Finnish politics of the

---

24. Dr. Fagerholm related in his interview with the author in October 1967 how the Russians stressed that it was a "question of what you are today" when he pointed out to the Soviet Ambassador that Tanner was not against them in 1917 and that Kekkonen voted for the Winter War. He said that after World War II Tanner was "like a red flag to the Soviet Union."

25. Author's interview with Professor Bonsdorff, September 1972: Tanner was a really dominant old type of Social Democratic leader and in a sense symbolized the party; he had a tendency to be outspoken. Author's interview with Dr. Söderhjelm, September 1972: "Tanner was a spoiled man, a difficult man, and had to always get his own way."

26. See Rintala, "Väinö Tanner in Finnish Politics," p. 91. The speech was printed in the Social Democratic party organ *Suomen Socialidemokraati,* August 27, 1958, and touched off bitter denunciations in the Soviet press. See *Izvestia,* August 29, 1958. Rintala, who has done extensive research on Tanner, noted that it "was hardly a surprise. It merely reflected a lifetime of opposition to Russian policy."

previous year. Before the election of 1958 the Soviet press carried articles attacking the Social Democrats and Conservatives in this vein.[27] Soviet decision makers, like those of other countries, especially great powers, seem to have the propensity, in dealing with perception of threat, for desiring the elimination of even vague or remote potential danger in an effort to maximize security. Tanner's power in the Social Democrats and the association of his faction with the "extreme Right-wing Coalitionists," both adding up to a strong factor in the Fagerholm government, represented in the mind of Soviet leaders a clear and present danger which should not be tolerated.[28] Here was the rationale of the decision to interfere and was the basis of *perceived need. Opportunity* was provided by the fact that Finland was already in the Soviet sphere and dependent upon the Soviet Union for its status as a neutral. *Opportunity and facility* were found in economic vulnerability, political divisions in the country, and the Finnish reluctant willingness to accede to pressure in order to preserve whatever degree of independence was practicable under the circumstances.

After the resignation of Fagerholm the soft sphere system seemed suspended in a sort of limbo. While the Social Democrats, including the two Tanner men, had been ousted from power, the party was still a dominant one in Parliament and Finnish politics, with the Tanner faction still the ruling one. The Conservatives were likewise an important political force in Parliament and in the country. Finnish politics were marked by intense bitterness between the two major noncommunist parties of the country whose cooperation could impart a viability to the soft sphere system and serve the national interest.[29] The presidency had become con-

---

27. X.Y.Z., "Finland: A Survey, 1957–1960," *The World Today* (January 1961) p. 22. See for example P. Krymov, "Aggravation of Political Struggle in Finland" in "World Events," *International Affairs* (Moscow), (12), December 1957, pp. 131–132.

28. In the Soviet perception Germany's increased strength and renewed interest in the Baltic could be linked with internal Finnish political developments bringing Tannerites and Conservatives into the government to increase the danger from her old enemy—an hypothesis expressed by Mr. Lance Keyworth in an interview with the author in October 1967.

29. An indication of bitterness by a leading Social Democrat, Mauno Pelko-

troversial because of the role of Kekkonen in the crisis, and it seemed doubtful that he would succeed to the universal support enjoyed by Paasikivi; in a few years he would stand for re-election, providing the arena for another test of strength before the basic problem giving rise to the Nightfrost had been settled.

In the aftermath of Fagerholm's resignation President Kekkonen addressed the nation on two occasions, the first on December 10 shortly after the collapse of the government and the second on January 25 after a two day visit to Leningrad for private discussions with Khrushchev. Fresh from the meeting in Leningrad he averred that the crisis was deeper than he had realized, but he insisted that nothing was at stake if the Soviet government could have confidence in a government that could fulfill Finland's commitments. In fact the theme of Soviet confidence is writ large in both addresses. While he conceded that Fagerholm's government "had not made any decisions intended to produce changes in our foreign policy . . . the fact remains that our neighbor . . . no longer has confidence in our sincerity."[30]

In justification of Soviet insistence that they be convinced of good intentions he said on January 25, "The Soviet Union can . . . make a good case for its interest in having as its neighbor a friendly government which is able to guarantee the fulfillment of our commitments."[31] He was willing to pay this price for the benefits which the system provided and warned that "if it is only rights that we are talking about, nothing can prevent us from living in our country as we wish, but then we must be prepared to stand by the consequences of our actions."[32] The President reminded the nation of the guiding rule that "foreign policy always precedes domestic policy" and declared that it was regrettably

---

nen, was expressed in a speech on Finnish independence day a year later when he alleged that the Soviet Union decided on pressure "only because it was confident that the Agrarian members of the government would quit." See *New York Times,* December 7, 1953, p. 3.

30. "On the Beginning of Cool Relations," broadcast on December 10, 1958, in Kekkonen, *Neutrality: The Finnish Position,* p. 75.

31. "The End of Cool Relations," broadcast on January 25, 1959, in Kekkonen, *Neutrality: The Finnish Position,* p. 82.

32. "On the Beginning of Cool Relations," in Kekkonen, *Neutrality: The Finnish Position,* p. 76.

forgotten, causing the disturbance in Finno-Soviet relations.[33] He appealed for restraint in the Finnish press to set at rest Soviet misgivings over criticism and ridicule because these reflected hostility and undermined the Finno-Soviet system; Moscow and Kekkonen thereby extended the need for confidence to the Finnish press and the public at large.[34]

Despite the President's appeals and warnings, a second crisis was soon to cause another dysfunction of the system and further embitter internal Finnish Politics.

---

33. *Ibid.*, p. 77. On Kekkonen's position on "Relations between External and Internal Affairs" see Jouko Loikkanen, *"K"-Line* (in Finnish) (Helsinki: Akateeminen Kustaanusliike, 1967), pp. 9–13, where the author quotes the Kekkonen view that "the formation of a government is an internal affair. But it is not only that. The government has relations with other countries. Accordingly, its composition is also an external affair. In the year Cajander's government failed to get a reconciliation with the Soviet Union, it was necessary to change the government. In 1958, the same thing happened again."

34. "The End of Cool Relations," in Kekkonen, *Neutrality: The Finnish Position*, p. 81.

CHAPTER SIX

CRISIS AND DYSFUNCTION:
THE NOTE CRISIS OF 1961–1962

The Note Crisis occurred against a background of Cold War tensions and impending presidential and parliamentary elections, and continued for three and a half weeks. Even though the lengthy note dealt with problems of Finno-Soviet security posed by West German rearmament, the consequences for internal Finnish politics were as great as, if not greater than, those from the Nightfrost. The Note was delivered to the Finnish Ambassador in Moscow on October 30, 1961, in the wake of several prior months of sustained international tensions,[1] and proposed "consultations on measures for insuring defense of the frontiers of both countries from the threat of a military attack by Western Germany and allied states as it is envisaged by the Treaty of Friendship, Cooperation and Mutual Assistance."[2]

---

1. The tensions centered mainly around the Berlin question, disarmament, and nuclear testing: On August 13 the Berlin Wall went up, on September 9 the disarmament talks in Geneva broke up, Kennedy's summit meeting with Khrushchev in Vienna did little to relieve the atmosphere, and on the day the Note was conveyed, Soviet nuclear tests climaxed with the explosion of a 50 megaton bomb. See "The Baltic: Dangerous Plans" by A. Pogodin, pp. 78–79 of "International Commentary" in *International Affairs,* (Moscow), (4) April 1960, for an example of Soviet misgivings over projected Danish-German cooperation in the Baltic written over a year before the Note was sent.

2. See *New York Times,* October 31, 1961, p. 12, for the text of the Note. The proposed consultations invoked Article 2 of the treaty: "The High Contracting Parties shall confer with each other if it is established that the threat of an armed attack as described in Article 1 is present." See above for discussion of Paasikivi's meaning of this article.

German rearmament, the Note averred, constituted a threat to the Scandinavian and Baltic region, and Norway and Denmark, through NATO arrangements, were being "drawn into the sphere of military and political influence of West German militarism."[3] Taken at face value the contents and tenor of the missive seem to have been inspired by military officials concerned with defense interests in this area. The defeat of Germany in World War II opened the Baltic to Soviet primacy, which together with the spread of influence to Finland and the neutrality of Sweden helped to secure the northern marchland. As NATO members, however, Norway and Denmark were weak points in Russia's northern frontier and could be exploited by renascent German power. This was particularly so in view of Norway's contiguity with both Finland and the USSR, and especially with the presence of a NATO Baltic fleet in what the Kremlin regarded as a closed sea.

The thought of military consultations stirred apprehensions in Helsinki, for they could burden Finland with commitments that would undermine the cherished neutrality so painstakingly built and recently recognized. Finland would be thus drawn into Soviet bloc military-strategic planning and Cold War positions, and thus might more closely be enfolded into the Soviet orbit. Finnish misgivings also stemmed from the unilateral Soviet assertion that a *casus foederis* for Article 2 had arisen which was contrary to the interpretation of Paasikivi that both parties had to agree that such a threat existed.

President Kekkonen and Foreign Minister Karjalainen, sunning on the beaches of Honolulu on a visit to the United States at the time, exuded a mood of composure; the President refused to end his visit abruptly but dispatched the Foreign Minister back to Helsinki. Once back in the capital Kekkonen reassured the Finnish people and chided foreign analysts for gloomy speculation that Finland was under pressure to grant military bases and change the policy of the government, resulting in diminished independence. The Note, he pointed out, was directed at West Germany, the NATO powers, and to the Scandinavian NATO

---

3. *Ibid.*

members—Denmark and Norway; it was not a pretext for changes in Finland.[4] Privately the President was worried, for he had accurately assessed the danger to neutrality;[5] he chose a strategy of postponing the meeting for consultations and offered a substitute for military arrangements to reassure Soviet officials. In an address to the nation he unequivocally affirmed the country's determination to maintain neutrality and "pledged himself to defend Finnish neutrality to his last breath."[6] As an alternative to military arrangements he suggested a possible political approach by which Finland would give fresh indications that it could be relied upon to maintain its foreign policy, and secured an invitation for Karjalainen to proceed to Moscow for exploratory exchanges with Gromyko.

In his meeting with Karjalainen on November 11, Gromyko explained how the military leaders, reviewing the critical international situation, demanded that the government take up military consultations with Finland;[7] here seemed confirmation of the official purpose of the Note. He then shifted to Soviet misgivings over instability in the Finnish political situation and the desire for assurance as soon as possible "that the foreign policy of Finland will continue and that nothing would prevent the development of friendly relations between Finland and the Soviet Union."[8] He continued that since the Soviet Union "fully relies on Finnish foreign policy and trusts President Kekkonen . . . we have, so far, not acceded to our military circles' demand."[9] The implication

---

4. Jakobson, *Finnish Neutrality,* pp. 72–74. He counseled foreign journalists "not to sell the bearskin until the beast had been felled." See also *New York Times,* November 6, 1961, p. 1.

5. Mr. Heikki Brotherus in an interview with the author in October, 1967, was of the view that the Russian move really alarmed Finland.

6. *London Times,* November 6, 1961, p. 10. The President had affirmed in stronger terms than ever his dedication to neutrality, the realization of which "is part of my life work."

7. Jakobson, *Finnish Neutrality,* p. 74.

8. *New York Times,* November 15, 1961, p. 1. See also Jakobson, *Finnish Neutrality,* pp. 74–75.

9. T. Junnila, *Noottikriisi, Tuoreeltaan Tulkittuna* (Helsinki: Werner Söderström, 1962), pp. 73–82. See also *London Times,* November 15, 1961, p. 14.

behind the political feature which Gromyko now introduced[10] was that Soviet security was endangered as well by internal political developments in Finland; that if political uncertainties were removed, security concerns could be disposed of without military consultations.

Renewed Soviet anxieties over internal Finnish politics had been excited by the formation of the "Honka Front," a coalition of five parties seriously challenging Kekkonen's re-election in the January 1962 balloting. Initiated by the Social Democrats in order to provide an alternative to an easy victory for Kekkonen, the Conservatives, the Swedish Party, the Liberals, and the Small Farmers Parties united behind Olavi Honka, a retired Chancellor of Justice.[11] Why was there a switch to the political approach? Were Soviet decision makers taking heed of negative Finnish responses to military consultations which caused them to have second thoughts on insisting that they be held? Were they disposed to make a concession to Kekkonen and try the political alternative he implied? If the latter were so, the substitute for military consultations would support Finnish neutrality as a pillar for maintaining peace in Scandinavia and the Baltic. The pillar of neutrality, in the Soviet view, could best be held up only by Kekkonen; any threat to his position was a threat to neutrality and the general pro-Soviet tenor of Finnish foreign policy as pledged in the Paasikivi Line.

It may be asked, however, if the real intention of the Soviet leaders all along was to propose consultations as a smoke screen and use the threat to neutrality as leverage for the purpose of swinging the election to Kekkonen. Answers to these questions must at this time be speculative, but it seems plausible to this writer to give credence to the interpretation that Soviet military officials did in fact recommend consultations and that this was the original purpose of the Note. Such speculation is supported

---

10. The only reference to an internal Finnish matter in the Note was to certain anti-Soviet "organs of the Finnish press which . . . actively support the dangerous military preparations of the NATO member countries and thus contribute to whipping up war psychosis contrary to the foreign policy line adopted by Finland." *New York Times,* October 31, 1961, p. 12.

11. See Junnila, *Noottikriisi,* Chapters 1, 2, and 3, on the formation of the Honka Front.

primarily by the deeply ingrained fear of Germany by Soviet military and political leaders.[12] In response to expanded German military activity into the vital northern European and Baltic region, the Soviet military would logically be expected to approach Finland for common action or commitments pursuant to obligations under the treaty of 1948. As military officials they would probably value more highly military contributions from the Finns than the more subtle and indirect benefits from maintaining neutrality. After a review of political implications by political officials, original plans were changed.

It should be remembered that the Note, while proposing military consultations to Finland, probably had as collateral purposes convincing the West that it would go far towards solving the Berlin crisis, influencing Denmark and Norway to draw away from NATO arrangements, and cautioning Sweden to maintain her neutrality.[13] Pressure on Finland for consultations that would undermine her neutrality could well have the added advantage of a technique to apply leverage on her Scandinavian cousins, who were reluctant to see her so pressured, preferring a neutral Finland. In shifting to the political approach success would be insured by the effect of the Note on Finnish public opinion and disarray in the Honka Front.

Upon closer analysis the military and the political approaches were not mutually exclusive, but complementary, and Soviet political officials probably convinced the military to see it this way; thus the shift was not a drastic vitiating of the general purpose of the Note. The threat to neutrality, posed by consultations, could be employed by Moscow to yield desired political results. The approaches were complementary, in the Soviet view, because they would each operate to strengthen the USSR's security. True, each would deal with a different perceived threat, but the threats were also seen as complementary. Karjalainen in discussions with Gromyko and later with Kekkonen in Helsinki, while pleased with

---

12. The Note itself and the luncheon speech of Khrushchev at Novosibirsk on November 24 are replete with references which portray the Soviet image of "West German militarists and revenge seekers" and the machinations of "Hitlerite generals." See *London Times,* November 25, 1961, p. 6.

13. Junnila, *Noottikriisi,* pp. 66–72.

the prospect of dropping consultations, was ready to accede to the political approach as the lesser of evils, but challenged the accuracy of Soviet analysis concerning the internal Finnish threat to Soviet security.[14]

President Kekkonen, acting immediately to produce the desired political changes, dissolved Parliament and rescheduled the elections for that body for February instead of July; presidential elections in January would thus occur only a month before elections for Parliament.[15] The move would drastically reduce the period of uncertainty between electing a president and parliament from six months to one month, thus fulfilling Soviet desire for more stability. After parliamentary elections a stronger government replacing the weak minority Agrarian government was anticipated. Kekkonen's political fortune had suddenly been boosted, first by the Note, then by the Gromyko statement, finally by rescheduled parliamentary elections. The effect of all this had been to weaken the Honka Front[16] and shift Finnish opinion to the President in order to make the "right choice" for the good of the country.[17]

Kekkonen's strategy seemed to be working satisfactorily, but suddenly collapsed with a renewed Soviet request for military

---

14. In reply to Gromyko's claim that "a certain political grouping had emerged attempting to prevent the continuity of the present foreign policy" Karjalainen replied that while there were different political groupings in Finland, "as was well known also in the Soviet Union, all groups were adherents to the Paasikivi Line," and that the Finnish people wanted to continue the policy of friendship and confidence with the Soviet Union. See *London Times,* November 15, 1961, p. 14, and Jakobson, *Finnish Neutrality,* pp. 74–75.

15. *New York Times,* November 15, 1961, p. 1.

16. On the weakening of the Honka Front see Junnila, *Noottikriisi,* pp. 83–88: "The Note undermined the Honka Union and weakened its realization. It drew the nation's worried attention to external affairs. . . . The disintegration . . . started after the discussions between Karjalainen and Gromyko in Moscow."

17. *New York Times,* November 16, 1961, p. 19, and Jakobson, *Finnish Neutrality,* p. 77. The Social Democrats who had been leading the anti-Kekkonen Line were confronted with compounded difficulties: firstly, their creation, the Honka Front, was weakening; secondly, in parliamentary elections now so close to the presidential campaign they would be forced to compete with their Honka Front allies; thirdly, the shift in public opinion to Kekkonen would hurt them in both elections.

consultations two days after the rescheduling of parliamentary elections. Moscow's motives for the change were probably based on scepticism of the adequacy and effectiveness of Kekkonen's measures, for in the Kremlin view rescheduled parliamentary elections left uncertain the presidential outcome, which was, after all, the primary Soviet concern. The Honka Front, especially the Social Democrats, its initiators and most powerful backers, continued their resolution to elect the former jurist and pressed the campaign against Kekkonen. Continued NATO activity in Scandinavia and the Baltic, intensifying the situation identified in the Note, was cited in the renewed call for military consultations.[18]

Shaken by the latest turn of events, the President felt constrained to play one of his highest cards to avert consultations and preserve neutrality: a personal meeting[19] with Khrushchev where he could clarify the internal political picture and prospects of the elections,[20] appeal in positive, but confidential, terms for postponement of the military talks, and urge a restoration of the Gromyko approach. Khrushchev, who was on an agricultural tour, agreed to a meeting in Novosibirsk in Siberia. Coincident with the summit sessions in Siberia the founders of the Honka Front met in Helsinki for watchful waiting and discussion of the movement's future.

At mid morning on November 24 the luncheon speech of Khrushchev at Novosibirsk was heard in Helsinki with its denunciation of "Tannerites" and "right wingers" as friends of the

---

18. *New York Times,* November 17, 1961, p. 1. Attention was called to West German Defense Minister Franz J. Strauss's current visit to Norway, current Atlantic Alliance manoeuvers in the Baltic, and Danish newspaper reports of a contemplated combined West German-Danish Baltic Command.

19. Kekkonen, in addition to being the favorite Finn of the Soviet Union, had a good working personal relationship with Khrushchev. The latter attended the President's birthday party in Helsinki in 1960; they conferred in saunas and went hunting together. In their several meetings, routine, serious, or critical matters were discussed; for instance, after the Nightfrost, in Leningrad they discussed Finnish association with EFTA and the opening of the Saimaa Canal.

20. *New York Times,* November 17, p. 1, and Junnila, *Noottikriisi,* pp. 83–88. He could explain how his chances to win were always good, had been improved by the Note, Gromyko's disclosure, and the rescheduled parliamentary elections. A victory was now certain due to disarray in the Honka Front and the latest Soviet move.

German militarists; he charged that their activities, which were "directed toward undermining the Paasikivi-Kekkonen Line, arouse our grave concern."[21] The speech was the event which provided the final weight to crush the Front, for in a rump session of the group attended mainly by members of the Finnish Nationalist and Swedish parties the mood was predominantly for abandonment of the cause. Both parties conveyed to Honka that evening the withdrawal of their support, whereupon Honka renounced his candidacy.[22] Kekkonen and Khrushchev, it has been reported, knew nothing of the actual collapse of the Union as they completed negotiations.[23]

The winding up of the Note Crisis came with the climactic events in Novosibirsk and Helsinki; all that remained was to publish the Novosibirsk agreement and conduct the elections with the expected results. The crucial point in the agreement was the postponement of the military consultations, and a significant portion indicates how Kekkonen argued for deferment of the talks: "that initiation of consultations might cause anxiety and war psychosis in the Scandinavian countries"; that if postponed, public opinion in these countries would be calmed, leading "to a lessening of the need for military preparations not only in Finland and Sweden, but also in Norway and Denmark." Khrushchev, for his part, indicated the Soviet rationale behind the political approach and declared his confidence in Kekkonen's leadership "to maintain the Paasikivi-Kekkonen Line" and "Finland's course of neutrality which had the support of the Soviet Union." On a concluding note he expressed the wish that the Finnish government watch developments in the Baltic and Northern Europe and submit to the Soviet government what measures it thought should be taken.[24]

Kekkonen's basic strategy of diverting Khrushchev to the

---

21. *London Times,* November 25, 1961, p. 6.

22. Junnila, *Noottikriisi,* pp. 83–88.

23. According to Max Jakobson, whose official position in the Ministry of Foreign Affairs as Director for Political Affairs placed him in a position to know, Khrushchev and Kekkonen reached agreement hours before the withdrawal. See Jakobson, *Finnish Neutrality,* p. 78.

24. See *New York Times,* November 26, 1961, p. 4, for the text of the Novosibirsk statement.

political approach had prevailed. The Novosibirsk statement clearly implies, however, that the President played with skill the Scandinavian card, for he was apparently able to persuade Khrushchev to reflect on how military talks would be greeted in these countries, especially Sweden, where the preservation of Finnish neutrality was basic policy.[25] The Note also seemed to serve its purpose as a lever in the wider context of the cold war, for by the time of Novosibirsk, Khrushchev had switched to a different tack and was "receptive to the argument that putting off military talks with Finland was likely to reduce tension in Northern Europe."[26]

Another gain, it has been claimed by Finnish sources, was scored by Finland in the interpretation of Article 2 of the treaty of 1948 because of the Paasikivi construction that both parties had to acknowledge the existence of a threat of aggression before consultations could take place.[27] This interpretation was now, according to Max Jakobson, "in effect confirmed by the course of events" when the Soviet assertion that such a threat existed had failed to trigger consultations. The Soviet government had never either accepted or rejected the Paasikivi interpretation, but at Novosibirsk, according to Jakobson, it suggested that it was up to Finland to assume initiative for consultations, which seemed to shift their position closer to Paasikivi's.[28]

In Finland there was relief that the crisis had passed and cheer that neutrality had been preserved but not much comfort in the price that once again had to be paid for independence, namely, that it was unwise to exercise it too freely. The Social Democrats and their associates had to make the sacrifice a second time in three years. Khrushchev in Novosibirsk disclaimed any intention to interfere or that he had interfered in Finnish politics but

---

25. *Lecture by Mr. Max Jakobson, Director for Political Affairs, Ministry of Foreign Affairs, at a Meeting of the Foreign Policy Association of the University of Lund, Sweden, November 13, 1963*, pp. 10–11. (Photostat copy obtained from the Finnish Ministry of Foreign Affairs). See also Jakobson, *Finnish Neutrality*, p. 91, and Junnila, *Noottikriisi*, pp. 73–82, and Puntila, "Finland's Neutrality," p. 225.

26. Jakobson, *Finnish Neutrality*, pp. 79–80.

27. See Chapter 2, pp. 57–64.

28. Jakobson, *Finnish Neutrality*, pp. 78–79, and *New York Times*, November 27, 1961, p. 1.

maintained "we would be bad statesmen if we did not follow carefully the development of the political situation in a country along our frontier."[29] If there was no interference in a strictly technical sense, there was the assertion of the propriety of viewing with alarm, criticizing, and even accusing, political groups and developments in a border state with the *expectation of results* (anticipated reaction) all induced by the leverage of invoking a treaty provision which would jeopardize a core national policy.

The Soviet leaders got the results they sought as far as internal Finnish politics was concerned, but they rejected the opprobrium of the word "interference" for it would convey the impression of arrogance and dictation, just as the Finns rejected it for the impression of submissiveness and helplessness it would imply. Semantic rigamarole abounds in spheres of influence relationships, especially where pressure or interference occurs, because interference offends nationalistic sensibilities of the sphere state and brands the paramount state with the stigma of "imperialistic" or "aggressive" behavior.

At any rate, the Soviet Union's assertion of influence could be seen to operate: Once *perceived need* shifted to affecting internal Finnish politics, *opportunity* was provided by party differences and rivalry, the weakening of the Honka Front, and public disposition to bend to Soviet wishes for the national good; while the *facility* employed was pressure for consultations and the threat they implied for neutrality. In *degree* the influence, while indirect, moved back toward hard sphere practices and in *effect* there was a disruption of the political process in the most important election in the country which resulted in temporarily diminished independence. There was thus once again dysfunction of the system because of the magnitude of the effects upon it by Soviet influence.

Upon his return to Helsinki from the Novosibirsk sessions, Kekkonen urged objectionable public figures to retire from politics as a patriotic duty; if they did so, he emphasized, there would not be "the slightest doubt" that the country would continue neutral in "all situations." He stressed his own conviction, how-

---

29. *London Times,* November 25, 1961, p. 6.

ever, that these men had no desire to change foreign policy but underscored the fact that "Soviet officials cannot be convinced that such is the case."[30] V. Leskinen replied the next day that he had no intention of complying with the request, but would sit tight; "If we quit, who knows who will be on tomorrow's blacklist,"[31] he added. Tanner, who was eighty, announced that he would not seek re-election to Parliament but would hold on to his post as Chairman of the Social Democratic Party. Professor Nils Meinander, leader of the Swedish Party and a prominent backer of Honka, announced that he, too, would not seek re-election.[32]

President Kekkonen, expectedly, was elected for a second six year term by an overwhelming vote; not expected was the large turnout of eligible voters who went to the polls. A few weeks later the Agrarians won 53 seats in the parliamentary elections, for a gain of 5, to become the largest party in the Diet, replacing the SKDL. It is significant that no parties of the Honka Front lost seats in these elections: the Social Democrats gained one, the Conservatives four, the Liberals five, and the Swedish Party retained its fourteen seats. Losses were sustained by the SKDL, three seats, and the Opposition Social Democrats, fourteen seats.[33] It seems that under the circumstances the voters supported Kekkonen and the Honka Front parties but turned against the pro-Soviet left in a demonstration of independence.

---

30. *New York Times*, November 27, 1961, p. 1. Italics added. Kekkonen mentioned no names but there was no doubt that he referred primarily to Tanner and other Social Democrats. Compare "Broadcast on November 26th 1961, in Helsinki," pp. 102–108, in Kekkonen, *Neutrality: The Finnish Position*, which is a collection of recently published edited speeches of the President where this point in the address seems very much toned down.

31. *New York Times*, November 28, 1961, p. 3.

32. *Ibid.*, December 14, 1961, p. 41. There were no other retirements and Tanner did not resign as chairman of the Social Democratic Party until three years later when he was 83.

33. On the parliamentary election results and the new government see Forster, "The Silent Soviet Vote in Finnish Politics," *International Journal*, p. 351. Voters ignored the appeals of Agrarians in the campaign to reject those objectionable to the Soviet leaders, for V. Leskinen and K. Pitsinki, both Social Democrats of the Tanner faction, were elected. *New York Times*, February 6, 1962, p. 7.

Motives behind the Note, as in many such decision-making situations, were probably multifaceted and shifting. Indeed, there seem to have been three shiftings after the original purpose of asking for military consultations. We have a picture of Soviet decision makers weighing alternatives and oscillating from one tack to another as developments were seen to require changes. In weighing and shifting, the consequences for the soft sphere system must have come under serious consideration.

Until the matter is clarified by hard historical evidence, speculation or advocacy of hypotheses to explain Soviet motivation will persist. The first is the "shift hypothesis," that Khrushchev probably intended to pursue consultations urged by the military but later shifted to the course of influencing the elections. An "abandon hypothesis" can be discerned by those who stress, as in the "shift hypothesis," the genuine quality of Soviet strategic preoccupations, and emphasize that Kekkonen persuaded them to abandon consultations primarily because of concern for Finnish neutrality and Scandinavian reactions. The "abandon hypothesis" rejects any Soviet intention to interfere, on the ground that the Honka challenge was exaggerated and Kekkonen was slated to win anyway. An "engineered hypothesis" claims the Note had as its real objective all along to influence the course of Finnish political processes by an imaginative and flawlessly executed scenario; this group stresses continuity in Soviet motivation behind the doctrines of preferred or opposed persons, so forcefully brought home in the Nightfrost. The "shift hypothesis," it is evident, has elements in common with both other hypotheses. In both the "shift hypothesis" and the "abandon hypothesis" President Kekkonen is credited with a major diplomatic achievement, but under the "engineered hypothesis" he was the one exploited as well as the prime beneficiary.[34]

---

34. The hypotheses reflect sincere efforts to probe for the truth in view of inadequate data as well as reflection of possible partisan political stances or a desire to serve a national purpose in the belief that it is necessary to stress only positive accomplishments of the Kekkonen regime and avoid any acknowledgement of Soviet interference. Three who apparently follow the "engineered hypothesis" are: Forster, "The Silent Soviet Vote in Finnish Politics," pp. 341–352; Holsti, "Strategy and Techniques of Influence in Soviet-Finnish Relations," pp. 63–82; and Junnila, *Noottikriisi,* pp. 66–72. Two supporters of the

There seems, in the view of the writer, more reason to accept at this time the "shift hypothesis" and credit the President with effective diplomatic skill. Without Kekkonen's astute statesmanship, personal qualities, and position of confidence in Moscow, a successful conclusion of the crisis might not have been possible. Backed by support at home and ability to communicate with Soviet leaders he could wrest from them crucial concessions. In these respects he was truly the successor to Paasikivi. Kekkonen succeeded in changing Soviet perceptions of need for military consultations somewhat in the same manner as Paasikivi changed Stalin's perception of need in negotiations for the treaty of 1948.

For other reasons Olavi Honka also deserves Finland's gratitude for his timely sacrifice in the national interest, which made possible the unanimity behind Kekkonen that the Soviets were virtually imposing upon the country. He realized that the system of the soft sphere was tied to "confidence abroad" which was "more important than pacts and agreements."[35]

Khrushchev could also claim success for the *quid pro quo,* for dropping consultations was the guarantee of Kekkonen's victory. Indeed, as a result of the Note Crisis, as in the Nightfrost, Kekkonen's powerful opponents had been for the time being defeated or neutralized, and in the Soviet view the security of the USSR had been accordingly enhanced. Temporary dysfunction of the system could be borne with equanimity if the dreaded Tannerites and other *personae non gratae* were thwarted. But what of long term implications for the system? Would dysfunction and recurring crises become a permanent feature, infusing it periodically with elements of the hard sphere when the groups supporting the Fagerholm coalition of 1958 and the Honka Front seemed likely to achieve political power? Actually, the country had been split down the middle, and the Soviets in both crises had intervened to influence the course of internal politics in favor of one

---

"abandon hypothesis" are Jakobson, *Finnish Neutrality,* pp. 69–82, and Puntila, "Finland's Neutrality," also a transcript of a radio interview with Puntila conducted by Mr. Aaron Bell, an American political scientist resident in Finland, a copy of which was lent to the author.

35. From a speech by Honka in Denmark, February 10, 1962, quoted in *Uusi Suomi* the next day. Cited in Holsti, "Strategy and Techniques of Soviet-Finnish Relations," p. 79.

side. The Social Democrats, as one of the three major political parties, represented about one in four voters while the Conservatives, Liberals, and Swedish Party, who combined with and followed Socialist leadership in the Honka Front and the Fagerholm government of 1958, also represented about one in four of the electorate.

It is not likely that there were many qualms in Moscow over the anomalous situation in Finnish politics and dysfunction of the soft sphere system as it had evolved up to the autumn of 1958, for Soviet decision makers stressed other priorities. Nor was there, from the Finnish perspective, an end in sight for the internal cause of the crises and dysfunctions as long as there was not full support for the position of President Kekkonen, the Tanner faction maintained its hold in the Social Democrats, and the Conservatives retained their strength. Moscow could again be expected to invoke, with a heavy hand if need be, the pair of doctrines on the acceptance or rejection of persons and groups and exploit internal divisions to insure desired results.

Nevertheless, in the aftermath of the Note Crisis a degree of calm had been restored to the turbulent political waters of Finland. Kekkonen had been elected for another six-year term and the Social Democrats could be excluded from the government for some time. These were the fruits of interference and dysfunction and they made it possible to buy time, for no new crisis along the lines of 1958 or 1961 could be expected for at least four years when, in 1966, the next parliamentary elections were scheduled.

The era of crisis and dysfunction underscores the crucial significance of perceptions of both Soviet and Finnish policy makers. The operability of the soft sphere in Finland and the conditions upon which the security of the USSR depended were founded upon perceptions of reality in Moscow which were so deeply embedded and tenaciously held as to admit of no other interpretation. SKDL and opposition Socialist partisan charges tended to reinforce such perceptions and worked to perpetuate them.[36] Partisan Agrarian imprecations against the Social Demo-

36. Some of the persons interviewed by the author in 1967 and 1972 were of the opinion that Soviet media and officials relied rather heavily for impressions and information on Finnish politics from the Finnish Communists and opposition Socialists and were led to believe that the Finns were ready to throw out Kekkonen in the 1962 election.

crats accusing them of being less capable of dealing with the Russians or meriting their confidence tended also to confirm the validity of the image.

In the course of the Honka-Kekkonen campaign the debate between the President and his Agrarian supporters versus the Social Democrats and theirs revived the issues which had been raised in the Nightfrost. In the opinion of the latter party, partisan political differences should be confined mainly to domestic problems; the Socialists insisted that all Finnish parties were pledged to abide by the Paasikivi Line, but with some differences in emphasis and the spirit in which it should be interpreted.[37] The Socialists warned of a truncated independence and democracy if there was no free functioning of the political processes; they again urged that there existed an adequate basis for confidence and that it should not be withdrawn until overt decisions gave cause. Kekkonen and the Agrarians still stressed confidence in persons, irrespective of policies, and contended that even though the suspicions of the USSR were "unjustified and groundless, we cannot fail to take into account the possible political consequences of this suspicion."[38] The President, as in the Nightfrost, urged that the line between domestic and foreign policy could become indistinct and that relations between states are unavoidably determined as much by internal conditions as by foreign policy; a country like Finland, he emphasized, ignored this at its peril.[39]

In great power-small power relations, especially in a sphere of influence situation, what the small power does has an effect upon the great power, but what the great power does may have tenfold the effect upon the small power. If a great power has an itch which it must scratch, the small power is in danger of being torn to shreds if the great power scratches too hard.[40] The Soviet Union

---

37. See Nousiainen, "The Parties and Foreign Policy" in *Finnish Foreign Policy,* pp. 185–188, for a discussion of party differences in interpretation of the Paasikivi Line and "policy toward the east" in general.

38. *Lecture by Max Jakobson to the University of Lund, November 13, 1963,* p. 10.

39. Nousiainen, "The Parties and Foreign Policy," pp. 185–188.

40. This graphic metaphor was suggested by Mr. Jim S. Nut, Consul General of Canada, who told an audience in Denver, Colorado, "What we do economically affects you, but what you do affects us ten times over; when you itch, you scratch—and when you scratch too hard, we are in danger of being torn to shreds." *The Denver Post,* December 22, 1971, p. 2.

was irritated by the general itch of security and two specific itches: "Tannerites" and "rightists" in Finland on the one hand and West German militarists and revanchists on the other. In the Nightfrost the first specific itch was most vexing, but the others irritated in the background. In the Note Crisis all three flared up.

The Note Crisis pointed up how precarious the soft sphere system and neutrality would be in the face of international tensions and conflict. It is beyond the scope of this study to treat in detail the contingencies affecting the future of Finnish foreign policy. In a general way these contingencies were provided for in the treaty of 1948 and were discussed in Chapter 2. In the future, however, there might be good prospects for retaining Finnish neutrality if Sweden remained neutral and the Gulf of Finland was not the scene of hostilities. If, however, a war was expected to be general, or Leningrad, the Baltic, or northern Russia endangered, the prospects for neutrality would be grim indeed. Under such circumstances the Soviet military officials would be inclined to exert great pressure upon political officials to convert the treaty of 1948 into an out-and-out military alliance and integrate Finland as much as necessary into the complex of Soviet military activities. The peacetime face of the treaty serving Finnish interest in neutrality would thus have to give way to the wartime face serving Soviet interests in alliance.[41] The Note summoning Finland to military consultations offers some implication that Soviet military officials might think this way.

In conclusion, the two crises raised for Soviet decision makers some nagging questions concerning implications of her spheres of influence policy for Finland. How did Moscow assess the consequences of interference on the Finnish public, politicians, and opinion makers with whom they hoped to establish a relationship of "good neighborliness" or at least acquiescence to inclusion in the Soviet orbit? What effect would there be on world opinion to

---

41. See Holsti, "Strategy and Techniques of Influence in Soviet-Finnish Relations," p. 82, for a prognostication that Finnish neutrality would not likely be respected "by either side during a general European war conducted primarily by conventional weapons." Professor L. A. Puntila in a radio interview with Mr. Bell, cited previously, was of the opinion that if the "equilibrium of the great powers in the world and Europe . . . is maintained and no full scale war breaks out," Finland's neutrality will probably be maintained.

which claims had been made for the Finnish case as an example of coexistence and the showcase of different systems living in relative symbiotic peacefulness and cooperation?

Some disconcerting questions also nettled the Finns: The first was, obviously, how can democracy and independence be reconciled with the intrusion of foreign influence of such magnitude and frequency? What role in the political life of the country would there be for the half of the body politic which had been frustrated in the two crises? Would the Social Democrats not have to capitulate to terms required by Moscow if they were to be an effective force in Finnish politics? If the Social Democrats did bow to Moscow, what would be the consequences for the party and Finnish politics?

To answer the last three questions, it will be necessary to examine the Social Democrats' reassessment and response to the crises and dysfunction.

CHAPTER SEVEN

RESPONSE TO CRISIS AND DYSFUNCTION: THE SOCIAL DEMOCRATIC "FULFILLMENT"

Social Democratic policies, which had evolved since the end of the war and the development of the soft sphere system, had a significant degree of support in the country, were logically conceived, consistent with Finnish constitutionalism, and could justifiably be claimed to be consistent with the Paasikivi Line and the country's cherished stance of neutrality. The Socialists had offered alternative leadership to that of Kekkonen and their Agrarian rivals within the context of the soft sphere relationship, *as they saw it*, but their policies were not acceptable to Moscow, as evidenced by the outbreak of the two crises. Why? In view of what has been noted elsewhere, Soviet objections ostensibly centered on Tanner and his followers, especially Leskinen. The power of the Tannerites in the Social Democrats led to placing the whole party on the blacklist, including even Fagerholm, who had opposed Tanner and who had served as Prime Minister in two governments before his ill-fated coalition of the Nightfrost.

Moscow's attitude toward the Social Democrats, however, went beyond rejection of specific leaders and extended to essential features of the party's foreign and domestic policies. Soviet leaders insisted upon the orthodoxy of Kekkonen's version of the Paasikivi Line and considered Socialist pursuit of their own version and criticism of the President's as incorrect and threatening. The Social Democrats also erred, in the eyes of Moscow, by refusing to follow the Soviet approved role for Kekkonen as the prime mover or "universal providence" of Finnish politics. Instead they spearheaded a movement to oppose his re-election.

The Socialists were also a thorn in the side of Moscow's favored Finns because of the bitter and almost unremitting hostility they indulged in toward the Agrarians, Communists, and schismatic Socialists. To complete the catalogue of "offenses" and "errors" the Social Democrats were disposed to cooperate with the Conservatives and other detested bourgeois and rightist groups.

Aside from the Tannerites, who drew the heaviest fire of Moscow, the Social Democrats and the other parties of the Honka Front, although perhaps technically "correct" in their interpretation of the Paasikivi Line, were regarded with scepticism and coolness. The Socialists and their associates were thought to be more detached, inflexible, and less solicitous of Soviet sensitivity. The USSR seemed to prefer the more "active" version of the Paasikivi Line being elaborated by Kekkonen, as indicated by his "pajama pocket speech" for neutralization of Scandinavia and the denuclearization proposal for that region.[1]

The shock of the crises and resulting dysfunction dramatized the fact that the relatively free play of Finnish political processes was obstructed and the predilections of Soviet leaders intruded to affect the outcome. The functioning of the system of the soft sphere, which essentially assured that internal Finnish political processes would suffer no inhibition of any magnitude, was thus arrested. A major consequence of these lapses in the function of the system was to deprive the Social Democrats and their associated parties (amounting to at least half of the electorate) from effectively participating in the political life of the country.

In the aftermath of the Note Crisis the Social Democrats turned to review the past and assess the future. It was surely a sobering examination, for it involved effects upon the party and the country if no timely and adequate adjustments were made. Crisis and dysfunction would again be in store, thwarting Socialist ambitions and clogging the system, for Moscow seemed determined to cling to her predilections and again interfere if a set of similar circumstances were to occur. If no changes were made, the Socialists could look forward only to continued exclusion, relegation to a permanent opposition, and the bearing of a share of responsibility for continued embitterment of Finnish politics. On

---

1. See Chapter 9, pp. 159–162.

the other hand, if they did change, what would be the fate of the policies which had been espoused? Could it not be said that if the Social Democrats came to terms with the leaders of the USSR, a major political movement would founder? Socialists must have experienced a sense of frustration and remorse when it is considered that they would have to do this because of the fears of the Soviet government; they had, after all, done nothing wrong except to oppose President Kekkonen and choose certain party leaders. If governments of small states are fain to accept the harsh necessity of expedient capitulation in dealing with great states, political parties in small states would, it seems, have to do likewise.

In coming to terms with Moscow there would have to be soundings taken to determine whether some selected timely concessions would be sufficient or if major retreat or even unconditional surrender would be required. At any rate, the Soviet leaders would, for the most part, call the tune in these proceedings. Thus the remedy of crises and dysfunctions, as far as Socialists were concerned, would be virtually dictated by Moscow. In the end, while the soft sphere would be restored to a normal functioning along the lines to which it had evolved by 1958, and the impasse in Finnish politics as well as the impotence of Social Democrats terminated, it should be acknowledged that a price had to be paid by the Social Democratic Party in particular and Finland in general.

Political parties respond to the need for change not only in view of harsh necessity but also in anticipation of opportunities for gain. During the post crisis period in Finland both motives converged in the Socialist reassessment as flexibility and expediency gained the upper hand. As the conditions for a *modus vivendi* with the Soviet Union unfolded, a favorable political climate for the party seemed to develop in the country, while painful divisions and frequent compromises took place within the party as the opposition to change grudgingly gave ground. The scales were tipped in favor of reform, and a degree of party consensus was restored when V. Leskinen, in 1965, renounced his former policies and attitudes as errors.[2] The earliest moves in the

---

2. See Kent Forster, "Finland's 1966 Election and Soviet Relations," *Orbis* (Fall 1968) p. 781. This is a most valuable article on the subject; Forster has used extensively Finnish, Russian, and American press reports including *Summary of the*

process of change and accommodation began, however, at the triennial congress of the party in June 1963 when Tanner, at the age of 82, retired as Chairman, and Rafael Paasio was elected to the post over V. Helle, Leskinen's candidate, by a vote of 99 to 63.[3] Although Paasio and his supporters also succeeded in removing Leskinen from the powerful Executive Committee, two other members of the Executive Committee, also on the Soviet blacklist, were re-elected unanimously. The party in 1963 thus made some significant initial overtures to end the impasse, but the new Executive Committee was composed of four Paasio supporters and eight who could be listed as Leskinen supporters.[4] For almost four years thereafter the process of change proceeded in response to indirect exchanges with Soviet leaders. There were debates within the party as well as exchanges with the Communists in Finland until February 1967.[5]

The desire to assume power was reinforced by signs that internal politics and socio-economic changes in the country presaged an enhancement of socialist strength at the polls, which was indicated by a favorable trend in the municipal elections of 1964. Hopes were also raised by the reinstatement of Emil Skog and several others who had bolted the party in 1957 in protest against the policies of Tanner.

Social Democratic participation in the government might help to remedy the somewhat anemic condition of parliamentary democracy which had set in due to the crises. This could be taken

---

Finnish Press prepared jointly by the Helsinki embassies of Great Britain, Canada, and the United States.

3. *New York Times,* June 17, 1963, p. 2. Paasio was a Social Democratic politician who was regarded as acceptable to Moscow, but he had not distinguished himself with a prior record of leadership. Especially when compared to Leskinen, some persons interviewed by the author in 1972 considered him as "colorless."

4. *Ibid.*

5. Forster, "Finland's 1966 Election and Soviet Relations" gives a detailed account of these exchanges and the changes which were adopted. For a brief reference see Uhro Kalevainen, "Soviet 'Non-Interference': Finland's Current Political Horizon and Finno-Soviet Relations," *International Peasant Union Bulletin* (January-May 1969) p. 29. One of the persons interviewed by the author in September 1972 offered the opinion that the Socialists anticipated what the Soviets wanted. He learned that when Leskinen met with Ponomarev in Moscow there were two main conditions which were indicated: 1) unequivocal support of Kekkonen and his policies and 2) inclusion of the SKDL in a new government.

by the Socialists as an opportunity as well as a responsibility as they prepared to institute changes in order to be in a position to assume power. Finally, the time was also propitious for possible new relationships due to ferment in the SKDL and the Communist Party's modifying rigid orthodox dogmas concerning pursuit of objectives through Parliament and collaboration with the Socialists.[6]

The Socialist reform resulted from a series of steps beginning in 1963 and ending in 1968 when they fulfilled a pledge to support Kekkonen for a third term. The process wrought changes in foreign policy, domestic politics, and internal party politics. The shift most significant in foreign policy was to drop the long and doggedly held version of the Paasikivi Line, which differed from that of President Kekkonen and the Agrarians. In 1965 it must have been pleasing to Soviet ears when *Sosialidemokraatti* editors endorsed an attack by Kekkonen on the American proposal for a NATO Multilateral Atomic Force, an attack which was accompanied by denunciations of U. S. actions in the Dominican Republic and Vietnam. The following year the party's Central Committee summoned all Socialists to "work for peace in Vietnam, the prevention of the spread of nuclear weapons, and the fostering of general disarmament—Soviet positions all—and expressed its 'delight' with the favorable development of Finno-Soviet relations."[7]

In domestic politics the Socialists accepted the principle of collaboration with SKDL and Communists as well as with the irreconcilably schismatic Simonist Socialists, thus reversing the decision of 1948 regarding collaboration with the Communists and Left Socialists. Next, a popular front including the Centrists, as the Agrarians were now renamed, was formed to resurrect the old Red-Green coalition of 1946–1948. The Soviet government at this time was hospitable to the popular front idea generally, but

6. See Kevin Devlin, "Finnish Communism," *Survey* (Winter-Spring 1970) pp. 49–69; Pertti Hynynen, "The Popular Front in Finland," *New Left Review* (September-October 1969) pp. 3–20; George Schopflin, "Finnish Communists in Disarray," *The World Today* (June 1969) pp. 231–234; and Forster, "Finland's 1966 Elections and Soviet Relations."

7. Forster, "Finland's 1966 Election and Soviet Relations," p. 782, citing *Helsingen Sanomat,* February 16, 1966.

their interest in this case seemed mainly to have been to bring the Communists back into participation in Finland's government for reasons peculiar to this situation.[8] Finally, the Social Democrats ended all opposition to Kekkonen politically and joined in supporting his election for a third term in 1968. This was the last crucial change of the fulfillment. Such a move was probably expected as supplementary to the espousal of Kekkonen's version of the Paasikivi Line and signaled a victory for the Soviet policy of grooming him as the successor to Paasikivi.

As to intra-party positions and politics the Socialists disavowed as errors earlier policies that led to the Nightfrost Crisis and their sponsorship of the Honka Front in 1961. Finally, Tanner, and others of his persuasion so odious to Moscow, were also disavowed.

The landslide victory of the Social Democrats in the Parliamentary elections of March 1966 seemed to confirm the wisdom of change, for as the largest party they would occupy a position of primacy in parliamentary politics and probably assume the major role in any new government.[9] Since nothing succeeds like success, doubts and remorse concerning the changes could more readily be glossed over; moreover, since the changes were made in order to exercise power, the times seemed most optimistic for the Socialists. Nevertheless, some were not reconciled to the shift, and they remained represented in party councils.[10]

---

8. See Forster, "Finland's 1966 Election and Soviet Relations." See also Devlin, "Finnish Communism," and Hynynen, "The Popular Front in Finland."

9. On the results of the election see *New York Times,* March 22, 1966, p. 1; Magnus Lemberg, "Finland: The Parliamentary Election of 1966," *Scandinavian Political Studies,* Vol. 2, 1967, pp. 247–252; and Forster, "Finland's 1966 Elections and Soviet Relations." The unprecedented victory of the Social Democrats netted them 27% of votes cast, which was the largest plurality cast for any party in the country's postwar electoral history. As the largest party they won 55 seats, a gain of 17 from the previous total of 38. The six other parties suffered reductions in Parliament and declines in popular vote: The Center declined to 49, a loss of 4 to make it second in strength; SKDL lost 6 seats and now had 41 to become third in strength; the Simonist Socialists declined from 7 to 2; the Conservatives went from 32 to 26, the Swedish People's Party from 14 to 12, and the Liberals from 14 to 9.

10. *New York Times,* November 29, 1966, p. 10, where no sweeping changes were made in the executive Committee.

Coalition negotiations began on April 14 and ended on May 21 with the establishment of the Left-Center government under Paasio. As Premier-designate Paasio encountered opposition in his own Socialist ranks over including the SKDL.[11] Communist bargaining strength was enough to get only three portfolios, although they had asked for four. The Center, on the other hand, could drive a hard bargain in the face of Social Democratic desire to balance the cabinet with their inclusion and the former party's reluctance to accord a prominent place in the government to the SKDL. Consequently, the Center wrested from the Socialists a farm subsidy program and were given five seats in the government, including the Foreign Minister. The Social Democrats took six seats, including the Prime Minister, and one seat was allotted to the Simonist Socialists. It was a strong coalition based on 152 seats in the 200 member Parliament.[12] None of the Socialists who had been objected to in the past had been included: Leskinen, even though he had renounced his former policies, Pitsinki, Lindblom, or Fagerholm.

At this juncture there remained the need for signs of positive Soviet responses to the turn of described events. In view of the fact that Soviet expectations had been kept well in mind—if not faithfully implemented—there should have been no surprise when within a month President Kekkonen received a state visit from Premier Kosygin, who conveyed praise and approval for the Socialist-led government. "We feel that because of this program," he declared on the second day of his official visit, "all those who seek to strengthen relations with the Soviet Union . . . can now continue with greater determination their work in the interest of both countries."[13] The Soviet Premier then augmented the positive response by extending an invitation to Paasio for a visit to

---

11. *Ibid.*, May 27, 1966, p. 3.

12. On the formation of the coalition see Forster, "Finland's 1966 Election and Soviet Relations," pp. 787–788; Devlin, "Finnish Communism," p. 56; Hynynen, "The Popular Front in Finland"; Magnus Lemberg, "Finland: Two Years of Left-Wing Coalition," pp. 230–231 in *Scandinavian Political Studies*, Vol. 3, 1968, a yearbook published by the political science associations in Denmark, Finland, Norway, and Sweden. Distributed by the Academic Bookstore, Helsinki, and Columbia University Press, New York, 1969; *New York Times*, May 22, 1966, p. 1, and May 28, 1966, p. 2.

13. *New York Times*, June 15, 1966, p. 15.

Moscow in November. Later, in the Soviet capital on his visit, Paasio reiterated his determination to strengthen the Paasikivi-Kekkonen Line.[14] The official communique which was published in full by *Izvestia* pointed out with

> great satisfaction . . . that the relations between Finland and the Soviet Union are good and that the interaction between both countries in the most difficult fields has continued to bring about valuable results. The good neighbourly relations between Finland and the Soviet Union are evidence of the application of the principles of peaceful coexistence in practice.[15]

The Socialist Party and the new coalition had passed muster, but Moscow maintained pressure until it gained unequivocal support for Kekkonen in his re-election bid in 1968.[16] Moscow also indicated that further changes in the governing council of the party should be made to conform to the spirit of the new orientation. On the eve of the Social Democratic Party Congress in 1966, *Pravda* warned against powerful "rightist" forces that wanted to undermine the new direction, and implied that a change in the twelve man Executive Committee would be desirable.[17] For its part the Socialists made no sweeping changes in the Executive Committee but re-elected Paasio as Chairman by acclamation. Resolutions were passed on NATO and Vietnam echoing the Soviet viewpoint,[18] but Moscow persisted in criticism.[19] Attempting to still the criticism, the fifty-five Socialist members of Parliament issued a statement emphasizing that it was important for the Finns to develop "especially active friendly relations with their big

14. *Finnish Features*, No. 16/66, "Speech by Prime Minister Rafael Paasio at the Luncheon in Honour of the Delegation of the Government of Finland, Moscow, November 15, 1966."

15. *Finnish Features*, No. 20/66, "Finnish-Soviet Communique on the Occasion of the visit to the USSR of the Finnish Government Delegation on November 15–19, 1966."

16. See above p. 131, and Forster, "Finland's 1966 Election and Soviet Relations," pp. 789–790.

17. *New York Times*, November 26, 1966, p. 12.

18. *Ibid.*, November 29, 1966, p. 10.

19. *Ibid.*, December 13, 1966, p. 15.

neighbor."[20] The criticism did not subside, however, until almost two months later, in March 1967, when party secretary Erkki Raatikainen formally announced the party's support for Kekkonen's re-election as proof of its support of the country's foreign policy.[21]

The Social Democratic fulfillment should be ranked among the most significant developments in the evolution of the Finnish soft sphere of influence, for it served to work toward completion of the process of delineating the nature of the system. In the soft sphere context Finland was supposed to enjoy internal self-government, but this could be hobbled if one of the major political parties was inhibited from playing a role commensurate with its power. With the change the Socialists could now fulfill such a role. In a soft sphere the hegemon should have no serious misgivings or hostility toward a major political movement in a sphere state unless that movement is palpably inconsistent with the basic understanding and seeks changes to this end. The Social Democrats did not intend to behave in this way, but it took the fulfillment to induce Moscow to go a long way toward changing its perceptions of them. In a soft sphere, influence should be subtle, indirect, and not bring about effects of such magnitude as to disrupt the system, which actually amount to removing the silk glove and exposing the mailed fist. The fulfillment resolved differences which caused such conditions. In a soft sphere the cement of good will, reciprocal advantage, and mystique seals the relationship between the parties. This had been true of only half of Finland. With the fulfillment the Socialists decided to institute changes in their party and policies that would make possible such a relationship with the paramount power.

The accommodation was one of the Socialist Party *to* the Soviet Union. As far as Moscow was concerned the Socialists had to be "de-Tannerized" before any accommodation so that the country could be fitted into the preferred version of the Paasikivi Line. In this sense the Kekkonen spirit would at last prevail in the post-Paasikivi era, while the Tanner spirit would be disavowed.

---

20. *Ibid.*, January 2, 1967, p. 7.

21. Forster, "Finland's 1966 Election and Soviet Relations," p. 790. Kekkonen was elected for a third term in January 1968, and the Socialist support proved crucial, for he received 61% of the vote.

From another perspective, however, the Socialists were not *compelled* to make the accommodation; the party could have continued in opposition. Such a role would have had to be permitted given the degree of constitutional and political independence exercised even under the incomplete soft sphere due to the dysfunction. But the banning of so large a party from the full use of its political power would have highlighted the defectiveness of the soft sphere. There would always be the prospect of threatened new interferences, and if the issue remained unresolved it could fester and poison relations between the Soviet Union and Finland—to say nothing of the Soviet Union and the Socialists. It would also continue to work its pernicious effect upon the volatile character of Finnish politics in general.

Once the accommodation was made its considerable consequences affected all parties involved. The Social Democratic Party itself changed some features of its national image, disavowed cherished positions, and reshuffled leadership, but these changes were primarily in the realm of foreign policy and political tactics. Their basic substantive program to achieve a socialist-planned economy and a "welfare state" remained unaltered.[22] Differences within the party over the degree of change to be made created conflict on all levels, but the changes facilitated reunion with most of the dissident left, including Emil Skog, restoring strength to the party as it again took up the reins of government. The era of isolation and a political role restricted to opposition[23] had ended, and the new orientation eliminated the prospect of crisis and frustration if the party again attempted to assume major political initiatives. In the process the Social Democratic Party moved leftward in intra-party policy and leadership as well as in foreign policy and choice of political collaborators. The Socialist shift meant that it would abandon the political grouping it had led under Tanner's leadership in efforts to steer the course of national policy. The Social Democrats had actually veered toward the side they had opposed, leaving the Conservatives as the only party of significance to continue the opposition.

---

22. See Nousiainen, *The Finnish Political System,* pp. 85–86.

23. See a statement in *Finnish Features* No. 18/66 titled "Before the Social Democratic Party Convention, November 26–28, 1966": "It can be said that throughout the 1960's the SDP led an abnormal existence, 'hermetically sealed' considering the strength of its support in the country."

It was, however, to be an opposition confined to domestic affairs, for the Conservative-backed opponent of Kekkonen in 1968, Matti Virkkunen, tried to avoid foreign policy, urging that all Finns must work for good relations with the USSR. Kekkonen would not let the issue subside and again stressed that the confidence of Moscow in the Finns to maintain the postwar foreign policy was at stake. The candidacy of Virkkunen drew only a few adverse allegations in the Soviet press that he was a "militarist."[24]

Socialist transformation and the return of the party to power as a coalition partner with the Center deprived the latter of the opportunity to lash them with the old charge that they should be kept out of power because of lack of confidence in Moscow. Accommodation with Moscow opened the door to Communist participation in government for the first time in eighteen years and saddled them with responsibilities for policies hammered out in the compromises of coalition cabinets, which did not help to heal factionalization over ideology and tactics which had recently wracked the party.[25] A politics of consensus and compromise centering around the Social Democrats was made possible by joining the Communists and Left Socialists on one side with the Center on the other, ending rivalries which had embittered and frustrated Finnish politics. The triumph of Kekkonen's version of the Paasikivi Line and his election to a third term which established him as the heir to Paasikivi were most significant consequences of the fulfillment, affecting internal Finnish politics as well as Moscow's view of Finland's soft sphere system.

---

24. On the matter of probable Soviet interference the *London Times* correspondent wrote that the "ever-present factor in the political climate in Finland is the wind from Moscow. During the campaign it has been moderate and the storm expected by some did not come." *London Times,* January 16, 1968, p. 5. Veikko Vennamo, who headed a splinter Agrarian Party, also ran for the presidency in a Poujadist-like campaign of wide-ranging criticism of domestic politics as well as some criticism of the country's foreign policy. The two candidates against Kekkonen received a combined 39% of the vote: 11.3 for Vennamo and 27.7 for Virkkunen, not a particularly good showing for the incumbent, who had the support of the three major parties and the blessing of Moscow. All pro-Kekkonen parties had a reduction in popular support, but the socialists suffered the heaviest losses, with only 15.5% of the vote. See *ibid.,* January 17, 1968, p. 6, and March 10, 1970, p. 6.

25. On the factionalization in the Communist Party and the SKDL see Devlin, "Finnish Communism"; Hynynen, "The Popular Front in Finland"; Schopflin, "Finnish Communists in Disarray"; and Forster, "Finland's 1966 Election and Soviet Relations."

The Soviet Union harvested some consequences of considerable significance, for the USSR could henceforth be more certain that the soft sphere system would function as she desired. For some years in the future it would not be necessary to precipitate crises which bring on dysfunctions and cloud Soviet claims of good neighborly behavior. Specifically, the Social Democratic accommodation to Moscow was in effect an acknowledgement of a sort of prerogative of Moscow to interpose the twin doctrines regarding the acceptability of persons and groups in the soft sphere system. Accordingly, the debate between the Social Democrats and President Kekkonen and the Agrarians over whether Soviet confidence should extend to the composition of a government regardless of policies pursued by it was to all intents and purposes decided in favor of the latter. Finally, military and political leaders in the USSR could breathe more easily with the termination of the Tannerites' hold on the Social Democrats because, in their view, the security interests of the Soviet Union had been served.

When it is considered that accommodation was the only viable alternative open to the Social Democrats, it could be argued that the Socialist fulfillment was good for the party as well as good for Finland. In terms of the soft sphere system its importance cannot be overestimated, for it removed the basic cause of the crises and dysfunctions and made it possible to return to the system as it had developed by 1958. If the fulfillment had not been consummated, the period of crisis might have been prolonged with continued hard-sphere-like effects upon the system.

For the future there was a better understanding of what the level of Soviet tolerance for the operation of internal Finnish politics would be. The Finns knew better what restraints they would have to institute on their own political behavior. Kekkonen, who had pleaded the need for such wisdom to his fellow Finns, could now feel vindicated by the Socialist conversion. One of the effects of the new Social Democratic position could be seen in the campaign for President by the Conservative-supported candidate in 1968, M. Virkkunen, who deliberately attempted to remove the issue of foreign policy from consideration.

Socialist rapprochement with Moscow left the National Coalition as the only major permanent political movement which had not come to terms with the USSR. It is beyond the scope of this study, but an appropriate topic of speculation arising from it is to consider the prospects of a "National Coalition fulfillment." The

Conservatives have not been included in any government since the Nightfrost and the Note Crisis; some of the persons interviewed by the author in September 1972 were of the opinion that it was due to Moscow's lack of confidence. Since 1968 some developments in Finnish politics indicate the possibility of lessened Soviet opposition to inclusion of Conservatives in a government, while other developments point to perpetuation of Moscow's apprehensions and possible opposition to their participation.

As noted above, the Conservative candidate for President in 1968 endeavored to lessen Soviet apprehensions and establish a basis for acceptability and tolerance if full trust could not be accorded. Soviet misgivings concerning the Right in Finnish politics were aggravated, however, by sharp increases in the Conservative vote in the parliamentary election of 1970 which swelled their number from 26 to 36. Such augmented strength placed the National Coalition as one of the four major political parties in Finland. In the same election the spectacular rise of Vennamo's rightist "Poujadist-like" Rural Party from 1 to 18 seats marked the strongest rightward shift since the end of the war.[26] Soviet leaders may have greeted this development with the same suspicions and apprehensions they had earlier reserved for the Social Democrats.

President Kekkonen's abrupt announcement that Finland would not join NORDEK, after all negotiations had been virtually completed, seemed to at least one distinguished Scandinavian analyst of international relations to have been tied to the election outcome which "appears to have been the decisive factor which

---

26. On the results of this election see *London Times,* March 18, 1970, p. 6, and March 20, 1970, p. 13. The "landslide of the right" also resulted in the Swedish Party and the Liberals holding their own, at 12 and 8 seats respectively. The four parties composing the government under Socialist leadership all lost: the Socialists lost only 2 to hold on to 52 seats, but the Center sank to 36, with a damaging loss of 14; the SKDL was reduced to 36 by a loss of 6, and the Left Socialists' 6 seat representation was wiped out. The "Popular Front" of Socialists, SKDL, and Center had enough votes to continue control of the government, but Center-Right coalition was a possible and logical grouping given the political shift. Center leaders, in view of the attitudes of the President, restored cooperation with the Left, and anticipated responses from Moscow would obviously not consider such a move.

tipped the delicate balance against the decision to go ahead with NORDEK."[27]

The Socialist fulfillment seems to indicate, however, that Soviet leaders will feel secure with nothing less than complete support for Kekkonen, his candidacy as well as his policies. The National Coalition took a significant initiative in this direction when on January 18, 1973, it joined the six other parties in the Parliament for an overwhelming vote to extend the President's term for an additional four years.[28]

Finnish-Soviet relations in the soft sphere context should be examined in terms of the wider compass of Finland's relations with the expansion of European economic integration and her affinities with Scandinavia in order to focus upon the primary external relationships affecting the system.

---

27. Birnbaum, "Soviet Policy in Northern Europe," pp. 231–232. By the end of March, he continued, " . . . a crucial point had apparently been reached in the *Finnish assessment of Soviet perceptions* as a result of a number of circumstances," including the election and some of Vennamo's revanchist remarks regarding Karelian territory ceded to Russia by the peace treaty.

28. See Chapter 8, pp. 145–146.

CHAPTER EIGHT

THE AFTERMATH OF THE SOCIALIST FULFILLMENT: THE EEC AND ACTIVIST NEUTRALITY, 1968–1974

Finland, the Soviet Union, EEC, and Comecon

After the Socialist fulfillment, the Finnish-Soviet system remained intact, and bodes well to remain unimpaired for the foreseeable future. The system soon had to come to grips, however, with an occurrence of the first magnitude, the enlargement of the European Common Market to include Britain and other members of EFTA with whom Finland was closely linked in trade. Resourcefulness and patience were required to maintain the system in the face of the new economic realities from December, 1969, when at The Hague Summit Conference it was agreed in principle to enlarge the Common Market, to November 16, 1973, when the Finnish Parliament ratified the trade agreement with EEC.

As early as April, 1970, before negotiations for full membership of Britain, Ireland, Norway, and Denmark were to take place, President Kekkonen expressed concern for adjustments Finland would have to make:

> Our struggle to mind our economic interests . . . presupposes the maintenance and improvement of our competitive powers everywhere and in all directions. . . . The question of the European Economic Community has opened a possible change in the European market constellation. In this situation we must safeguard the preconditions of our competitive ability in this direction as well.[1]

---

1. UAL, 1970, pp. 16–17. See also Aimo Pajunen, "Finland's Security Policy in

As EFTA dissolved, the Finns needed to find an alternative, but full membership in the EEC was out of the question for it would jeopardize her neutrality and raise the hackles of Moscow. The Soviets would certainly view full association with the Common Market as beyond the level of tolerance of the exercise of Finnish sovereignty, because Common Market membership was more than a free trade area like EFTA. This would touch off a new crisis and disruption of the system. Yet some sort of a trade agreement was needed, for Finnish trade with EFTA was about 45% of the total; and if these countries moved behind the Common Market tariff wall, the results could be very serious, particularly for trade with Britain, Finland's biggest customer, one that took nearly a fourth of the exports of her wood and paper industries.[2]

Accordingly, Finland in company with other neutrals— Sweden, Austria, and Switzerland along with Portugal—entered into negotiations for Special Relations Agreements at the time Britain, Ireland, Norway, and Denmark sought full membership. These negotiations began in November, 1971, and were concluded in July, 1972; in the other countries they were ratified and went into effect on January 1, 1973. The Finnish ratification was delayed for a year, and the agreement went into effect on January 1, 1974. From the time the negotiations were entered into for Finnish association with the EEC to the formal approval by Parliament, the operation of internal Finnish politics and the process of securing Soviet acquiescence revealed the characteristics of the sphere state-paramount power relationships that had developed between Finland and the USSR through almost three decades.

Internally, a strong base of political support had to be established before the Russians could be approached for positive responses to an agreement with the Common Market. Although there was grumbling about some of the terms of the agreement that had been negotiated in July, 1972, almost all of the noncom-

---

the 1970's: Background and Perspectives," *Cooperation and Conflict,* 3/4, 1972, p. 52.

2. *London Times,* February 8, 1972, p. 17. See also *Finnish Features,* No. 6/71, "Finland European Integration," speech delivered by Olavi J. Mattila, Minister of Foreign Trade, at the Society of Business Economics in Helsinki, February 5, 1971.

munist members of Parliament arrived at the sober conclusion that some sort of trade agreement was necessary. The Communist Party continued to hold an adamantly ideological position, insisting that the EEC was a tool of the West serving capitalist ends and that a closer economic tie-up with the Soviet Union and Eastern Europe should instead be pursued. A strong coalition headed by the Social Democrats and including the Center, Swedes, and Liberals resolved the problem of internal political support for an agreement. The government was pledged to seek some modifications favorable to Finland, however, especially to reduce the transitional period for elimination of barriers from twelve to fewer years; this was eventually reduced to eleven years.

Efforts to persuade Soviet leaders to view favorably an agreement with the EEC should be traced in terms of the system of inter state influence that operated in Finno-Soviet relations.

Even though full membership was not sought by Finland, *any* agreement or association with the Western European economic integration movement would be sure to evoke a chilly and suspicious response in Moscow. Cold War perceptions still clouded the Soviet view of the EEC, and a Finnish agreement of any kind with Western Europe could be taken as a step in Finland's drifting toward the West away from the moorings seemingly so firmly established with the East. Because of Finland's historic background, there was always an apprehension in Moscow that, if given an opportunity, the Finns would turn to the West. For this reason, even though Finland was not a full-fledged satellite, a degree of "sealing-off" of Finland was desired by the USSR—enough to preserve the system. Indeed, it could be said that Finland's "neutrality" actually helped to further the policy of partial isolation, and Soviet acknowledgement and support of it is thus made more explicable. In the minds of Soviet leaders, if not in actuality, a dynamic and expanding Western Europe might work to supplement or replace Soviet influence and thus undermine the Finno-Soviet system. In this regard it was surely noted in Moscow that Soviet-Finnish trade had declined in the previous decade, while Finnish-Western European trade had increased.[3]

---

3. The Soviet share of Finland's foreign trade diminished from about 17.5% in 1954 to 12.7% in 1972. Kekkonen in a speech on April 4, 1973, said that this should be remedied and that he wanted to see a growth of trade with the Soviet

The burden of Finnish diplomacy was to devise a formula of concessions and assurances that would be acceptable in Moscow and lead to a reversal of the Soviet position. Bearing in mind the pivotal importance of the "favored Finns" to the Soviet Union, we should begin with the role of President Kekkonen in this process. The President was in the crucial position of guiding the process by which Soviet approval was to be secured. The doctrine of trust-acceptance-assistance applied especially to Kekkonen, and as President he had cultivated effective personal diplomacy with decision makers in Moscow. If Kekkonen stood for a definite position in favor of an agreement with the EEC and if he had strong political support within the country, it would prove to be the decisive factor in withdrawing Soviet objections, particularly if adequate compensatory arrangements were included to help dispel misgivings in Moscow.

As early as April, 1970, noted above, Kekkonen broadly implied a possible Finnish-EEC agreement. This view persisted, and in his 1973 New Year's speech he stressed that the process of integration of national economies taking place in Europe "has faced Finland with decisions that will have sizeable repercussions on the economy. . . . Finland must preserve its national competitiveness and in this way safeguard its exports."[4] Finland was moving toward a relationship with the EEC, and the President's task was to utilize the resources at his command and the established procedures to remove Soviet opposition. This was done for the most part by personal diplomacy when he made several official and unofficial visits to the USSR.

The package by which the Finns eventually procured Soviet acquiescence included: 1) some specific features of the agreement, 2) a new Soviet-Finnish economic and trade agreement, 3) a collateral agreement with Comecon, 4) the premature extension of the Pact of 1948 for 20 years, and 5) the special procedure by which Kekkonen would serve for an extended term without election.

Efforts to induce a reversal of opinion in Moscow would get

Union and Comecon. See *The Current Digest of the Soviet Press,* Vol. XXV, No. 14, April 3–9, 1973, p. 15.

4. *Finnish Features,* No. 1/73, "New Year's Address by the President of the Republic," January 1, 1973, p. 3.

nowhere, however, if Kekkonen failed to impress upon the Soviets how vital to Finnish economic life an EEC agreement was. If Moscow persisted in opposing a Finnish agreement with the Common Market, it would place the paramount power in the position of inflicting a serious injury to the sphere state by an inflexible negative attitude serving selfish unilateral ends. In spheres of influence situations, especially in a soft sphere system, a paramount power should accede to that which serves a primary or even middle-range interest of the sphere state unless it disrupts the system or conflicts with a primary or middle-range interest of the paramount power itself.

The President would also get nowhere in Moscow if he lacked firm public commitment from a wide spectrum of opinion in Finland. The main obstacles here were the Social Democratic and SKDL efforts to attach as a condition for approval of the EEC agreement the passage of a series of measures for greater economic control to deal with the effects of the agreement upon the country. The Socialists and the SKDL insisted upon the passage of the economic controls as a condition precedent to the approval of the EEC agreement. Kekkonen succeeded in persuading the Socialists at least to drop their insistence upon directly linking the two issues. He accomplished this by acknowledging that the effects of the agreement were not entirely favorable and that there were "good grounds for giving the government better methods than those offered by present legislation to regulate the effects of foreign trade."[5]

When the question of linking the two issues was resolved, the right wing parties shifted to support for for the EEC agreement, which left only the Communists and the SKDL in opposition; their internal ideological cleavages, however, weakened the force of their opposition. In the end, though, they maintained a voting unity of 36 votes in the Parliament against the agreement.[6]

---

5. See F. Singleton, "Finland, Comecon, and the EEC," *The World Today* (February 1974) pp. 70–71, and Pajunen, "Finland's Security Policy in the 1970's: Background and Perspectives," pp. 52–53.

6. See Singleton, "Finland, Comecon, and the EEC," pp. 68–70. Taisto Sinisalo, leader of the orthodox wing of the Communists, was adamantly opposed to the agreement, but Aarne Saarinen, the party chairman and leader of the revisionists, and Ele Alenius, chairman of the SKDL, seemed reluctantly resigned to the agreement.

Soviet acceptance of limited Finnish association with the EEC required that the Finns give iron-clad assurances that Finland's foreign policy would not be altered, especially her obligations to the USSR. Ever mindful of the Soviet predilection for persons they preferred to be in control of the Finnish government, it is not unwarranted to assume that Moscow wanted Kekkonen to remain at the helm beyond 1974, when his third term would expire, and during the early years of Finland's association with the EEC. Kekkonen, however, had stated in 1968 that he would not seek another term, and if he did there might be the divisive effect of a presidential campaign.

A device to resolve the matter was indicated when Mr. Karjalainen, a close associate of the President and leader of the Center Party, informally proposed in February, 1972, two years before the expiration of Kekkonen's third term, that all political parties agree to an extension of the President's term.[7] Kekkonen a few months later declared that he would be willing to remain in office beyond his present term if a majority of the Finns agreed; he also said that he would not run as a candidate in an election campaign. By the summer of that year a majority of the political parties declared in favor of an exceptional prolongation of the President's term.[8]

Preparations seemed well in hand for the passage of an extraordinary bill requiring a five-sixths majority because it represented a constitutional change. On December 14, 1972, however, the President announced he no longer felt bound by his previously expressed willingness to remain in office beyond 1974. The reason was that a "leak" had revealed a betrayal of trust by some of his senior advisers and rendered his position as head of state "questionable." Kekkonen said that he believed that he had lost the confidence of the Soviet Union and could no longer function usefully as President of the republic. The leak in question appeared in the Stockholm daily *Dagens Nyheter* on October 31, 1972, and was said to be based upon a documentary record of a Kekkonen-Brezhnev meeting in August of that year. The Soviet leader was reported to have set forth serious reservations about a Finnish-EEC agreement and the Finnish President to have de-

---

7. *New York Times*, February 9, 1972, p. 2.
8. *Keesing's Contemporary Archives*, January 29-February 4, 1973, p. 25708.

nied that the agreement would have any negative effects on the relations of the two countries. When he returned from a further visit to the Soviet Union on December 23, 1972, Kekkonen said he had been convinced that the leak had not harmed his rapport with the Soviet leaders; therefore he could accept the prolongation of his term of office for four years.[9]

All seven major parties, including the Party of National Cohesion, which was formed by twelve dissident members of Vennamo's Rural Peoples Party, supported the bill submitted to the Diet to extend the President's term for four years. The vote for passage was 170 to 28 on January 18, 1973; its opponents would have needed 34 to defeat the measure.[10]

A trade agreement with the expanding Common Market was accorded the highest priority to meet Finnish economic needs, but it was early perceived in Helsinki that the route to Brussels led first to Moscow, where Soviet misgivings over the tie-up with Western Europe could be reduced by collateral economic agreements with the USSR and Comecon. Although these negotiations with the East were supposed to "balance" the agreement with the West and were conducted "parallel" with the Soviet/Comecon negotiations, it is suggested by the time table that Finnish strategy, if not necessity, was to complete the Eastern agreements first.

The Finnish-Soviet Treaty on the Development of Economic, Technical and Industrial Cooperation was signed in April, 1971. It projected long-range trade, economic cooperation, and development of production cooperation and specialization. It was to run for ten years, and specific recommendations were to be prepared by the Soviet-Finnish Inter-Governmental Commission on Economic Cooperation.[11] Almost a year later considerable progress had been made in planning to implement provisions of the treaty. Talks had been held for common efforts, including the

---

9. *Ibid.*, and July 16–22, 1973, p. 25992. See also Singleton, "Finland, Comecon, and the EEC," p. 67.

10. Vennamo's Rural Peoples Party, reduced to 6 members, and a minuscule rightist party, the Christian League, opposed the bill as parties; there was one abstention. See *London Times,* January 19, 1973, p. 7, and *New York Times,* January 19, 1973, p. 5.

11. *The Current Digest of the Soviet Press,* Vol. XXIII, No. 17, May 25, 1971, pp. 10–14.

production of a series of standard models of equipment and machinery for the lumber, wood processing, pulp and paper, machine building, electronics and other industries. There were plans to construct, with Soviet technical assistance, iron and steel manufacturing facilities in the Finnish city of Raahe. There were also plans for the construction, with Finnish participation, of an ore-enriching combine in the Soviet Union for processing ores from the Kostomuksa iron ore deposits in the Karelian Autonomous Republic. On the Finnish side, progress was made on the construction with Soviet assistance of the first atomic power station near the city of Lovisa. The two countries signed contracts for the designing of a gas pipeline from the Sovet Union to Finland and for later deliveries of natural gas to Finland for 20 years beginning in 1974.[12]

Negotiations for an agreement with Comecon came on the heels of the conclusion of the Soviet-Finnish treaty of April, 1971. Talks were thus conducted at the same time in both the East and the West, for Finland and the five other European countries not seeking membership in the EEC opened discussions for an agreement with the expanding Common Market in December, 1971. Negotiations in Brussels were completed on July 22, 1972, before those for an agreement with Comecon. But Finland only initialed the EEC agreement, because, as noted above, internal political obstacles had to be overcome and a favorable attitude in Moscow had to be induced. It thus became urgent to complete negotiations for the agreement with Comecon.

Talks for a treaty with Comecon proceeded to the point of a draft proposal submitted by Finland, and by mid-March, 1973, negotiations were concluded when an agreement was initialed which was subsequently signed in May. The Comecon treaty and the Soviet-Finnish treaty of April, 1971, were complementary in that the Soviet Union was the key country in Comecon, and it was anticipated that the kind of Soviet-Finnish economic cooperation growing out of their own treaty would extend eventually to Comecon as a whole.[13]

The Finnish-Comecon treaty provided for the first non-socialist government to associate with the organization; but unlike

12. *Ibid.*, Vol. XXIV, No. 12, April 19, 1972, pp. 20–21.
13. *Keesing's Contemporary Archives*, July 16–22, 1973, p. 25993.

arrangements between Yugoslavia and Comecon, the agreement did not include membership rights for Finland.[14] Comecon is composed of eight full members—USSR, Poland, Bulgaria, Czechoslovakia, Hungary, Romania, Eastern Germany, Mongolia, plus Yugoslavia as an associate member. Economic cooperation within Comecon does not take the form of a customs and monetary union, as within the EEC, but is more directed toward a division of labor, long-range planning, communications policy, etc.

The agreement signed in Moscow provided for establishment of a joint commission consisting of the Comecon members and Yugoslavia with Finland. The commission would work on detailed proposals for economic, scientific, and technological cooperation. It was expected that agreement would be sought with about 10 of Comecon's 23 permanent commissions—those concerned with standardization, statistics, finance and currency, light metals and chemicals. It was reported that Finland was interested in Comecon's International Investment Bank as a source of medium and long-term credits for her development projects.[15]

The negative Soviet attitude toward a Finnish-EEC treaty persisted despite the agreements with Moscow and Comecon. Kekkonen nevertheless felt constrained to make another unofficial visit to the USSR on September 2–3, 1973, to plead his country's case for approval of an agreement. Finland had only three remaining months before the expiration of the deadline set in the EEC agreement for her signature. This time the persevering Finnish President was apparently given the coveted green light,[16] for a month later in an extraordinary meeting of the Cabinet on October 3, 1973, he authorized signature of the EEC agreement.[17] On November 16 the Parliament ratified the free

14. *Ibid.*, and Singleton, "Finland, Comecon, and the EEC," p. 65.

15. See *Current Digest of the Soviet Press,* Vol. XXV, No. 11, March 15, 1973, p. 26, and *Keesing's Contemporary Archives,* July 16–22, 1973, p. 25993.

16. Kekkonen's visit to the USSR was reported in *Pravda,* September 4, 1973. See *Current Digest of the Soviet Press,* Vol. XXV, No. 36, p. 11, where it was reported that in the Finnish President's talks with Kosygin "a great deal of attention was devoted to examining the prospects for trade and economic cooperation in Europe."

17. *Finnish Features,* No. 18/73, "Statement by the President of the Republic to the Minutes of the Cabinet Meeting Presided over by the President on October 3, 1973."

trade agreement with the EEC and the European Coal and Steel Community by a vote of 141 to 36, with only the Communists and SKDL voting in opposition.[18]

The Finnish treaty with the EEC differs in some respects from those concluded with the other EFTA countries, reflecting her special relationship with the Soviet Union; the provisions of the Finnish treaty were part of the package which was put together in order to reassure Moscow. The Finnish agreement is strictly limited to the lowering of trade barriers, and it had no "evolutionary clause" by which the parties at a future date extend their cooperation into other fields. The treaty also excludes "both membership in the Community and any form of association or any commitment that might eventually lead to membership."[19] The Finns in their treaty were obliged to give only three months' notice of withdrawal, whereas the other EFTA countries were required to give twelve months.

The tenor of Kekkonen's private assurances to the Soviet leaders was reflected, in part at least, in his public statements. In November, 1972, he pledged that if trade with the East was reduced to a disturbing extent, the EEC agreement would be abandoned and the three months' notice of withdrawal would be given.[20]

As part of the public record of assurances and interpretations deemed necessary by the Finns, Kekkonen in a commentary affirmed the EEC agreement was "purely commercial" and aimed at ensuring Finnish competitiveness. The treaty was consistent with all Finland's international obligations, he declared, and added, "We have been able to establish our foreign policy on good neighbourly relations and strict observance of the agreements we have concluded. In this respect nothing has changed and nothing will change."[21]

Formal commitment to these assurances, with details spelled

18. *Keesing's Contemporary Archives,* December 17–23, 1973, p. 26252.

19. See *Finnish Features,* No. 9/73, "Mr. Pentti Uusivirta, Head of the Commercial Policy Department, Ministry of Foreign Affairs, at the Conference 'Scandinavia, Britain and the European Community' on May 3, 1973, in Copenhagen."

20. See Pajunen, "Finland's Security Policy in the 1970's: Background and Perspectives," p. 53.

21. *Finnish Features,* No. 18/73, "Statement by the President of the Republic to the Minutes of the Cabinet Meeting Presided over by the President on October 3, 1973."

out, was submitted in the motion of the government asking for ratification of the agreement by Parliament where it pledged that

> the agreement concluded with the EEC in no form binds Finland politically, and . . . Finland will in the future, too, continue to observe the Paasikivi-Kekkonen line in her foreign policy . . . the customs agreement will in no way affect Finland's earlier international obligations. In this connection the Government places special emphasis on the YYA Treaty [the Finnish-Soviet Treaty of Friendship, Cooperation and Mutual Assistance], in which Finland agreed not to participate in any alliance directed against the Soviet Union.
> . . . The Government holds the view that if the application of the EEC agreement causes damage to Finnish-Soviet co-operation so that co-operation does not develop in the way laid down in the Finnish-Soviet agreements, Finland will use her right to give three months' notice to cancel the agreement.
> The Government states that the concessions made by Finland to the EEC countries will also be granted immediately to the Soviet Union for any parts not covered by the customs agreement between the two countries.[22]

Due to the delays in Finland's case, her agreement with the EEC went into effect a year later than the agreements with Austria, Iceland, Portugal, Sweden, and Switzerland. The Finnish agreement, therefore, provided for a 40% cut in tariffs of industrial goods to bring the timetable of tariff reductions for Finland in line with the timetable already in operation between the EEC and the other EFTA countries. The Finnish-EEC treaty included arrangements to safeguard Finland's paper and forest industry exports to EEC countries and especially to Britain. Duties on industrial products were gradually to decrease over a period of four years, but agricultural products were not included. This put Finland in a more difficult position because of Britain's membership in the EEC; the treaty, however, left the door open for negotiations on this matter.[23]

---

22. Quoted in Singleton, "Finland, Comecon, and the EEC," p. 68.

23. See *Keesing's Contemporary Archives,* December 17–23, 1973, p. 26252, Singleton, "Finland, Comecon, and the EEC," p. 64, and Pajunen, "Finland's Security Policy in the 1970's: Background and Perspectives," p. 52.

There was to be equal treatment on tariff questions for Finland, and her traditional special trade arrangements with the USSR were to be protected, although some of these imports from the East would have to contend with tougher competition in the future. Finnish exports in turn would have to compete with the increased volume of Western exports to Soviet markets.[24] Above all, the EEC pledged respect for Finland's policy of neutrality.

In all probability the decisive reason behind Soviet acquiescence to the EEC-Finnish trade agreement was the fact that the Finns—especially President Kekkonen—had won over the Soviet leaders to the view that a strictly economic agreement with the EEC was a *sine qua non* for the future economic life of Finland. In addition Moscow was disposed to assume the risks of this limited arrangement with the EEC because the Finno-Soviet system at the time enjoyed favorable stabilizing features: the leadership of Kekkonen as President was extended; the Socialist fulfillment removed apprehensions from that quarter; and the Treaty of 1948 had, in July, 1970, five years before its expiration, been extended for another term of twenty years.[25] The international climate of détente provided another stabilizing feature, and a stubborn rejection of such an agreement would not have set well with world opinion at a time when the Conference on European Security and Cooperation was in progress, for which the Russians entertained high expectations. As will be seen below, Finnish initiative was preparing for the conference in Helsinki.

Just as Moscow acceded to the necessity for harmonizing her relationships with EFTA and the Scandinavian subsystem with her relationship to the Soviet Union, Moscow had to acknowledge grudgingly the need of Finland to harmonize her relationship with the EEC and the USSR.

---

24. See Pajunen, "Finland's Security Policy in the 1970's: Background and Perspectives," p. 72.

25. In a statement shortly after the extension of the treaty, President Kekkonen noted that the premature extension was based on a desire "to remove any possible doubt about the consistency of our policy." He then directly linked the extension of the pact to a possible trade agreement saying, "this is all the more important in view of Finland's vital interest in maintaining her trading position *in all markets.*" (Italics added.) See UAL, 1970, pp. 16–17. See also *The Current Digest of the Soviet Press,* Vol. XXII, No. 29, August, 1970, pp. 14–16, for the joint communique of the two countries on the occasion of extending the treaty.

Finland's Activist Neutrality

A. The All-European Conference on Security and Cooperation. After the Socialist fulfillment, Finnish foreign policy aimed to contribute in a direct and positive way to lessened international tensions and enhancement of favorable prospects for détente. Such an atmosphere, policy makers in Helsinki believed, would serve to safeguard if not strengthen Finland's neutrality and independence and thus be the most favorable milieu for the functioning of the Finnish-Soviet system. This conception had earlier inspired Kekkonen's 1963 proposal to make of Scandinavia a nuclear-free zone and before that his famous "pajama pocket" proposal that the Scandinavian countries follow a policy of neutrality similar to that of Finland and Sweden. Moscow had approvingly responded to these prior efforts for a more active neutralism.[26]

Finnish activist neutrality was to a considerable extent complementary with Soviet policy, which would account for its favorable reception in Moscow, but it was undertaken because it was perceived to be genuinely in Finland's interest. Here once again was a happy occurrence where the cement of common interest bonded the two countires in support of the same policy. Keen Soviet interest in Finnish efforts to sponsor the All-European Conference on Security and Cooperation was expressed on several occasions, and there were undoubtedly discussions of the Finnish initiative in private meetings Kekkonen and others had with Soviet officials.[27]

Finland's sponsorhip of the All-European Conference on Security and Cooperation was her boldest move in activist neutrality. Such a conference had been proposed earlier by the USSR and the Warsaw Pact countries,[28] but the time chosen by Helsinki

---

26. See below pp. 158–162.

27. See, for example, *The Current Digest of the Soviet Press,* Vol. XXII, No. 29, August 18, 1970, pp. 14–16, where it was noted that "The Finnish and Soviet leaders stated their satisfaction that the proposal to convene an All-European Conference on Security and Cooperation had received broad international support. The Soviet side noted Finland's initiative in the question of the conference and her role in helping to carry out this proposal."

28. See Lawrence L. Whetten, *Germany's Ostpolitik, Relations between the Federal Republic and the Warsaw Pact Countries* (London: Oxford University Press, 1971) especially Chapter 4, "European Security Problems: The Multilateral Approach in West German-Warsaw Pact Relations."

was more propitious for a favorable European response. In addition there was now a better prospect of success, for the United States and Canada were invited. As host, Helsinki could claim an advantage over most other European capitals because it was a location which would probably be acceptable to all the parties concerned.

The initial memorandum was distributed to the invited governments in May, 1969, and early the next year Ralph Enckell was chosen as roving ambassador to conduct exploratory consultations. In November, 1970, Helsinki proposed bilateral discussions at the ambassadorial level in the Finnish capital to smooth the way to hold the preparatory conference.[29] The bilateral exchanges, which lasted until 1972, took place in a favorable international atmosphere, for it was a time when diplomatic developments leading to normalization of East-West relations took place. The Soviet and Polish treaties with West Germany were negotiated, as were the Four Power Agreement on Berlin and the "Basic Treaty" between the two German states.

The preparatory talks which opened on November 22, 1972, were concluded in June, 1973, and provided for a conference in three stages. The first would be the development by the Foreign Ministers of an agenda based upon recommendations arising out of the preparatory sessions. The second stage would consist of substantive work of committees to bring forth recommendations, and the third would provide for the formal adoption of the final conference documents.[30]

The Foreign Ministers completed the first phase on July 7, 1973, and adopted the recommendations of the Preparatory Conference as the agenda for the second stage. Four main topics thus comprised the agenda for the important second stage: 1) questions relating to security in Europe, 2) cooperation in the fields of science and technology and of the environment, 3) cooperation in humanitarian and other fields, and 4) follow-up to the conference.[31]

---

29. UAL, 1970, p. 74.

30. *Keesing's Contemporary Archives,* July 30-August 5, 1973, pp. 26013–26015. The First stage was to take place in Helsinki in July, 1973; the second in Geneva in September, 1973; and the third was scheduled for Helsinki in the spring or summer of 1974.

31. *Ibid.,* p. 26013.

The second stage of the conference convened in Geneva on September 18, 1973, and remained in session until December 14 when it adjourned for a month's vacation. Talks reconvened in mid-January, 1974, and continued into the summer. Draft agreements on the sovereign equality of states and renunciation of the use or threat of force had been ascribed to, but the conference was stalled on the issues of the "inviolability" of postwar European frontiers desired by the Soviet Union and which the West was prepared to accept if in exchange the Russians gave concessions on human rights issues.[32]

Finnish activist neutrality also utilized the United Nations for opportunities offering international responsibility. Finns assumed the chairmanship of United Nations committees, and in 1968–70 Finland was elected to membership on the Security Council. Max Jakobson, the head of the Finnish delegation to the General Assembly, was in 1971 a serious contender for the post of Secretary General. The following year Helvi Sipilä, a Helsinki lawyer, became the first woman to hold the post of Assistant Secretary General of the United Nations.[33] Finland hosted the SALT negotiations to contribute to efforts for arms control, and the first session opened in Helsinki in November, 1969, while subsequent sessions were divided between Vienna and Helsinki. By 1974 it seemed that Helsinki would share with Vienna, Geneva, and The Hague the reputation of pursuing a constructive internationalist policy and sponsoring appropriate conferences to that end. Given its relationship with the Soviet Union and Moscow's favoring such activities in the 1970's, Soviet leaders were undoubtedly favorably impressed by the success of Finnish activist neutrality.

B. Diplomatic Relations with the Two German States. The German problem throughout the Cold War years remained a matter of dispute between the great powers, and the Finnish position on the question reflected the characteristic policy of neutrality: to steer clear of involvement in the quarrels of the great powers. Accord-

---

32. See *Facts on File,* September 16–22, 1973, pp. 777–778, and April 27, 1974, p. 319. See also *New York Times,* May 26, 1974, IV, p. 15.

33. Pajunen, "Finland's Security Policy in the 1970's: Background and Perspectives," p. 44.

ingly, Finland repudiated both the Western view that only the Federal Republic of West Germany represents the German people and the Soviet doctrine of two states. Although Finland did not recognize either the East or West German governments, trade missions were maintained in both German capitals. The Finns thus adopted the principle of equal treatment of both Germanies, and the commercial representatives were able to take care of economic as well as other matters between Finland and these two governments in a satisfactory manner.[34] Finnish attitude toward the German question was guided by this policy until September, 1971, when it was perceived in Helsinki that Chancellor Brandt's "Ostpolitik" had begun to make obvious progress. In particular the Four Power draft text on the status of, and access to, Berlin was agreed to less than a month earlier, and the two German states were about to enter into serious negotiations for a "Basic Treaty" in the wake of the signature of the Four Power Pact on Berlin.[35]

As the international picture changed, Finland was determined to move quickly and normalize her relations with both German states; in so doing she would be the first nonsocialist country to recognize the two of them. If, among other things, the German governments, in treaties of recognition to be negotiated, explicitly recognized Finnish neutrality, it would be a legal acknowledgement of her status desired in Helsinki. Inclusion in the body of a treaty would provide a coveted *legal* claim for neutrality greater than would inclusion in the preamble of a treaty.[36]

Taking the lead in recognizing the reality of the existence of two separate German states was consonant with activist neutrality; for if both were recognized simultaneously, Finland could avoid being embroiled in the conflicts of these two states as well as the ideological conflicts between "East and West." If full diplomatic relations were established with both Germanies simultaneously, it

---

34. See Hannu Vesa, "The Problem of Germany in Current Finnish Foreign Policy," pp. 41–43 in *Essays on Finnish Foreign Policy* published by the Finnish Political Science Association. See also Aimo Pajunen, "Finland's Security Policy," p. 14 in the same work.

35. See *Keesing's Contemporary Archives*, September 11–18, 1971, p. 24813. Actually, discussions between East and West Germany had begun as early as November 27, 1970.

36. See above, pp. 58–64.

would be possible for Helsinki to retain its eligibility as one of the few capitals where both German states were represented at the same level.[37] A probable additional motive to establish diplomatic relations with both Germanies was the fact that the USSR and the Warsaw Pact countries favored such a move and would regard it as evidence that even if Finland were to sign a trade agreement with the EEC, it would not slide too precipitously toward the West.

On September 10, 1971, the governments in Bonn and East Berlin received a draft treaty from Finland designed to establish a "comprehensive ordering of relations between Finland and the two Germanies which would come into force simultaneously."[38] The communique which accompanied the document noted that the European atmosphere had been improved by the preliminary agreement on Berlin and proposed that the two governments should:

1) acknowledge Finland's policy of neutrality;
2) renounce recourse to force or threat to use force;
3) conclude a settlement that would compensate Finland "for the destruction wrought by troops of the German Third Reich in 1944–45."[39]

It was evident from discussions which took place in July and August of 1972 that the government of East Berlin was ready to conclude an agreement; the desired treaty was initialed the following month on September 6. Bonn, however, expressed regret that the Finns had decided to pursue the matter at a time negotiations between the two German governments for a "Basic Agreement" were in progress; the latter took precedence over a treaty establishing diplomatic relations with Finland.[40] This obstacle was eliminated with conclusion of the "Basic Agreement" on November 6, 1972.[41] Accordingly an agreement was signed between Bonn and Helsinki on January 7, 1973, establishing diplomatic relations at the ambassadorial level. The initialed

---

37. *London Times*, September 9, 1972, p. 15.

38. *Facts on File*, September 9–15, 1971, p. 707.

39. *Finnish Features*, No. 19/971, "Communique of the Finnish Government," September 11, 1971.

40. *Keesing's Contemporary Archives*, October 7–14, 1972, p. 25516.

41. *Ibid.*, December 16–23, 1972, p. 25612.

Helsinki-East Berlin agreement was duly signed on December 8, 1972, also establishing diplomatic relations at the ambassadorial level, and went into effect on the same day as the other treaty.

The agreement with Western Germany was not so satisfying as the one with Eastern Germany, for Bonn was unwilling to include a settlement on reparations for damages caused in Lapland by German troops in 1944–45.[42] Thus ended the 16 month effort to normalize relations with the two German states. Finland had steadfastly refused to accede to West German insistence that it spoke for all Germans. In a public speech almost a year later President Kekkonen credited Chancellor Brandt's statesmanship for his "Ostpolitik"[43] which laid the groundwork for an almost completely successful Finnish policy toward the two German states.

The shift to a policy of establishing diplomatic relations with both parts of partitioned Germany in Europe led almost immediately to the application of the principle to partitioned Asian countries. On January 25, 1973, Finland recognized North Vietnam and declared its intention to do the same with the Saigon government when the situation in that state had cleared.[44] A few months later the five Nordic countries agreed to establish diplomatic relations with North Korea.[45]

---

42. *Ibid.*, February 5–11, 1973, p. 25717.

43. *Finish Features*, No. 2/73, "Speech by the President of the Republic at the Meeting of the Paasikivi Society, December 19, 1973," p. 2.

44. *Keesing's Contemporary Archives*, March 12–18, 1973, p. 25777.

45. *Facts on File*, June 3–9, 1973, p. 479.

CHAPTER NINE

THE PRIMARY EXTERNAL RELATIONSHIP: FINLAND, THE SOVIET UNION, AND THE SCANDINAVIAN SUBSYSTEM

A principal endeavor of Finnish foreign policy has been to harmonize her obligations to the USSR in one subsystem of which she is a part, while pursuing an involvement in expanding Scandinavian regional cooperation in another subsystem of which she is also a part.

The cardinal concern of Finland regarding the Soviet Union and Scandinavia has been her primary obligation to the former in Article 1 of the pact of 1948, which insists she must fight to repel an attack on her own territory "or on the Soviet Union through Finnish territory" by Germany or any country allied with her. Scandinavia is the obviously probable direction from which such an attack could be mounted. Hence, if conditions in that region were such as to reduce or eliminate the occurrence of such an attack, Finland's obligations under this provision would be largely on paper, and *pari passu* the neutrality features of the treaty would assume greater significance. Correspondingly, the possibility of Soviet invocation of Article 2 of the pact calling for consultations regarding the obligation in Article 1 would also be reduced. With diminished Soviet apprehension over Scandinavia,[1] the soft

---

1. On the relationship of Finland's obligations to the Soviet Union and the pivotal position of Scandinavia thereto see Göran von Bonsdorff, "Soviet-Finnish Relations and Peace in Northern Europe," *International Affairs* (Moscow) (6) June 1957, pp. 41–42, where he notes that "aggravation of world antagonisms might

sphere would have favorable international conditions under which to be sustained.

For almost his entire postwar career Kekkonen has assigned the highest priority to achievement of these objectives; he reasoned that the most effective device for reducing or eliminating the threat of an attack upon Finland or the Soviet Union through Finland was the neutralization of Scandinavia. If this could be achieved, the Finnish objective would be attained and so would Soviet interests, for it would mean the withdrawal of Norway and Denmark from NATO. Neutrality would thus function as the basis for harmonization between Finland's obligations to the Soviet Union and her membership and participation in the Scandinavian subsystem. Thus, while Finland integrated her Soviet and Scandinavian policies, the Soviet Union would be integrating her Finnish policy with Russia's Scandinavian objectives.

Kekkonen's earliest effort to realize the neutralization of Scandinavia was on January 23, 1952, in his noted "pajama pocket" speech which in effect proposed that Norway, Denmark, and Iceland—the Scandinavian members of NATO—switch to a policy of neutrality similar to that of Finland and Sweden.[2] Not only was the idea rejected out of hand by the Nordic NATO allies,[3] but it drew a spate of criticism in Finland and abroad and raised the

---

lead to greater danger of military complications" by which the Northern countries might be used as bridgeheads for attack against the USSR through Finland. Temptation to use them as bridgeheads would be reduced if relations between the Soviet Union and the Scandinavian countries are improved—something it is in the interest of Finland to cultivate.

2. See Kekkonen, *Neutrality: The Finnish Position,* pp. 53–56, for the text of the speech. See Göran von Bonsdorff, "Finland as a Member of the Nordic Community," in *Essays in Finnish Foreign Policy,* pp. 63–65, for an analysis of lines of discussion concerning security issues in Scandinavia, including consideration of Finland's special position therein. See also Hodgson, "Postwar Finnish Foreign Policy: Institutions and Personalities," p. 90, and *New York Times,* January 24, 1952, p. 2.

3. Studies of Norwegian and Danish foreign policy can be consulted, among other things, for their refusal to leave NATO. See for example Arne Olav Brundtland, "Norwegian Foreign Policy," *Cooperation and Conflict,* 3, 1968, pp. 169–183; Johan Jörgen Holst, "Norwegian Security Policy," *Cooperation and Conflict,* II, 1966, pp. 64–79; Erling Bjøl, "NATO and Denmark," *Cooperation and Conflict,* 2, 1968, pp. 93–107.

issue of Kekkonen's modification of the Paasikivi Line.[4] Kekkonen was accused of departing from the original passive version of the Paasikivi Line and converting it to a more activist one which sought to provide a more favorable milieu in which neutrality would thrive. In the course of time it was called the Passikivi-Kekkonen Line to underscore the fact that the latter was not only the heir of the originator, but perpetuator and contemporary interpreter of the Line as well.

Eleven years later, as President Kekkonen again tried to reduce the possibility of Scandinavia's becoming the scene of great power conflict with untoward consequences for Finland, he focused on a single tension-producing problem. In a demarche to the Scandinavian countries in May 1963 he proposed that the region be made a nuclear-free zone. It was based on a proposal advanced in November 1961 by Östen Undén, who was the Foreign Minister of Sweden. There were no nuclear weapons in any of the Scandinavian countries at the time Kekkonen offered his proposal, nor was there an imminent prospect of their being introduced. Indeed, Norway and Denmark from the inception of their NATO membership had adhered to a "no bases policy" on their territory. Kekkonen, however, urged his plan with the object of making certain that the region *remain* nuclear-free and that this status not depend upon unilateral policies of four countries but be affirmed through mutual undertakings.[5]

---

4. Hodgson, "Postwar Finnish Foreign Policy: Institutions and Personalities," pp. 90–91, where he notes how the issue centered on how Kekkonen violated the principle of keeping out of great power quarrels, which had become the paramount principle of Finnish neutrality and the Paasikivi Line in its original interpretation. Speaker K. A. Fagerholm implied disapproval of the speech in his address at the opening session of Parliament, and *Helsingen Sanomat,* a leading national daily newspaper, criticized it editorially.

5. See *London Times,* May 28, 1963, and Jakobson, *Finnish Neutrality,* p. 95. See also *Finnish Features,* No. 38/64, for remarks of Kekkonen given in an interview to Dr. H. Zilk of Austrian Television where he stated that his proposal "proceeds from the idea that positioning of nuclear weapons in areas previously without them is a very dangerous proceeding, bound to increase international tension. The purpose of my proposal was to ensure that Scandinavia remains outside of this field of tension."

Soviet interest in an atom-free zone for Scandinavia was published about ten months before Kekkonen offered his proposal. See A. Pogodin, "Make Northern Europe a Peace Zone," *International Affairs* (Moscow) (7) July, 1962, pp. 27–31. See *ibid.,* (8) August, 1963, "International Commentary" where V. Golubkov in "Fin-

The appeal for a nuclear-free Scandinavian zone was also greeted with coolness, suspicion, and some hostility by the Nordic NATO allies. Their Foreign Ministers, meeting in September 1963, discussed the idea but took no positive action. Norway, in particular, argued that its nuclear policy was strictly its own concern and not the subject of Scandinavian discussion.[6] In an interview about three years later Kekkonen ascribed to bipolar thinking present in the Scandinavian region the negative attitude toward his plan.[7]

The President could, nevertheless, within fourteen months draw satisfaction from the fact that the Norwegian and Danish governments had in effect concurred with the essence of his proposal. Their approval could be clearly inferred, he claimed, from a joint communique of these countries and the Soviet Union upon the conclusion of Khrushchev's visit there in July 1964. The Soviet government at that time declared its appreciation for the refusal of the two Scandinavian NATO members to permit the stationing of nuclear weapons on their territory and seemed pleased that the usual reservation that this would apply only in time of peace was not included.[8] Kekkonen could then optimistically assert that his country's international position was greatly improved by the "fact that the Soviet Union, in contrast to its attitude of only a few years ago, now looks upon the Nordic area as a region of peace."[9] Not only was the President vindicated in his

---

land: President Kekkonen's Important Initiative," p. 107, lauds Kekkonen's initiative.

6. Jakobson, *Finnish Neutrality*, p. 97.

7. Concerning unfavorable reactions to the plan see "Interview with the President of the Republic, Mr. Kekkonen, in *Dagens Nyheter* on September 27, 1966." The interviewer was Ulf Brandwell. It was sent to the author by the Embassy of Finland, Washington, D.C. In one response Kekkonen stated, "This proposal of mine, like many other proposals, was examined only from the standpoints of either East or West. It was not perceived, or there was no desire to perceive, that one of its focal aims was to give the first visible example of prevention of the proliferation of nuclear weapons." See also Jakobson, *Finnish Neutrality*, p. 97, where he relates how Kekkonen was accused not only of meddling in the affairs of others but "worse still, promoting the Soviet cause at the expense of the security of Finland's western neighbors."

8. *New York Times*, July 26, 1964, pp. 1 and 2, and Jakobson, *Finnish Neutrality*, p. 97.

9. *New York Times*, July 26, 1964, pp. 1 and 2.

nuclear-free zone endeavor, but it might be contended that he had, in a substantial degree, also attained the aims of his "pajama pocket" speech a dozen years earlier.

A year later, in the autumn of 1965, Kekkonen attempted to deal with a specific source of potential Finnish-Norwegian irritation when he broached the subject of a Finno-Norwegian treaty to assure that the common border in Lapland would remain peaceful in the event of a conflict between NATO and the Warsaw Pact. He sought by this means to stress the defensive nature of Finnish commitments in the treaty of 1948 and hoped "to remove Norwegian fears that Finnish Lapland might be used as a staging area for Soviet aggressive action against Norway."[10] Although no agreement resulted from Kekkonen's effort, he surely conveyed in clear terms to his Scandinavian neighbor the Finnish construction of her obligations in the Nordic region to the Soviet Union—which was not lost on the Soviets.

In tandem with Finland's concerns issuing from commitments to the Soviet Union was the concern for enhancing associations with her sister Nordic countries and assuming initiative to expand cooperation among them.[11] When Finland became a member of the Nordic Council, it could be taken as an affirmation of her soft sphere status and a reinforcement of it. This can be inferred from the characteristic of the soft sphere where the country, or region, if that is the case, is opened for increased outside relations. If Finland were a hard sphere, like the satellites of Eastern Europe, the Soviet Union would probably have maintained a more exclusive sphere of influence wherein the sphere state is "sealed-off" and integrated with the paramount power.[12]

Finland's membership in the Scandinavian family was fortuitous, for as a soft sphere state she could readily expand relations with a compatible group of countries in geographic proximity. The Finns were also fortunate in their Nordic kinship because the Scandinavian subsystem offered an alternative to isolation and

---

10. Jakobson, *Finnish Neutrality,* p. 98.

11. See Stanley V. Anderson, *The Nordic Council, A Study in Scandinavian Regionalism* (Seattle: University of Washington Press, 1967), pp. 9–10. In the post World War II period the Finns have replaced the Danes as the ones most eager to strengthen ties with the rest of Scandinavia.

12. See the Introduction for the contrasts between the hard and soft sphere.

dependence in the Soviet orbit despite the soft sphere status, for such a sphere might not thrive in isolation and dependence. Given the early Soviet decision to institute the soft sphere in Finland and Moscow's perception that Finland's Nordic nexus would serve the USSR's interest, it was only a matter of time before the Finns would be drawn into the web of Scandinavian ties. All Helsinki had to do was to observe certain caveats prescribed by her commitments to the Soviet Union and the Paasikivi Line.

Even though she had one foot in the Soviet orbit, Finland could fit well into the Scandinavian subsystem because it is so loosely structured, the processes are informal, and there is a rigid adherence to regard for the individual sovereignty of members.[13]

The Council is composed of sixteen deputies of Parliament from Finland, Norway, Denmark, and Sweden with an allotment of five from the Parliament of Iceland. About thirty governmental representatives are also included, comprising the Prime Minister, Foreign Minister, and other cabinet members. Annual meetings are held in different capitals each year and they last about a week, during which the members are divided into four committees: juridical, cultural, socio-political, and economic. The work of the Council is directed by a Speakers' Committee made up of one representative from each country, and the host country's member on the Council serves as presiding officer. Parliament members and governments alike have an unrestricted right to put motions, but the Council can make recommendations only to the governments, who are obligated to report subsequent actions to the succeeding session of the Council.

In addition to the Nordic Council several permanent organs of cooperation were created earlier in the postwar period to examine current problems. Commissions were established for social problems, general legislation, cultural matters, coordina-

---

13. For general studies on the Nordic Council, see Franz Wendt, *The Nordic Council and Cooperation in Scandinavia* (Copenhagen: Munksgaard, 1959); Anderson, *The Nordic Council, A Study in Scandinavian Regionalism*. See also *Finnish Features,* No. 32/63, "Finland and Nordic Cooperation," and No. 60/61, "Finland in the Scandinavian Family Circle"; also Chapter X, "The Scandinavian Balance," pp. 91–101, in Jakobson, *Finnish Neutrality* and Paul Dolan, "The Nordic Council," *The Western Political Quarterly* (June 1959) pp. 511–526.

tion of communication and removal of travel restrictions, and economic cooperation. Finland participated in an unofficial capacity in the work of all but the last before she became a member of the Nordic Council.

Although there is no limitation on subjects which may be considered by the Nordic Council, differences in foreign policy have led to selective exclusion of a topic from the agenda; but outside of the Council the Foreign Ministers meet twice a year, mainly for the purpose of coordinating policy in the United Nations and exchanging views on the international situation. Since 1967 the Defense Ministers of Denmark, Finland, Norway, and Sweden have had regular annual meetings; "they deal exclusively with matters relating to Scandinavian preparations for, and participation in, United Nations peace-keeping operations."[14]

Attesting to the proposition that a high degree of coordination and integration can be attained by states without a central government if a highly developed community exists among them despite their separate sovereignties, "the Scandinavian nations have gradually achieved a greater degree of integration than probably any other group of sovereign states."[15]

Moscow's assessment of Finland was not only in terms of a border state but also as a vital part of the strategically important adjacent Baltic-Scandinavian region that was staked out for the assertion of defensive interests. In Soviet theory the Baltic was a *mare clausum* where the "coastal states . . . have a right to control in-going and out-going naval traffic, denying outside powers military access to the Baltic waters, and keeping the straits open to their own maritime units."[16] The other Baltic states would, accordingly, have to "accustom themselves to think in terms of Russian rather than German predominance in the Baltic."[17]

---

14. Jakobson, *Finnish Neutrality*, p. 101.

15. *Ibid.*, p. 99.

16. Erling Bjøl, "A Soviet View of Northern Europe," a review article of Vl. Prokofiev, *Severnaya Evropa i Mir* (Moscow: Izdatelstvo "Mezhdunarodnye," 1966) in *Cooperation and Conflict,* II, 1967, pp. 112–115. For several years the Russians have referred to the Baltic as "a sea of peace."

17. Albin T. Anderson, "The Soviets and Northern Europe," *World Politics,* July 1952, p. 475. See also Bonsdorff, "Soviet-Finnish Relations and Peace in Northern Europe," p. 42, where he notes that the Northern countries, especially

Three points of strategic importance were identified by Moscow: the western outlet of the straits, the Aaland Islands, which dominate access to the Gulf of Bothnia as well as approaches to the Gulf of Finland, and the islands and waters of the latter.[18]

Soviet concern in the area extended also to the foreign policy options of countries located there. Moscow's foremost concern during the fluid period of 1948–1949 was to safeguard her sphere of influence in Finland,[19] and to prevent, if possible, the adhesion of any Nordic countries to NATO at the time of its inception. Sweden proposed an exclusive Nordic Defensive Alliance in 1948, which fell through mainly because Norway favored linking the Nordic grouping with the projected Atlantic Alliance. In the end Sweden stood by her traditional neutrality while Denmark, with some reluctance, followed Norway into NATO. In a move to prevent Norway from so doing, the USSR offered her a treaty of nonaggression, which was rejected, but Moscow succeeded in eliciting from Norway the "no foreign bases" pledge, to which Denmark also adhered.[20]

The Soviet Union, although constrained to bear the intrusion of NATO influence in the region, had prevented a full-bodied presence in the form of American or Western European bases. Moscow strove to maintain these abridgements of NATO influence in the 1950's and 1960's and to encourage Nordic tendencies toward neutrality and demilitarization to reduce the possibility of international tension and conflict in this corner of the world. In this she was heartily joined by Finland, for her own purposes.

A renewed but different approach to Scandinavian unity was broached by Denmark in 1951 and led to the creation of the Nordic Council the next year.

Representatives from the Finnish Parliament joined with

Denmark, Sweden, and Finland, together with the Soviet Union are "united in a great common interest . . . namely, maintenance of peace and security in the Baltic area." Such common interest, he concluded, would help to make the Baltic an "inland sea of peace."

18. Anderson, "The Soviets and Northern Europe," p. 475.

19. Birnbaum, "Soviet Policy in Northern Europe," p. 228, notes that Soviet leaders were cool to a Nordic Alliance which by its very existence could exert an attraction to Finland with whom the pact of 1948 had recently been signed.

20. Arne Olav Brundtland, "The Norwegian Balance, Past and Present," *Cooperation and Conflict*, II, 1966, pp. 31–32.

those of the four other Scandinavian countries to endorse unanimously the idea of expanded Nordic cooperation. Fagerholm, as speaker of the Parliament and head of the Finnish delegation, put forth reservátions that reflected anticipation of negative Soviet reactions to Finland's membership in the Council.[21] The Finns, not wishing to obstruct the work of forming the organization, remained to participate in drafting the statute of the Nordic Council but when completed stated that they could not accept membership at that time.[22]

By its reluctance to join the Nordic Council, the Finnish government "had either assumed or known that the Soviet Union would in no case regard an organization like the Nordic Council with favor." The Finns may have been apprehensive that forms of cooperation would be discussed, which Finland could not take part in " . . . out of regard for her general principles of foreign policy."[23] It was no secret in Helsinki that Soviet leaders harbored general suspicion of Scandinavian cooperation, and the Nordic Defensive Alliance of 1948, which was opposed in Russia, was still fresh in mind.[24] There should have been no surprise, therefore, when the Soviets heaped abusive accusations on the Nordic Council when it was founded in 1952 and for three years thereafter. It was charged with being an instrument for anti-Soviet purposes to subvert the region to NATO and American influence, and with being particularly aimed at hauling Sweden into the Atlantic Alliance.[25] Efforts to include Finland in the organization, it was said, were "inspired by reactionary and imperialist circles in

---

21. Törnudd, *Soviet Attitudes towards Non-Military Regional Cooperation,* 2nd revised edition, p. 115. The full text of the reservation reads: "It is quite clear—I do not think I have to explain it in more detail—that the position of Finland in such an organ of cooperation may become somewhat delicate. We have our special problems and our special considerations, which we must pay regard to, and I fear that in an organ of cooperation of the kind outlined by Mr. Hedtoft such questions may come on the agenda which we on the Finnish side simply do not find it possible to deal with. Such questions have in recent years been before us in Nordic cooperation—I suppose that I do not have to give any examples of that here—and such problems will of course appear later on as well."
22. *Ibid.*
23. *Ibid.*
24. *Ibid.*
25. *Ibid.*

the West which wanted to damage friendly relations . . . " between Finland and the Soviet Union.[26]

In 1955 a more positive appraisal of the Nordic Council succeeded the initial vituperation in Moscow and, reversing itself, the Finnish government applied for membership, a decision seeming to reflect the new Soviet evaluation of the institution.

Soviet leaders probably took into account five facets of the situation in their reassessment of Finland's joining the Council. The first facet may have been one of a series of cognate decisions taken at this time to loosen the reins and make concessions to Finland after President Paasikivi visited Moscow and agreements were concluded for the withdrawal from Porkkala and the renewal of the pact of 1948. Actually, Kekkonen, as Prime Minister, on September 18, 1955, conveyed to Soviet leaders Finland's desire to apply for membership. In reply the Soviet leaders related "that they had been hesitating in their attitude to the Council but that they had no observation to make in connection with the Finnish intention to join."[27] Moscow in the same context may also have concluded that it would serve no useful purpose to prolong its interdiction of Finnish membership, if it had ever explicitly done so, especially in view of the ardent desire of the Finns to associate with their fellow Scandinavians. Then too, consistent with their soft sphere decision in the case of Finland, the time had probably come to let that country take up these relationships, for by 1955–1956 the soft sphere had well established its credibility and it seemed much less probable that Finland would be drawn away from her obligations to the Soviet Union. If anything, the Finns would probably at this time be strongly motivated to correlate their Soviet relations with their new Scandinavian ties.

In the second facet a broader scope of considerations may well have affected Soviet attitudes toward Finnish membership in the Nordic Council, for Moscow's appraisal of the world situation in 1955–1956, which was symbolized by the "spirit of Geneva," culminated in statements made at the Twentieth Party Congress

---

26. *Izvestia,* September 19, 1954, cited by Hodgson, "Postwar Finnish Foreign Policy: Institutions and Personalities," p. 87.

27. Törnudd, *Soviet Attitudes toward Non-Military Regional Cooperation,* 2nd rev. ed., p. 115.

referring to a "zone of peace" with the Socialist camp as its nucleus. Accordingly, Soviet contacts abroad were to be expanded, and there would be more participation in institutions of international cooperation. Moscow would no longer harbor the notion that if a country is not with her, it is against her.[28] Such new perceptions would weaken suspicion and induce examination of opportunities that could fetch dividends from Finnish membership in the Council.

As to the third facet, decision makers in Moscow could well have calculated that with Finnish membership the neutral component of the Nordic Council would be augmented to offset the presence of the three NATO allies. This would be only partially accomplished, for although Finland was striving to be classified as a neutral, she had known commitments to the USSR and had prudently to maintain a solicitous regard for good relations with her eastern neighbor. Yet, with Finnish inclusion, the strictly Scandinavian character of the body would be emphasized and would work to dilute the NATO identification. If the Finns joined, the neutralism of Sweden could be reinforced and the latent neutralism of Norway and Denmark encouraged. Moscow, in its new assessment of the Nordic Council and Finnish membership therein, thus sought to exert influence to shape it nearer to its heart's desire rather than continue condemnation. Finnish desire to join the Council hence coincided with Soviet interest to change its direction.

The fourth facet of USSR reappraisal of the Nordic Council and Finnish membership in it was the examination of the true nature of the organization. Moscow could easily see the loose structure, that the sovereignty of its members was safeguarded, and that foreign policy and controversial political subjects were avoided. There was, therefore, little danger that Finland would be drawn into matters which would conflict with her obligations to the Soviet Union. Nevertheless, the government of Finland in its application for affiliation with the Council expressed reassurance to Moscow, clarified for public opinion at home, and put in the record for the other Scandinavians that:

---

28. *Ibid.,* pp. 120–122. See also Hodgson, "Postwar Finnish Foreign Policy: Institutions and Personalities," p. 87.

If the Council, at variance with its practice, were ever to take up questions relating to military policy or which might result in commitments of conflicts of interests between Great Powers, the representatives of Finland should not take part in the discussion of such questions.[29]

In the fifth facet of reassessment it could be seen that Soviet leaders in 1955–56 had reason to revise earlier perceptions of the Scandinavian organization based on the suspicion that it was little more than a catspaw for NATO. For one thing Norway and Denmark had comported themselves in ways to relieve such anxieties. In particular these two NATO countries had faithfully adhered to the "no base policy" by refusing in time of peace to allow foreign bases on their territory, which substantiated the unprovocative and restrictive character of their NATO identification.[30] By 1955–56 it may have seemed quite plausible to Moscow that prospects for this condition to be sustained and even expanded were fairly good. Soviet policy makers may probably have hoped that northern Europe would continue to develop along the lines of "a thinned-out zone, an area of reduced ten-

---

29. Törnudd, *Soviet Attitudes toward Non-Military Regional Cooperation*, 2nd rev. ed., p. 115. See Bonsdorff, "Finland as a Member of the Nordic Community," p. 68, where he notes that "the attitude of the Soviet Union changed toward acceptance of the Nordic Council, which may be a consequence of the experiences gained of the activity of the Council and also of the modified Soviet outlook on neutrality."

30. Norway's pledge that it would "never join in any agreement with other states that contains obligations for Norway to open bases for the military forces of foreign powers as long as Norway is not attacked or subject to threats of attack" was given to the Soviet Union in a diplomatic note on February 1, 1949, in answer to a Soviet note a few days earlier on her position toward the proposed North Atlantic Pact. For the text of the Norwegian note see *Current History* (March 1949) Vol. 16, No. 19, pp. 170–171. See also Brundtland, "The Nordic Balance," pp. 31–32, and footnote 2, p. 57. In practice the Danish government has followed the same policy but has not made a formal pledge. In March 1949, however, the Danish Foreign Minister was quoted as saying that NATO membership would not mean foreign bases on Danish soil. In 1953–1954 the Danes refused permission to NATO authorities when they claimed it was necessary to station American airmen in Denmark. See Lyman B. Burbank, "Scandinavian Integration and Western Defense," *Foreign Affairs* (October 1956) p. 145.

sions and an example of partial disengagement."[31] Although her first choice for the area might have been for all Scandinavians to follow the example of Finland, or at least Sweden, Soviet leaders reckoned that the course of realism was to settle for a *partial denial* to the West of the Nordic region.

As she took her place in the Nordic Council, Finland fulfilled a cherished national aspiration, indeed, one which Paasikivi had included among the principles of his formula for the country's postwar foreign policy. Her membership was cordially greeted by the other Nordic countries, for without Finland the system was not fully functional; if Finland was attracted to Scandinavia, the attraction went the other way as well. For their part the original members readily "recognized" the special and delicate concerns of the Finns' relations with Russia; but actually there was no serious problem in this regard, for matters of foreign and defense policy had always been studiously omitted from the agenda, and the Finnish reservation made the matter explicit. The reservation did, however, assist Finland in her effort to maintain the duality of association with the two subsystems.[32]

In the course of time the Scandinavian subsystem flourished despite the divergent paths to security taken by the members in 1948–49, when all but Sweden assumed some degree of obligation to outside powers. Nordic cooperation accentuated common interests, blurred differences, and to some extent overlay outside commitments of the members. Finland's neutrality, Norway's and Denmark's "no bases policy" and denuclearization, Sweden's no alliance policy, and traditional propensity to neutrality, all worked to foster an *inward* Scandinavian orientation.

Whether the Scandinavian system which had developed along these lines to provide a degree of insulation from the vicissitudes of international conflict could endure the outbreak of a major war, re-intensification of the cold war, or the flaring up of serious

---

31. Brundtland, "The Nordic Balance," p. 30. See also Bjøl, "A Soviet View of Northern Europe," pp. 114–115, where he refers to Prokofiev's view that Danish and Norwegian policy inside NATO has a specific character; that they try to maintain some kind of unprovocative "low key membership in the Alliance."

32. To facilitate the task of reconciling her membership in the two subsystems Finland hoped to ease Scandinavian suspicions of the Soviet Union. *Finnish Features,* No. 38/64, "President Kekkonen [on] aspects of Finnish Foreign Policy."

crises affecting that part of the world is questionable. The Scandinavian system, like the Finnish-Soviet relationship, has better prospects for survival in the absence of such conditions.[33] Hence, the movement toward great power détente, the spirit that nurtures it, and agreements that result from it serve the interest of the Scandinavians and their system.

Although Soviet leaders perceive Russian interests as being served in some ways by Finland's Nordic association, some of Moscow's original suspicions still linger that these ties will dilute, or conflict with, Finnish obligations to the Soviet Union. Finns are thus obliged to summon their ingenuity to devise practical formulas to integrate their obligations to the eastern neighbor while pursuing closer ties with their Nordic neighbors. Negotiations for Finnish association with EFTA, which went on for two years, reflect a successful balancing on the tightrope. The Finns were less successful, however, when it was thought prudent to reject membership in the Nordic Economic Union after elaborate negotiations to create the organization.[34]

The "Nordic Balance"

It is appropriate to conclude with an evaluation of the widely discussed "Nordic Balance" theory, for it is intimately related to the subject of this chapter, if not the entire study. In essence the theory postulates that Norway and Denmark, Sweden, and the Soviet Union all observe restraints in basic regional policy in order to achieve a balanced status quo for the area that serves their common interests. Norway's and Denmark's restraint is the no bases and nonnuclear policy, Sweden's is her alliance-free policy and refusal to join the Atlantic Alliance, and the Soviet Union's is the policy of moderation toward Finland, which could have been militarily occupied or completely satellized after the war. As a result of these self-imposed limitations, the theory goes, the region enjoys the "low profile" character described above. Lastly, the theory posits the maintenance of the balance by the conscious and deliberate pursuit of checks and balances by the parties in order to avoid unwanted consequences. For example, if

---

33. See p. 158 above.
34. See p. 138.

Russia moves to harden its sphere in Finland to a degree objectionable to the others, Norway and Denmark will terminate their no bases and nonnuclear policy and Sweden will forsake its neutrality to enter NATO. Conversely, if Norway and Denmark move to renounce their restraints, Moscow will respond by terminating her policy of moderation toward Finland. The theory has effects beyond the Nordic region, for it is proposed that, as a consequence of its operation, a stand-off will result between the United States and the Soviet Union regarding their direct involvement in the area.

Nordic Balance theorists like Brundtland refer specifically to the Note Crisis of 1961, where fear of responses by Norway and Sweden were said to induce Soviet abandonment of proposed consultations, as illustrative of the theory in practical operation.[35] Several authorities on relations between Finland and the Soviet Union who have been cited throughout this study, while not proponents of such a full-blown theory, refer in a general way to some restraints, especially Soviet restraint toward Finland in the face of possible Swedish switching to NATO, if steps were taken to satellize Finland.

Since its publication the concept has drawn the fire of noted Scandinavian foreign policy and defensive strategy authorities.[36] The author initially offers his own critical observations of the theory adduced mainly from this case study. Fairness requires it be noted, however, that those who critically analyze theories in foreign policy have advantages over theory builders, for the former have mainly to probe for flaws. Theories that posit mechanical or deterministic interactions among states are especially susceptible targets, for the complexities of foreign policy and the subjective element in decision making have rendered such theory building a difficult and hazardous undertaking.

One of the main burdens of Chapter 1 of this case study is an

---

35. See Chapter 6, pp. 113. See also Brundtland, "The Nordic Balance, Past and Present," which is a comprehensive exposition of the theory.

36. Nils Övik and Niels J. Haagerup, The Scandinavian Members of NATO, *Adelphi Papers,* No. 23, December 1965 (London: Institute of Strategic Studies); Holst, "Norwegian Security Policy" and Erik Moberg, "The 'Nordic Balance' Concept, A Critical Commentary," both in *Cooperation and Conflict,* 3, 1968. See also Jakobson, Chapter X, "The Scandinavian Balance," in *Finnish Neutrality.*

analysis of the reasons why Finland was not satellized on the hard sphere model after World War II. Although there was a complexity of factors considered in the decision, the crucial one was the fact that Soviet leaders perceived the USSR's interest in Finland and the Scandinavian region as defensive and decided that these interests could be safeguarded without satellizing Finland. The Nordic Balance theory implies, however, that nonsatellization of Finland is accounted for by restraints *imposed* upon Stalin, who would have preferred to impose a hard sphere such as he eventually forced upon the countries in Central Europe. It is implied from this case study, however, that Stalin did not have to be restrained from doing what he decided not to do.

Additional support for the position that Soviet policy for Finland as a soft sphere did not have to be induced by threat of Scandinavian reprisals is found in other sections of this case study which delineate the steadily evolving soft sphere from 1948 through 1955–56. These sections indicate how Soviet decision makers found confirmation of the original decision for the soft sphere and were convinced that it should be continued. Thus, in attachment to their theory, Nordic Balance analysts, it seems, may have inadvertently overlooked evidence pointing to other interpretations and concentrated on evidence supporting their own. Among the other evidence overlooked is the fact that the soft sphere status for Finland began with the armistice of 1944 and was brought to a dénouement in 1948, before Norway and Denmark joined NATO and could impose restraint upon the Soviet Union by threats to end the "no-bases" pledge.

Several authorities on Finnish-Soviet relations cited in this study refer to possible Swedish renunciation of neutrality in 1948, about the time of the Czechoslovak coup and Stalin's letter to Paasikivi proposing a defensive pact as a deterrent inducing Soviet moderation toward Finland. At first glance this seems to confirm the Nordic Balance thesis, but none of these writers link it with an intricate scheme of reciprocal constraints. We lack needed Soviet souce materials to settle the question, but the thesis of Chapter 2 of this study is that Stalin and Molotov accepted the Paasikivi draft for the treaty of 1948 largely because of skillful Finnish diplomacy, and that the treaty was a reaffirmation and continuance of the soft sphere decision of Stalin taken in 1944 and kept up to 1948. Soviet leaders concluded on the basis of the crucial years of 1944 to 1948 that Paasikivi's leadership and his new policy for Finland warranted retention of the soft sphere decision and its formalization in 1948. A possible abandonment of Sweden's alliance-free policy was in all likelihood taken seriously in Moscow, and as such it may have been *contributory* to Soviet decision making in 1948, but in the view of the author there is no available evidence to conclude that it was decisive.

In the Note Crisis, which figures in expositions of the Nordic Balance theory, there was probably a complexity of considerations influencing the final decision to drop the request for military consultations pursuant to Article 2 of the 1948 treaty. The Soviet leaders shifted away from their original request for military consultations in the face of a firm stand by President Kekkonen, who, skillfully utilizing personal diplomacy, succeeded in persuading Khrushchev of the high value Finland placed upon neutrality. It was at this point that Khrushchev switched to the breakup of the Honka Front and assurance of the continuity of Kekkonen's leadership and foreign policy as the safeguards to Soviet interests. Kekkonen, in appealing to Khrushchev, invoked concern for opinion in Scandinavia which seemed to impress the Soviet policy makers. Here again it seems reasonable to infer that Scandinavian restraint was *contributory* and important, but probably not exclusive and decisive in the Soviet shift. It should also be noted that Scandinavian deterrence did not operate to induce restraint on Soviet interference in the internal political processes in either the Note Crisis or the Nightfrost.

Within the context of spheres of influence analysis, the Scandinavian countries have "recognized" Finland's special position in the Soviet orbit, as have the United States and its NATO partners, even though it is a tacit recognition.[37] Under such circumstances the probability of outside intervention in the sphere of a great power is usually rather remote, despite condemnations to score propaganda points. The United States refrained from intervention in 1956 and 1968 when the Soviet Union had crises in her Eastern European sphere, and it seems reasonable to assume that she would not intervene in the case of Finland. Moreover, what would—or could—Norway do in the face of American reluctance

---

37. See the Introduction on recognition of spheres of influence.

to establish bases there as a part of a Nordic retaliation against harsh Soviet treatment of Finland? In all likelihood Norway and Denmark have adopted their no base and nonnuclear policies for purposes of their own unrelated to concern for curbing the Soviet Union in Finland. These countries probably would be sympathetic if their fellow Nordic country were to be the victim of harsh Soviet treatment, but whether such sympathy would lead to reversal of their policies is very difficult to say.

The foremost criticism of the critics of the Nordic Balance is the supposed automatic operation of reciprocal restraints upon the countries involved. Although some restraints exist, they do not stem primarily from the existence of counterrestraints that will unfailingly be invoked.

The issue of credibility is stressed by most writers. Would Norway, Denmark, and Sweden *actually* take the responses called for in the theory, once they weighed the risks and costs? There is, too, an issue of credibility in United States and NATO commitments to supply men and material for bases under such circumstances.

Holst raises a question of symmetry. Is there in fact an equal "distribution of the potentialities for compensatory adjustments both in the context of the Nordic regional system and the bipolar great power dominant system?"[38] He also raises the issue of short term dangers for Norway, or Denmark, of provoking immediate Soviet countermeasures against the long-term impact of Finland's new position in the event of a Soviet forced change in her status.[39] Holst also poses the problem of *adequacy*: Would Norwegian or Danish compensatory actions be sufficient to offset the advantages gained by the Soviet Union in concessions wrested from Finland?[40] Lastly he raises for decision makers the problems that would result from small incremental changes that could, in the aggregate, materially change the status quo.[41]

In conclusion, a relatively satisfactory set of interrelationships was developed among the Finns, the Soviets and the Scandinavians to resolve the delicate and complex problems arising from

---

38. Holst, "Norwegian Security Policy."
39. *Ibid.*
40. *Ibid.*
41. *Ibid.*

Finnish involvement in two rather distinct communities. Finland had been a special case in the Soviet orbit, but with membership in the Nordic system, this condition had a greater prospect of becoming assured and accentuated. The Finns also became a sort of special case in the Scandinavian subsystem because of pledges to the Soviet Union. Finnish membership in the Nordic system, however, contributed to the system's development, which, in turn, accentuated Finland's Scandinavian proclivities. Thus, Finland's cultivation of her Scandinavian ties not only served to fulfill cherished national aspirations and bring various practical benefits, but also worked to promote the Nordic system and to anchor more securely the soft sphere system for Finland. The success of this country's association with Scandinavia may have contributed to Soviet disposition to accept other extra-orbit relationships, such as the EFTA and the trade agreement with the expanded European Common Market; and other outside relationships might also be given favorable consideration in the future.

CHAPTER TEN

A NOTE ON "FINLANDIZATION"

On both sides of the Atlantic, "Finlandization" has been raised as a specter to frighten people into believing that Western Europe could be reduced to a form of hegemony resembling, or even worse than, that of Finland. According to the standard version, the Western Europeans will be mesmerized into passivity and will not only be lulled into unwariness by interminable reiteration "of slogans about relaxation of tensions and the end of the cold war, but coaxed into a state of irresolution so that they can be heavily leant upon and induced to move at Russia's bidding."[1] A more dreaded version of the alarm was sounded by the American Secretary of Defense, James R. Schlesinger, who offered the frightful prospect that the Soviet Union and its allies "without making use of their armed forces, will be able to dominate the policies of the countries of Western Europe" in a way more like the satellites of Eastern Europe than Finland if the disparities in military posture were to favor the Soviet Union.[2] Indeed, under these terms "Finlandization" would be a blessing beside the possible calamity of "Czechoslovakianization."

Those who anticipate the "Finlandization" of Western Europe base it upon some highly improbable contingencies—there are

---

1. "What Finlandization Means," *The Economist* (August 4) 1973, p. 16.
2. Schlesinger gave a rather full explication of his meaning of "Finlandization" in a speech before the National Jaycees in Arlington, Virginia, on December 15, 1973. *News Release, Office of the Assistant Secretary of Defense (Public Affairs),* December 15, 1973.

just too many "ifs" in their analysis. Moreover—and crucial to evaluation of "Finlandization"—is the application of the Finnish model to the entire region of Western Europe. It is very dubious, if indeed not out of the question, that the model can be replicated for Western Europe, for it represents a special relationship between a giant neighbor and a small country on its periphery. The Finno-Soviet relationship arises out of the historic and geopolitical dynamics affecting these two countries. It is the kind of relationship a small country or group of small or middle-sized countries might have with a regional paramount power.

Those who argue the "Finlandization" hypothesis lack understanding of at least two important features of the Finno-Soviet system that account for the degree of independence Finland enjoys even though it is a species of sphere state. The steady amplification and Soviet acknowledgement of Finnish neutrality is the first, and probably more important, of the two. Under the present rather salutary international climate it describes in significant degree Finland's world status and works to render the commitments of the Treaty of 1948 largely formal and academic. Despite her special relationship with the USSR, Finland can be classified as one of the company of European neutrals for many purposes.

Those who posit the "Finlandization" hypothesis also fail to understand, it seems, that while the Finno-Soviet system provides for the projection of influence *from* Moscow to Helsinki, there have been several significant instances of influence transmitted from Helsinki *to* Moscow, as brought out in this study. The system could not survive repeated sacrifice of national interests and economic injury to the sphere state by an inflexible and unilateral paramount power.

The notion that the countries of Western Europe would be subjected to such a degree of Soviet influence as to render them pliant and subservient hostages to Moscow is ill-conceived and misleading.[3] The overriding factor of Finland's presence in the path of expanding Soviet influence in the wake of the postwar

---

3. For a severe criticism of "Finlandization" similar to that of the author's see George F. Kennan, "Europe's Problems, Europe's Choices," *Foreign Policy*, No. 14 (Spring 1974) p. 9, where he concludes that "the analogy applied to the term 'Finlandization' turns out to be absurdly overdrawn and unsuitable."

redistribution of power required that the Finns get the best terms they could from Russia. Compared to other countries in Eastern Europe these were exceptionally favorable terms.

To institute a form of dependency such as would result from "Finlandization" of Western Europe, it should be ascertained that the potential hegemonic power *desires to do so* (perceived need), is confronted with *few effective impediments to doing so* (opportunity), and *has the resources to establish and maintain the degree of influence required* (facility). It is highly improbable that under foreseeable conditions these criteria would apply to Soviet establishment of such an ascendancy, qualified though it may be, over Western Europe. Four of the countries of Western Europe—France, Germany, Great Britain, and Italy—are big industrial countries, and when joined to the other countries of the region form an aggregation of formidable economic power. Western Europe also has basic military capability and the potential to expand it, and possesses political and diplomatic power to assert its interests and withstand Soviet pressure to install sufficient Soviet influence to reduce to quasi-satellites. Any meaningful analysis of possible expansion of Soviet influence in Western Europe should go beyond the comparative military postures of the USSR and Western Europe and account for historical, political, economic and psychological factors as well.

For the USSR to establish a sphere of influence on the model of Finland in Western Europe, it would have to replace the influence now exercised by the United States. Even though American influence has been declining in Western Europe, it would be fantastic to assume that Russia could accomplish this feat. Influence from across the Atlantic, while declining, is not about to be extinguished; its decline is evidence of European revival and ambition to assert more and more independence. It is far-fetched, indeed, to believe that Soviet influence could be expanded significantly while the Europeans are so assertive in Atlantic relations. The North Atlantic Alliance, although shaky, is still a political fact and it has endured for twenty-five years. Nor is there any prospect in sight for the large countries of Western Europe opting for neutrality as Finland has.

While it is true that the Western Europeans have difficulties in perfecting and maintaining their unity along with the fact that the U. S.-Western European relations are in the doldrums, it is simply not true that these factors have so weakened Europe as to expose her to quasi-hegemonization by Moscow. Likewise, it would have to be demonstrated that Soviet power has so expanded that it could mount so great a degree of influence. It should be conceded, however, that some conditions might arise that could result in an increment of Russian leverage in the give and take of diplomacy, but it would be extravagant to postulate that conditions exist—or are foreseeable in the immediate future— for the extension of Soviet sway over Western Europe à la Finland. To suggest that these countries might be satellized like Czechoslovakia is ludicrous.

An hypothesis of "Finlandization" would be more useful as a description of future prospects for the Soviet satellites of Eastern Europe, in which case it is more a specter to terrify the leaders of the USSR. As noted in the Preface, the desire for softening by the Eastern European satellites has plagued Moscow and will probably continue to do so. When Soviet leaders accede to assertions of independence by these countries, it could be argued that a process akin to "Finlandization" has taken place. But the USSR has intervened to prevent anything approaching the degree of independence exercised by Finland. The recurrence of a Dubcek or a Tito, of revolts such as in Poznan or Hungary, or of defection, such as in Albania, haunts Moscow's decision makers.

It may help to understand the "Finlandization" phenomenon if it is viewed as an invention of skeptics and opponents of détente who may have been more comfortable with cold war modes of thought and interaction with the Soviet Union. Thus it may be more explicable to account for this conception as a facet of internal politics re détente on both sides of the Atlantic than as a description of Western Europe's destiny.[4]

---

4. See F. Singleton, "Finland, Comecon, and the EEC," p. 71, wherein it is noted that Franz-Josef Strauss of the oppostion CDU attacked former Chancellor Brandt's *Ostpolitik* and accused him of submitting Germany to a process of "Finlandization." In America it has been well known that Secretary Schlesinger had withheld full support for the Kissinger-Nixon détente endeavors.

RECAPITULATION AND CONCLUSIONS

Finno-Soviet relations were examined in this case study in an effort to utilize relevant empirical data for the basic purpose of employing, testing, and refining the concept of the soft sphere of influence.

Conclusions of one kind or another are presented where appropriate throughout the book and should be considered as part of the basic findings of this research; some of them will of necessity be repeated here. Conclusions here, however, will focus on the general findings relating to the basic purpose and will refer to specific features of the soft sphere model and other conceptual devices for analysis of influence set forth in the Introduction.

Employing the Soft Sphere Model

The concept of a soft sphere of influence and its opposite, the hard sphere, existed in only bare outline at the time work on this book began. Necessity thus required that research on the case study be conducted coincident with the fuller formulation of the soft sphere and the other conceptual devices. It soon became evident that some serious problems of feasibility arose from the multiplicity of ancillary analytical concepts to be employed together with the soft sphere model and the breadth of the thirty year period of Finno-Soviet relations. In a rather loosely-structured "plan of research" it was decided that general study had to precede systematic research and later alternate with it. General study was indispensable for needed historical perspective, knowledge of sources, and elaboration of the soft sphere model and the other conceptual devices.

The problem of feasibility was settled by deciding to center attention on the essential character of the soft sphere model. The other analytical devices could then be assigned auxiliary functions as required, but especially to probe the process of decision making and to make distinctions in classification of hardness and softness.

Decision-making situations were encountered in every aspect of this study. In a soft sphere, decision making has characteristics which complicate the process and color it with its own peculiarities because of the subtleties of indirect influence.

Not only the soft sphere model, but all the other devices assisting in the investigation of this phenomenon were fruitfully employed in this study. In particular, the formula for establishing a sphere of influence, perceived need plus opportunity plus facility, was useful when "applied to important decisions affecting an established sphere. . . ." The same can be said for means, degree, and effect of the operational scheme for implementing a sphere of influence. The Soviet system of influence in Finland described in Chapter 4 was also a scheme for analysis of decision making in Moscow for the Finnish sphere. The modes for exercising sphere state influence, treated below, which are refinements of the conceptual design indicated by this study, are in goodly measure an outline of considerations that guided Finnish decision making.

The main uses of classification were to chart the origin, nature, and development of the soft sphere in Finland as well as the effects of the crises and dysfunctions that afflicted it.

The basic structure of the case study, which emerged from the preliminary studies, was the identification of two rather definite patterns in the Finno-Soviet relationship, which are usually referred to as "systems" in the book. There were also distinguished the outlines of rather distinct periods of time that indicated the effect of some significant historical occurrences upon the systems. Hence, the soft sphere as depicted in the origin, nature, development, and changes in these "systems" during these periods is the heart of this case study. Proceeding from this basic structure it was possible to facilitate systematic research, for the organization and subtopics of the book were thereby implied, and these in turn became the basis for collection and classification of data as well as for ascertaining the problems, issues, developments and positions which would be dealt with.

The system of Finno-Soviet relations reflecting the essentials of the soft sphere model is the foremost of these basic patterns. Next in importance, and derived from the system of Finno-Soviet relations, is the schematic depiction of Soviet influence in Finland. Phases in the evolution and functioning as well as dysfunction of the Finno-Soviet system are represented in the basic organization of the case study. Finally, the Finno-Soviet system is viewed in its interaction with the Scandinavian subsystem.

Some expected attitudes were encountered in gathering data because of the usual reluctance in both the sphere state and the paramount power to admit the existence of a sphere of influence of any kind. In the Finnish case this was abetted by the fact that it is a soft sphere where influence is diluted and disguised. In a soft sphere of influence there is not much awareness of the paramount power's role if it functions well; there is greater cognizance of influence, however, with the intrusion of elements of the hard sphere leading to dysfunction and hybridization of the sphere. The Finns have been prone to stress their independence, neutrality, and obligations of the Paasikivi-Kekkonen Line whereas a sphere of influence is usually seen as a hard sphere, satellite situation.

The picture has been clouded in the Soviet Union by ascribing spheres of influence as a mode of behavior peculiar to capitalistic states. Geopolitical thinking, although obviously pursued in the USSR, is also masked in several ways. Moscow's frequent allusions to Finland's "maintenance of foreign policy commitments" and her criteria for "good neighborly relations" between the two countries are for the most part euphemisms for the *expected* behavior of the Finns.

It is possible to conclude on the basis of this research that *there is* such a phenomenon as a soft sphere of influence. It is possible, therefore, to employ the concept for research and analysis in the general context of international relations or as part of the framework of concepts for the study of spheres of influence. The soft sphere concept can also be utilized in the study of internal sphere state or paramount power politics.

Testing and Refining the Soft Sphere Model

As treated here, *testing* means the investigation of correlations between the soft sphere model and historical experience. Refinements are those revisions of the model indicated by testing.

An affirmative answer to the question "Is Finland an example of a soft sphere?" obviates the necessity to ask if Finland is in the Soviet sphere of influence. Actually, Finnish inclusion in the Soviet sphere of influence, as distinct from what kind of a sphere it was to become, was confirmed in Chapter 1, relating to "the decision of World War II" and "Why did the Soviet Union want Finland in its sphere of influence?"

General Correlations with the Soft Sphere Model. The overall conclusion of this case study is that a positive correlation, with some exceptions to be noted, was found to exist between the Finno-Soviet relationship and the essentials of the soft sphere model. The period from the end of World War II to the autumn of 1958 was one of cumulative softening leading to a high degree of approximation to the model. From 1958 to 1962 dysfunctions set in because of the intrusion of stimuli into the system; and when the disturbing factors were gradually removed between 1963 and 1968, the system was restored more or less to normal. The system accommodated itself to the need for Finland to deal with economic imperatives in the wake of the collapse of EFTA and the enlargement of EEC after 1968.

Although the Finno-Soviet relationship, in most important respects and to a substantial degree, is a soft sphere, an intimate association posited in the ideals of partnership, amity, equality, and cooperation did not develop to any great extent. Moscow seemed to be more concerned with hard-headed questions dealing with who could be trusted to exercise power in Finland consonant with the pro-Soviet policy and obligations. For the Finns, the relationship was dictated by taking pragmatic account of geographic location and the harsh lessons of history.

According to the model, a soft sphere is genuine "if there is truly a substantive change that endures, and this is more likely to occur when a new set of relationships has been established which conditions perceptions, instills expectations, and guides decisions." The case study disclosed a high correlation with these criteria. A new set of relationships has been established that includes

changes in the foreign policy of Finland as well as the new undertakings of the Paasikivi Line, which have resulted in Finnish
acceptance of a system of Soviet influence. Evidence that perceptions were conditioned in Finland is found in abandonment of the
former "outpost of the West" mentality and pledging in good
faith her obligations to Moscow. The Finns had to redefine not
only the nature but the extent of justifiable Soviet interest in
Finland. Moscow in turn had to regard Finland as different from
her eastern European satellites and reciprocated by acceptance in
good faith of the changed Finnish outlook. Moscow decision
makers found, however, that they would not extend good faith to
Finland under certain conditions, which indicates that a full correlation with the model did not exist on this point.

Expectations were instilled by the new pattern of Finno-Soviet
relations as the soft sphere achieved stability. Both countries, with
a few exceptions to be noted, understood and accepted the rules
and limits which were reflected in rather definite mutual expectations; the decision-making process in both countries was facilitated thereby. Soviet exercise of indirect influence counted heavily upon Finnish political leaders' ability to anticipate Soviet responses based upon these expectations. In foreign policy the
Finns invariably succeeded in anticipating Moscow's responses,
but in domestic matters the Finns differed in some respects
among themselves, and with Moscow, on the rules, limits, and
expected Soviet responses, as was brought out in the Nightfrost
and the Note Crisis.

Soviet decision makers have accorded due regard to the Finnish expectation to avoid involvement in the conflicting interests
of the great powers. In the Note Crisis, for example, Soviet regard
for this expectation of the Finns led to a reversal of Moscow's
original request for military consultations between the two countries due to the German role in the Baltic Command of NATO.

Moscow accepted the soft sphere alternative in the belief that
the system would function satisfactorily. Soviet decision makers,
however, have found it necessary to facilitate the satisfactory
functioning of the system by influencing the conduct of internal
political processes in Finland. Such Soviet activity was not in
concurrence with the soft sphere model in which Finland's expectation was that her internal political processes would function
freely. Divergences from the model for this reason, however, did

not always result in effects of such magnitude as to cause dysfunction in the system.

In another set of criteria ". . . reciprocal advantages, respect for sovereignty, and a 'mystique' that unites the paramount power and sphere state in common purposes and ideals" are designated as underlying principles of the model. There were substantial reciprocal advantages. Finland was fitted into the Soviet defense and security system, and Moscow's anxieties arising from possible menace to the Baltic-Scandinavian region were reduced. Although Finland resigned herself to becoming a pro-Soviet buffer state, she did reap advantages accompanying the soft sphere condition, enjoyed a form of neutrality with many benefits, and was able to cultivate ties with the Nordic countries and EFTA. There was respect for sovereignty inherent in Finnish control over internal affairs, but this depended upon whether Soviet decision makers were confident that persons and groups in Finnish politics merited their trust. There was little "mystique" to unite the countries in common purposes and ideals, for they were united in common purposes by the bonds of expediency.

Finland's joining the Nordic Council and becoming involved in Scandinavian integration as well as her agreement with the EEC correlates well with the characteristic of a soft sphere whereby the country ". . . is exposed to an increase in outside relationships, thus reducing the isolating effects of exclusiveness, sealing-off, and integration with the paramount power found in the hard sphere." Yet, Finnish relations with Scandinavia also corroborate Finland's circumspect regard for Soviet influence.

The Concern for Sphere State Interests. When the time came for Finland to join the Nordic Council, a significant perspective on the way a paramount power *should* treat a soft sphere state was brought out. A paramount power will be unduly severe and in effect impose a hard-sphere-like condition upon the sphere country if the paramount power persists in objecting to a policy deemed in the national interest of the sphere country, and one not strongly objected to by the paramount power. An action of such severity by the paramount power is probably a sort of dysfunction because of the magnitude of the effects which might occur in the sphere state.

Although this principle is alluded to under "Concessions and Gifts" in the system of Soviet influence in Finland, it should be identified as one of the refinements of the model based upon this research. Finland's association with EFTA is another example of Soviet acquiescence to Finnish interests in the period covered in the case study. The trade agreement with the EEC is another, but the indefinite postponement of the implementation of a treaty for Nordic economic union, however, was in some respects a severity prompted by negative indications from Moscow.

When Is Influence Consistent with the Principles of the Soft Sphere System? The principles of the soft sphere model confine the exercise of influence by a paramount power to the degree where the effects are consistent with preserving the basic nature of the system. In practical operation, however, there seem to arise inescapable problems over the question of whether influence is of such a nature and extent as to be inconsistent with the principles of the model. The Finnish case offers a rich opportunity to trace manifestations of this apparently unavoidable and perplexing aspect of the soft sphere.

In Finland the main source of the problems were the two basic doctrines of the Soviet system of influence, which should best be considered as two sides of the same coin: the doctrine of trust-acceptance-assistance and its counterpart, the doctrine of distrust-rejection-opposition. In a soft sphere of influence that is relatively "pure" once the system has been instituted, the sphere state is entitled to carry on its internal political processes free of a degree of influence that would constitute interference. The paramount power in such a relatively "pure" system, having been given assurances by the sphere state as well as legal or informal commitments, accepts them in good faith and regards them as sufficient *until* there is palpable cause to consider these undertakings as having been violated by *actual policies* of the sphere state. Under these circumstances the paramount power does not really need either of these two doctrines unless they have been restricted to the expression of general principles. In this way such doctrines are more consistent with the soft sphere concept.

The second doctrine was interpreted in one significant instance along these moderate lines correlating with the soft sphere in what has been termed the "Stalin Precedent" of 1948. In 1958 and 1961 the same doctrine, narrowly interpreted, rejecting the Stalin precedent, became the basis for a degree of influence inconsistent with a soft sphere. Hard-sphere-like conditions for the functioning of the soft sphere were in this way imposed by the paramount power. The second doctrine when interpreted and applied in this way is tantamount to the assertion of a unilateral prerogative by the paramount power to determine *how* the soft sphere was to function in the face of certain conditions. These actions on the part of Moscow provide reason to believe that Soviet leaders did not really want an unencumbered soft sphere for Finland.

The narrow interpretation of the distrust-rejection-opposition doctrine and nonapplication of the Stalin Precedent resulting in dysfunction of the system provide some serious tests for the Finnish soft sphere model. Finnish political life had constantly to take into account the parameters assigned by Moscow. Nor was there developed a consistently utilized effective means to resolve this problem short of crisis for the country and virtual capitulation by a major political party. There were two reasons for this: the Finns offered no united resistance and the Soviet leaders were so strongly suspicious of Tanner and his followers that it was very difficult for them to contemplate suspending judgment as prescribed by the Stalin Precedent.

The Socialist "fulfillment" seemed to be the only way a restoration of the soft sphere system could be made. In this way the Finns could end a hard-sphere-like condition that might have stretched into a prolonged lapse of the soft sphere. This sort of thing, however, smacks of unilateral revision of the terms under which Finland was to be free to conduct the internal political processes.

The Level of Tolerance Problem. The point to which a sphere state is entitled in a soft sphere to carry on its internal political processes free of a degree of influence that would constitute interference is related to the determination of the level of tolerance of the paramount power. The level of tolerance problem is inherent in spheres of influence and reflects the paramount power's expectation of behavior in the sphere state. In soft spheres the range of tolerance is wide, but there *is* a limit because the paramount power has been given commitments and expects its interests, though broadly conceived, to be served. The degree of independence enjoyed in soft spheres can lead to the tendency of the sphere state—and even the paramount power—to overlook the limits of tolerance and regard them as very flexible. Such disregard of limits might be a source of conflict, especially if paramount power leaders harbor anxieties and sensitivities not perceived as such in the sphere state.

The level of tolerance problem reflects political conditions in the sphere state and will vary with the anxieties of paramount power decision makers evoked by sphere state politicians and political movements. Conversely, the level of tolerance will reflect sympathetic understanding and confidence resulting from effective communications between leaders of the two countries. Communication is more effective if it is conducted as a *regular* process. The level of tolerance also reflects international tensions or improved world conditions. It can change with the vagaries of the personalities in charge of government in the paramount power or reflect internal political conditions of the time.

A possible explanation of the Tanner faction's behavior was their endeavor to extend the level of tolerance to higher reaches in order to test how far they could go. To accomplish this the Tannerites probably thought it unnecessary, if not inconsistent, to maintain communications that would lead to greater sympathetic understanding on both sides. The Tannerites also seemed to regard Finnish commitments as a sufficient basis for tolerance by Moscow and subscribed to the view that the government of Finland should be extended tolerance *until* overt policies clearly indicated otherwise. Such an attitude proved to be disastrous in the wake of the crises and dysfunctions, and from 1963 onwards the Socialists, including Leskinen, improved relations and communications with Moscow.

The Finnish case indicates that when the level of tolerance declines there will be a tendency on the part of the paramount power to interpret narrowly the doctrine of distrust-rejection-opposition and to pursue more actively the doctrine of trust-acceptance-assistance; the Stalin Precedent under these circumstances will probably be ignored. On the basis of the Finnish experience it can be pointed out that a soft sphere thrives best with the absence, or minimal influence, of leaders and groups in the sphere state who will not maintain good relations with the paramount power. Under these conditions paramount power leaders are more disposed to raise the level of tolerance to where the commitments of the sphere state and assurances of its government would be accepted in good faith. If any doubt existed, paramount power leaders would suspend judgement until policies of the sphere state government were patently inconsistent with the system. As noted above, this position is more consistent with a "pure" soft sphere system and was, incidentally, essentially the position of Fagerholm in the Nightfrost.

Combinations, Degrees, and Changes. The problem of the level of tolerance and the problems arising from degree and effects of influence relate to "Combinations and Degrees" and "Changes" dealt with in the Conceptual Design.

In the course of the thirty year period covered in this case study, the immediate postwar years from 1944 to 1948 can best be described as years of trial and transition in which were present elements of a hard sphere causing a hybrid condition. From 1948 to 1958 the soft sphere was firmly set and experienced a decade of progressive development. The soft sphere, it seems appropriate to conclude on the basis of this study, was instituted, developed, and abided by in good faith by Moscow. It was not "an expedient change of form . . . for the deliberate purpose of a facade . . . where the silk glove will be removed at the appropriate moment to reveal the mailed fist."

Yet, there was an intense period of lapse into a hybridized sphere where the silk glove was removed in the autumn of 1958 and the autumn and winter of 1961–62. The lapse into hybridization, in the opinion of the author, was not a capricious or cynically high-handed modification of the system by the paramount power. The misgivings of Soviet decision makers leading to the lapse were genuine, although based upon a questionable "definition of the situation" after the rise of Tanner in 1957. The lapses indicated a need for adjustments in the system at a time when, in the view of one of the parties, the conditions upon which it would function satisfactorily were open to considerable uncertainty.

A process of restoring the system lasted from the autumn of 1963 until the spring of 1968. As noted in another context above, a hard-sphere-like condition resulted from the fact that the

Socialists were virtually required to institute particular changes which in turn affected internal Finnish politics. In retrospect, however, it can be said to have been ". . . an affirmation and adjustment in response to changed conditions and new problems." The Social Democrats made political gains and have assumed a pivotal role in the governments since 1966. The Soviets withdrew objections and ceased interference, and the internal political processes functioned more or less as before. Moreover, there resulted a better understanding in Helsinki regarding the need for communications, the level of tolerance, and the problem of adjustments—or appeasement when necessary—with the paramount power.

Sceptics and the Viability of a Soft Sphere. The intrusion of hard-sphere-like conditions by the paramount power are grist for the mill of sceptics who dismiss the soft sphere as a facade. The sceptics can also allude to the "inherent dilemma—perhaps flaw—in the soft sphere arising from disparities, often very great, in the political, economic, and military capabilities existing between hegemonic and sphere countries." There can be little doubt that these disparities contributed to Soviet ability to induce dysfunction and impose the conditions for the restoration of the soft sphere after the Socialist "fulfillment." We have been deprived of an example of Soviet response in the face of united Finnish assertion that the composition of a government and the election of a president were *internal* matters, that the doctrine of distrust-rejection-opposition should be broadly interpreted and the Stalin Precedent applied.

There are times when a paramount power backs down or revises its position in anticipation of responses in the sphere state. In the face of unity and firmness tactfully conveyed, together with reassurances, Moscow decision makers might not have mounted the pressures on the Fagerholm government of 1958. In 1961 Khrushchev revised his position on military consultations but was adamant in his opposition to the Honka candidacy.

In the final analysis, however, the invoking of superior capabilities by the paramount power is determined by the combination of factors in any particular situation. If Moscow felt strongly enough it could dictate to Helsinki even if there were unity in the country; that was settled by World War II. Moscow could also destroy a sphere state government like that of Dubcek or crush the rebel Hungarian regime. In Yugoslavia's case a successful withdrawal was possible, despite the paramount power's superior capabilities, because of a favorable combination of factors for the withdrawing sphere state.[1] Finland does not enjoy such a favorable combination of factors for defiance of the USSR.

In conclusion it can be noted that the disparities of power can affect the sphere state in many possible ways, but this does not preclude sphere state capability for resistance or for inducing favorable adjustments from the paramount power. Nor does it mean that the paramount power will invariably act without restraint. Disparities in power do not mean that there cannot be a soft sphere under a favorable combination of circumstances. This case study indicates that there can be such a phenomenon.

The Personality Factor in Leadership and Decision Making. Viewed from several angles, the Finnish case study provides a vivid illustration of the personality factor in decision making concerning the soft sphere. In both Moscow and Helsinki it was acknowledged that it takes leadership with distinctive qualities in a soft sphere state to institute the system and successfully maintain it. Throughout the entire period covered in this study Stalin and the two groups of his successors consistently viewed the Finnish soft sphere through the spectrum of the types of persons who would wield power in that country. Soviet preference for Kekkonen as the new Paasikivi, and dread of the influence of a forceful and venerated nationalistic figure like Tanner, indicated that a ruling principle of the system was Moscow's concern for *which* Finns took charge.

Men like Paasikivi and Kekkonen convincingly assured the Russians that they knew concessions had to be made and that the paramount power's desires and antipathies would be anticipated. As sphere state leaders they developed the facility to wheedle concessions from paramount power leaders, but upon occasion they had to be prepared to throw their weight behind a move by decision makers in Moscow which had untoward effects upon the

---

1. See "Introduction" on *Withdrawal,* p. 20.

free functioning of internal Finnish political processes—as in the Nightfrost.

With men like Paasikivi and Kekkonen in authority ". . . the requisite set of perceptions and temperaments" existed in Finland for Moscow "to entertain the notion that a soft sphere is one they can live with—possibly even like—and one which can be made to function satisfactorily." There developed in the USSR decision makers who also could be relied upon to have sensitive regard for the tenets of the soft sphere. This case study is dotted with examples of "kindness and concessions" and the effective working relationship of political leaders in Moscow and Helsinki. Under exceptional conditions, however, as described under crises and dysfunctions, Soviet leaders could alternate between honey and vinegar.

In the overall period under study in this case, the soft sphere fared better because "decision makers with tact, restraint, and patience" were in authority in both countries and maintained "a continuous and effective system of communication." It was for the most part a soft sphere "founded on two-way trust and confidence" based upon pragmatic consideration of common interest. Nevertheless, the author finds that he must conclude that the system could have been spared the trauma of crisis and dysfunction if there were persons in power in the Soviet Union with more restraint, patience, and higher regard for the consequences of their actions. If the Soviet decision makers during the Nightfrost and the Note Crisis could have summoned the resolution to examine with greater care the accuracy of the "definition of the situation," they would have found that the menace they had construed did not comport with realities. They would have seen that they had allowed anxieties to cloud judgement and lead to the decision to invoke the narrow interpretation of the doctrine of distrust-rejection-opposition and to ignore the applicability of the Stalin Precedent of 1948.

The Demarcation of Domestic and Foreign Policy in a Sphere Country. Study of the experience of Finland as a soft sphere also shed light on problems growing out of the demarcation of foreign and domestic policy not altogether anticipated in the model. The matter arose particularly in relation to the crises and dysfunctions where it was asserted, especially by President Kekkonen, that the line dividing the two areas was shifting and indistinct. Soviet spokesmen, while making no specific reference to the problem, left no doubt that internal Finnish politics affected Soviet judgement regarding Finland's ability to abide by her commitments and implied that Finns should prudently take due account of the attitude in Moscow.

Of foremost concern here is the shifting line between the domain of foreign and domestic matters as related to basic principles of the soft sphere, such as degree of independence, reflected in the fact that the ". . . political processes function freely without the threat of interference or dictation." In a soft sphere, then, the area of internal policy should remain essentially intact; indeed, this is one of its chief attributes. If the line is altered to reduce significantly the scope of the internal domain, the soft sphere has been compromised. If the line is indistinct as well as shifting, there is the basis for pretexts that facilitate interference in internal matters.

Sphere state internal politics can be burdened by the expectation of paramount power assertion of special interest in these matters if the line between the two zones is shifting and indistinct. One of the results can be the conduct of sphere state internal politics anticipating approval or disapproval of the hegemon. Indeed, the very approval and disapproval can be an important issue of partisan politics. Once Soviet leaders formulated their two doctrines concerning acceptability of persons in Finnish politics, it seemed inevitable that at certain times there would be insistence upon linking foreign policy with domestic policy in order to justify interference (or an escalation of influence) without technically violating the soft sphere system.

Finland's foreign policy commitments opened the door to influence in the domain of foreign policy, but the soft sphere system preserved the area of domestic affairs from interference. Nevertheless, because of foreign policy commitments to the paramount power, a sphere state like Finland may find that its domestic politics *affect* its foreign policy and are a cause of concern in the paramount power. This leaves the matter still somewhat vague, for the issue can be argued as to *when* domestic policy really affects foreign policy and the *extent* to which it is affected. We are back to the problem of drawing lines, for people will differ on whether, or how much, foreign policy is affected by domestic policy and vice versa.

President Kekkonen in the Nightfrost argued that the com-position of a government is both an internal and an external matter because the government has relations with other coun-tries. In the Note Crisis he argued that the line could become indistinct because internal conditions determined relations be-tween countries. These positions answer in a very broad way the question of *when* foreign policy is affected, but leave rather indef-inite the question of when foreign policy *is not* affected. The issue of the extent to which it is affected should in these circumstances be given careful attention.

The Nightfrost and Note Crisis were in some respects contests between the paramount power and sphere state on the one hand, and two groups within the sphere state on the other, on where to separate the two jurisdictions. The internal differences in Finland prevented a fair test of strength with the paramount power.

The soft sphere model should be revised to include a formula to draw the line between domestic and foreign policy to prevent legitimizing incursions into the domestic area, especially those that interfere with the free functioning of internal political pro-cesses. There is need to clarify the nature and extent of paramount power influence on the ground that ". . . it continues to claim a stake in the area and exercises constant concern for what is done or not done." The position of Fagerholm and others, stated elsewhere, which in essence called for renewal of assur-ances by the sphere state and suspension of judgement on the part of the paramount power until concrete decisions proved a violation of foreign policy commitments by the sphere, offers the basis for such a clarification. Under the Stalin Precedent of 1948 there is a record of Soviet acceptance of the spirit of it.

Needless to say there are practical problems stemming from the need to retain flexibility in fixing the bounds between the two areas, but there is equally a need for a sufficient degree of cer-tainty to provide stability because there is a reliable basis for expectation in the interaction between the two countries. Exces-sive flexibility can serve the ends of the paramount power to subvert the soft sphere; excessive certainty, on the other hand, can lead to rigidity and insensitivity by the sphere state to legiti-mate paramount power concerns. In the end, however, in this problem as in others that may arise in soft spheres of influence, sphere state leaders would be well advised to cultivate good rela-tions and communications with decision makers of the paramount power instead of relying exclusively upon strict adherence to formulas of the model.

The Finnish experience also shed light on ways the sphere state exercises influence upon the paramount power. While there are indications of the existence of sphere state influence in it, the conceptual design of the Introduction is largely devoted to the exercise of influence by the paramount power.

Influence of the Sphere State. The independence, nationalism and pursuit of national interest, respect for sovereignty and rights are all objectives of and instruments for the exercise of influence by a soft sphere state. The avoidance of unilateralism, good will, common interests, and the cultivation of reciprocal advantages are also in the model and can be linked to the exertion of influence by the sphere state. The concept of sphere state influence was dealt with obliquely under "Concessions and Gifts" in the system of Soviet influence, but the model should be refined to include a definite description of this significant feature.

A first principle should be set forth, however, before sketching in the elements of this refinement as adduced from this case study: *that the extent to which there is a substantial soft sphere is the extent to which the sphere state has reasonably effective means for exercise of influence upon the paramount power.*

It was found that sphere state influence was achieved largely by inducing tractable attitudes on the part of paramount power decision makers leading to concessions, favorable changes, or backing down from less desired positions. Conditions more favorable for the exercise of sphere state influence obtained when paramount power interests were collaterally served. Good examples here are the elaboration of Finnish neutrality and membership in the Nordic Council. Sphere state willingness to make concessions can lead to reciprocation by the paramount power, which may bestow an even greater concession, such as Soviet withdrawal from the base at Porkkala in exchange for Finnish agreement to renew the Pact of 1948 in 1955, three years before it expired.

Alluded to in another context are certain restraints that act upon the paramount power to induce a disposition to accede to sphere state influence, such as the desire to avoid sphere state resentment by a negative policy toward its genuine national interests, especially in view of only marginal objections of the paramount power, which could be dealt with by reservations or special provisions. Finland's association agreement with EFTA and membership in the Nordic Council are examples of this. Another restraint upon the paramount power which might ease the exercise of sphere state influence is the concern of the paramount power to maintain the position of its favored sphere state leaders.

Restraints were felt by Soviet decision makers stemming from the probable unfavorable responses in Scandinavian countries (especially Sweden) which Finland could invoke for the exercise of influence. Such restraint would be evident in Moscow even though there did not exist a scheme of automatic reciprocal restraints as proposed in the "Nordic Balance" theory.

Anything that cements good relations between the two countries can promote the disposition for paramount power acquiescence to sphere state influence. Kekkonen made deposits in the Soviet bank of good will by his proposals for neutralization and denuclearization of Scandinavia even though these efforts served Finnish interests as well. Sphere state restraints can help cement these good relations; such were Paasikivi's appeals for the end of residual anti-Soviet attitudes and Kekkonen's pleas for restraint by the Finnish press.

Some periods of time may be more opportune than others for the exercise of sphere state influence due to changes in government or outlook of the paramount power; some changes, however, can bring the reverse effect. Changes in the government of the sphere state may likewise affect favorably or adversely the exercise of influence. Improvements in international politics may also contribute to making the time ripe for favorable changes, and sphere state leaders should be prepared for opportunities as they were in 1955–56 when the times were auspicious.

Successful exercise of sphere state influence depends upon effective representations by sphere state leaders and diplomats who have nurtured paramount power confidence and maintained a working system of communication and personal diplomacy. Effective representations should be facilitated by "doing the homework," for the situation may call for painstaking negotiation to devise formulas acceptable to the paramount power. Finland's association with EFTA and EEC and the visit in 1948 of the delegation to Moscow to present a well-formulated Finnish counterproposal to Stalin's plan for a mutual defense treaty are good examples of effective representations.

Sphere state exercise of influence in a critical situation may require unity at home to impress paramount power leaders with sphere state resolution and dissuade them from the temptation to exploit internal differences. Finnish unity was rewarded in negotiation of the Pact of 1948, and there is some basis for belief that it might have succeeded in the Nightfrost. Firmness backed by unity must nevertheless be tempered by prudence to avoid overplaying the hand; for although bluffing sometimes wins, the cards held by the sphere state are not, in the nature of things, as high as those in the hand of the hegemon.

The analysis of pursuit of influence by sphere state leaders can also utilize with profit the devices for operational analysis of influence. Perceived need, opportunity, and facility as well as means, degree, and effect, as well as conditioning with appropriate transpositions are applicable to sphere state influence as well as paramount power influence.

To sum up, despite the presence of some hard-sphere-like characteristics and, on occasion, the accentuation of these features, the Finnish case study seems clearly to indicate that softness is the general attribute and long-term propensity of the Finnish sphere of influence.

POSTSCRIPT: FUTURE PROSPECTS

It seems apposite to have this study run its full course by a venture into the "tenuous and precarious undertaking" of prediction, which, it was claimed in the Introduction, would be rendered more accurate by use of the analytical devices employed in this study. The estimate of future prospects will be mainly in terms of hardness and softness in the system, and the projection is for only ten to twelve years.

Several factors seem to favor the durability of the softness in the system, which was re-established after the Social Democratic "fulfillment":

1. The possible refinement and continued use of the devices of sphere state influence.

2. The willingness of President Kekkonen to accept an extension of his third term, which will provide a stabilizing effect until 1978.

3. Softness and stability will also be enhanced by general cooperation of the Social Democrats, the Center Party, and the SKDL. These parties enjoy the trust-acceptance-assistance of Moscow and as a group will probably continue to enjoy a preponderance of power in Finnish politics. This will persuade Soviet leaders that the system is working satisfactorily.

4. The National Coalition as the leading party of the right has prudently shown restraint and cooperativeness, and Soviet misgivings toward it may accordingly be toned down.

5. The rightist movement led by Vennamo seems to have

been weakened, for the time being, if not longer, by divisions and defections.

6. The "low tension" quality of the Baltic-Scandinavian region aids the maintenance of Finnish neutrality and ties with the Nordic countries and thereby reinforces softness in Finland.

7. Cold War anxieties of the Soviet Union have been lessened to provide a more stable international atmosphere to sustain Finnish neutrality and softness.

Even as the soft sphere enters a period of bright days with the persistence of the foregoing favorable signs, the twin doctrines will be kept in reserve by Moscow to deal with the rise of a strong rightist-nationalist leader or movement or the recrudescence of international tensions. Under the favorable conditions foreseen, however, the doctrine of trust-acceptance-assistance will be applied as the general rule, and the doctrine of distrust-rejection-opposition will be held in reserve. The Soviet decision makers will also be more disposed under these favorable conditions to accept at face value the assurances of the Finns that they are loyal to the Paasikivi-Kekkonen Line and will abide by the commitments to the USSR. If in the face of these assurances uncertainties persist, Soviet leaders will be more likely to suspend judgement until concrete decisions are taken by the Finnish government. The level of tolerance will rise, and influence will be indirect and without significant effect upon the system.

All of these developments point to a relatively unencumbered soft sphere with a clearer demarcation of domestic and foreign policy that protects the legitimate preserve of the former. In 1978, if not before, Moscow will, however, probably actively seek to influence the choice of Kekkonen's successor. The Soviet decision makers do not show the slightest inclination of changing their view that the key to the satisfactory functioning of the system as desired by the USSR is the "sphere state leader" of the stamp of Paasikivi and Kekkonen.

Two matters that affect the prospect of softening are in the delicate area of international affairs. The first involves the future of neutrality and the obligations of the Pact of 1948. If the favorable international climate lasts, the Finns will probably find stronger legal expression and acknowledgement of their status as a neutral and Soviet commitment to it. The Russians may in time accede to such firmer legal underpinning of Finnish neutrality because it is a concession ardently desired by Helsinki and would cost Moscow very little.

It may be a very long time, however, before Finnish neutrality takes an undiluted form, for Moscow will probably continue to regard highly Finland's obligations in the Pact of 1948. Continued Soviet insistence upon Finnish military commitments in the Pact of 1948 will be made despite the long duration of Finnish loyalty to the Paasikivi Line and even though these commitments are under present and future international conditions largely on paper. Moscow views the Pact of 1948 as a formalization of the relationship between the two countries and deems it as imparting greater viability to the general obligations of the Paasikivi Line; besides, why surrender an insurance policy for future adverse contingencies without a *quid pro quo*?

There is thus no termination of the soft sphere in sight that Moscow would approve. A termination of the soft sphere would be greeted in the USSR, we might conjecture, as setting Finland adrift. If Finland is set adrift, Soviet leaders believe that nationalistic, rightist, revanchist, anti-Soviet latent tendencies may be revived. The influence of others might be established, or Finland might be drawn into a Scandinavian neutrality-defensive system or join the expanding EEC. The Soviet Union will thus probably continue to look upon Finland as a marchland that has been pre-empted to serve her defensive interests and one whose neutrality is consonant with those interests. Moscow will not be ready for some years to look upon Finland as a neutralized buffer like Sweden.

Thus, although the softness of the system seems assured, there will be no evanescence of Soviet influence, but rather retention of it for the period ahead in order to derive benefits for the USSR in international situations in which she is concerned.

The expanding European Common Market is the second long-range international concern affecting the future prospects of the Finnish soft sphere. The reverberations of the evolving continentalization of the European economy were felt in Moscow and Helsinki and after almost four years were reflected in the Finno-EEC trade agreement. For the next few years the Finns, having established this beachhead, will have to be circumspectly content with these trade relations.

It is possible, however, that in the course of time Soviet decision makers might review their negative assessment of Finnish membership in the EEC as they did their assessment of Finnish membership in the Nordic Council and association with EFTA. Such a revision of Russian perceptions of the new Europe and Finland's relation to it would have significant consequences for the economic future of Finland as well as Finnish relations with the Soviet Union. Two long-range tendencies draw Finland closer economically to the new Europe: 1) the attraction this enlarged economic entity has for *all* Europe will undoubtedly be felt in Finland, and 2) Scandinavian countries will be drawn to this burgeoning economic giant; and Finland, as part of Scandinavia, will feel the additional magnetic pull.

Securing the national interest means that the substance of nationalism and independence will be enjoyed—these are the hallmarks of the soft sphere. Kekkonen and his successor can acclaim the system, for the benefits assured are worth the price to be paid—a price hitherto unavoidable. There will be no need to deviate from the Paasikivi Line, for it would only stir new Night-frosts and Notes. The system will endure for the foreseeable future; there is no Finnish leader or political movement in prospect that will upset the apple cart. A danger, if there is one, will be rigidity and negative unilateralism of a pronounced character in Moscow detrimental to Finnish interests. Such a development could estrange the parties now enjoying confidence in Moscow, if not raise up a new Tanner. The Soviet record of timely adjustment to Finnish nationa needs is a good one, but it has been contingent upon their confidence in the men in Helsinki. For the men of Helsinki, necessity will continue to induce the wisdom of clasping the hand with a silk glove rather than taking the blows of a mailed fist. Politics—including foreign policy—is the study of power, but it is also the study of wisdom—or the lack of it—in the use of, or response to, power.

INDEX

WH/   O/N725J

VLOYANTES